AF557828

TAMING The DRAGON

Since the clashes in 2020, India-China relations have been poised in the limbo between hope and dread for five years. Stepping bravely into a policy and strategy void, Manoj Kewalramani and his fellow authors from the Takshashila Institution have given us a perceptive, rigorous and constructive prescription for India's policies towards China. This manifesto is based on deep study of the structural dynamics driving India-China relations, and looks forward rather than back. A new and promising generation of Indian China scholars urge a dual policy of self-strengthening and engagement with China, based on strategic discipline, asymmetric responses to China's military challenge, de-risking the trade and economic relationship, and using the changes in the international situation. This is a book that deserves to be widely read, not only those in policy circles, who would do well to heed its advice, but by all those interested in India's future. It is a major contribution to the strategic conversation in India.

—Shivshankar Menon
former National Security Advisor of India

A lucid, unsentimental guide to India's China dilemma. Manoj Kewalramani has marshalled with his co-writers a practical framework for stability in relations with our largest neighbour, grounded in Indian strength and disciplined engagement.

—Nirupama Menon Rao
former Foreign Secretary, Government of India

Manoj Kewalramani and his colleagues point to a pragmatic Indian path to engaging China amid Delhi's growing power asymmetry with Beijing and an increasingly volatile international environment. The clinical and unsentimental essays in 'Taming the Dragon' offer incisive new approaches to India's trade, security and political challenges in its China policy. As India's relations with China enter the post-Galwan phase, this volume offers an insightful window into the shifting dynamic between the two Asian giants.

—C. Raja Mohan
Strategic Affairs Expert and Columnist

Rare to see such a clear-eyed view, not long after the fog of conflict between India and China ended. While the volume edited by Manoj Kewalramani primarily attempts a roadmap for the future of India-China ties post-Kazan, it is also necessary stock-taking of the mistaken perceptions of the past few years pre- and post-Galwan. Kewalramani et al. remind us that a return to status quo ante is unrealistic, even as the two countries essay a new engagement between them.

—Suhasini Haidar
Diplomatic Affairs Editor, *The Hindu*

TAMING The DRAGON

A Manifesto for a New Modus Vivendi with China

Edited by
MANOJ KEWALRAMANI

RUPA

First published by
Rupa Publications India Pvt. Ltd 2026
161-B/4, Gulmohar House,
Yusuf Sarai Community Centre,
New Delhi 110049

Sales centres:
Bengaluru Chennai
Hyderabad Kolkata Mumbai

P-ISBN: 978-93-7646-367-1
E-ISBN: 978-93-7646-817-1

First impression 2026

10 9 8 7 6 5 4 3 2 1

Printed in India

To the policymakers and professionals who have shaped India's foreign policy, and to the new generation of thinkers and doers who will redefine India's China policy in the years ahead.

Contents

Editor's Note

Often, books dealing with current affairs, particularly the India-China relationship, are descriptive. Some explain the historical antecedents of the present-day predicament. Some elaborate the evolving political, economic, social and policy paradigms. And some detail the intricate, often behind-the-scenes, interactions between the actors involved, highlighting the role of personalities and institutions. However, essentially, each in their own way defines the problem. This book is unlike any of them. This is a prescriptive book. It details the strategic challenges and opportunities within the India-China dyad, places them within broader national and geopolitical contexts and recommends specific policy measures for the Indian leadership. In that sense, this book is a guide to action. Or as the title states, it is a manifesto.

After five years of tensions following the standoff in eastern Ladakh in 2020, India and China are once again embarking on tentative steps towards engagement. The current process is unfolding amid a historic churn in the global balance of power. The post-Cold War world order is history, and it is still unclear what's likely to replace it. The US remains the preponderant global power. But its systemic stability, economic dynamism and global appeal are under significant strain. Europe is struggling to cope with the flames of war in Ukraine, along with the twin challenges of populism and policy stasis. Russia remains a declining but still tremendously significant international actor. China, meanwhile, continues to be at the heart of global industrial and supply chains, despite its domestic economic challenges. At the same time, it is also rapidly expanding its military capacity and ability to shape regional orders and global norms. In this process, China has been working to mobilize much of the developing world to align with its agenda.

In essence, the world is at an inflection point. It is, thus, imperative for India's political elite and strategic affairs community to deliberate about the pathways that India must pursue to fulfil the goal of Viksit Bharat, i.e., the goal of India becoming a developed country by 2047. One of the most critical components of this ambition is managing India's relationship with China or arriving at a new strategic balance. To do so, it is imperative to first ask: what is it that India desires from this relationship? What are the specific contours of this new, desirable state of affairs that we wish to arrive at? And what does India need to do to get there? These questions require deeper yet urgent reflection, for policy to proceed with purpose rather than being reactive. This is the gap that this book aims to fill.

The core argument of this book is that the paradigm within which Indian policy thinking must be located is that of *atma-shakti* or self-strengthening. This framework must then inform decisions about economic policy, military preparedness, external partnerships, trade and investment, and even engagement with China. Specific chapters in the book deal with these domains in great depth. In some cases, we argue that the current policy trajectory is aligned with this framework of self-strengthening. However, what may be needed is either a dialling up of measures or streamlining implementation. In other instances, we contend that the current policy direction is misaligned and needs to be overhauled along the lines of our recommendations. Of course, in this process, there are certain specific domains that this book does not address. For instance, it doesn't articulate any particular course of action with regard to the issue of Tibet and the succession of the Dalai Lama. Likewise, we do not delve into a detailed discussion on India's policy with regard to Taiwan. These are narrow yet important issues that can have strategic implications. And we hope that our articulation of the framework of self-strengthening will encourage other scholars to analyse these issues in context.

This book is the result of extensive research and ongoing conversations with colleagues, scholars and friends at the Takshashila Institution and within the broader public policy community in India. The interdisciplinary analysis and recommendations contained within the book reflect the richness of those engagements. The thoughtful, open and intellectually vibrant environment that Takshashila fosters is critical to this work. Of course, this is only made possible by the steadfast backing of the institution's leadership and community of supporters. In this regard, I am especially grateful to Ms Anjana Kaul for her unwavering support of the Indo-Pacific Studies Programme and for her commitment to nurturing future Indian scholarship on China through the Network for Advanced Studies of China Fellowship. I am also deeply thankful to the team at Rupa and our editor Richa Tewari for their guidance and support throughout this project.

Finally, for readers, this book is the product of deep work by dedicated policy wonks, who relish engaging with the complexity, paradoxes and intricacy of the real world. You will experience these woven throughout the different chapters, as each deals with urgent and pressing questions. While each chapter can be read on its own, the book is best approached from start to finish, as the early chapters establish the context on which the later ones build. As you encounter the ideas presented, some of which may appear counterintuitive, I recommend keeping the overarching framework of self-strengthening firmly in mind. It is the compass that will allow you to effectively navigate the terrain ahead.

Manoj Kewalramani
15 November 2025

Introduction

Asymmetry and Disorder: Why Is the India-China Relationship so Volatile?

MANOJ KEWALRAMANI

Not all conclusions arrive with a spectacle. Sometimes, the end mirrors the beginning—emerging with stealth and obfuscated by the clutter of routine activity. Quietly is precisely how the standoff between India and China in eastern Ladakh began in May 2020. A few months prior, Chinese forces had been carrying out routine annual exercises in western Tibet. By April, some of these Chinese combat forces began to move closer to the Line of Actual Control (LAC), a boundary between the two sides that has never been delineated on a map but has been observed and reinforced through presence and patrolling on the ground. Despite intelligence inputs, questions have been raised on the responses from the Indian side. As per reports, the Indian side fell short to respond adequately to the movement of Chinese forces, either because they misread the Chinese actions or owing to a communication gap in sharing intelligence[1]. But as journalist and scholar Manoj Joshi clarified and noted, the problem for the Indian side 'was not the lack of intelligence, but its assessment.'[2] By early May, Chinese soldiers

---

[1]Singh, Sushant, 'First intel on PLA came mid-April, long before Pangong clash', *The Indian Express*, 15 July 2020, https://tinyurl.com/yjpym45t. Accessed on 10 November 2025.

[2]Joshi, Manoj, *Understanding the India-China Border: The Enduring Threat of War in High Himalaya*. HarperCollins, India, 2022.

had occupied key positions and were blocking Indian patrols in several areas.

In the months and years that followed, these locations would acquire the nomenclature of friction points. Some witnessed violent exchanges. The most prominent of these was the Galwan Valley clash of June 2020, which resulted in the first loss of life in fighting along the India-China boundary areas since 1975. This shattered the already fragile bilateral trust, plunging the relationship to its lowest point since the 1962 war. Others witnessed intense tactical jockeying, as each side dug in its heels for the long haul. At the same time, both sides engaged in continuous diplomacy. In December 2024, External Affairs Minister S. Jaishankar told Parliament that since June 2020, 17 meetings of the Working Mechanism for Cooperation and Coordination (WMCC) took place and 21 rounds of Senior Highest Military Commander (SHMC) meetings were held at the corps commander level.[3] These resulted in disengagement through the creation of buffer zones at friction points along Pangong Tso, Galwan Valley, Gogra and Hot Springs. The last of these was agreed upon in September 2022. Talks thereafter continued, but yielded little. That was until the eve of Indian Prime Minister Narendra Modi's visit to Kazan, Russia, for the 16th BRICS Summit.

On 21 October 2024 came an understated announcement, buried in a routine briefing. After detailing the prime minister's agenda, in response to questions about potential bilateral meetings, Foreign Secretary Vikram Misri informed that India and China had agreed upon 'patrolling arrangements', 'leading to disengagement and a resolution of the issues that had arisen in

---

[3]Ministry of External Affairs, 'Statement by External Affairs Minister, Dr. S. Jaishankar in Lok Sabha', 3 December 2024, https://tinyurl.com/5n7n54xz. Accessed on 10 November 2025.

these areas in 2020.'[4] The two countries were turning the page on years of tensions. The details were sketchy but the stage was set for a meeting between Modi and China's leader Xi Jinping.

The signals that emerged from Kazan were positive. Both sides seemed keen to put the acrimony of the past few years behind them in order to explore a new balance in the relationship. From the Chinese perspective, the call was for India to adhere to the view that both sides are 'development opportunities for each other, and do not constitute threats to each other.'[5] The Indian side stressed that it sought engagement to build a 'stable, predictable, and amicable' relationship with China.[6] To this end, both agreed to resume all-round dialogue at different levels.

Expectations for a quick turnaround in the relationship, however, remained very low. This has been borne out by the slow grind of the process of normalization. Following Kazan, the early meetings between officials at the highest levels yielded few breakthroughs. This was the case despite negotiations focusing on what are terribly low-hanging fruits, such as the resumption of the Kailash Mansarovar Yatra, re-establishment of direct flight connectivity, issuance of visas, clearances for journalists and data sharing on trans-border rivers. For instance, in November 2024, the two foreign ministers met on the sidelines of a G20 meeting in Rio de Janeiro. This was followed by the 23rd Meeting of the Special Representatives on the boundary issue in Beijing in

---

[4]Ministry of External Affairs, 'Transcript of Special Briefing by Foreign Secretary on Prime Minister's Visit to Russia', 21 October 2024, https://tinyurl.com/524275v6. Accessed on 10 November 2025.

[5]Ministry of Foreign Affairs of the People's Republic of China, 'Xi Jinping meets with Indian Prime Minister Modi', 24 October 2024, https://tinyurl.com/4ydjwke3. Accessed on 10 November 2025.

[6]Ministry of External Affairs, 'Meeting of Prime Minister with Mr. Xi Jinping, President of the People's Republic of China on the Margins of the 16th BRICS Summit', 23 October 2024, https://tinyurl.com/mvyhu6t2. Accessed on 10 November 2025.

December 2025—the first such meeting in five years. Thereafter, in late January, Foreign Secretary Vikram Misri travelled to Beijing to meet Chinese officials. Each of these meetings referenced the goal of restoring basic connectivity between the two countries, but tangible progress remained elusive. The first significant achievement, however, came after a five-year hiatus in June 2025, with Indian pilgrims returning to Tibet for the Kailash Mansarovar Yatra, which was halted after the 2020 Galwan clash and travel restrictions owing to Covid-19. The two sides continued to maintain high-level official dialogue through the summer. Defence Minister Rajnath Singh and National Security Advisor Ajit Doval, followed by External Affairs Minister S. Jaishankar, travelled to China to attend meetings under the Shanghai Cooperation Organisation (SCO) framework. These visits offered opportunities for direct contact with their Chinese counterparts. This process eventually yielded some fruit during Chinese Foreign Minister Wang Yi's brief visit to Delhi in August. The visits resulted in agreements to establish an expert group to explore early harvest in boundary delimitation in the India-China border areas, a working group to advance effective border management, and the creation of General-Level Mechanisms in the Eastern and Middle Sectors of the boundary. Both sides also agreed to resume border trade through the three designated trading points, while committing to put economic, people-to-people engagement and other issues back on the bilateral agenda. The Chinese side characterized this as a 'dual-track' approach.[7] This implied that both sides would progress on thorny issues related to the boundary while pursuing broader easing in the relationship. Nevertheless, both sides have retained the large troop deployment along the LAC, with de-escalation still elusive.

---

[7]Ministry of Foreign Affairs of People's Republic of China, 'China and India Hold Special Representatives' Talks on the Boundary Question', 19 August 2025, https://tinyurl.com/3ubsn4yp. Accessed on 10 November 2025.

Wang's visit also paved the way for Modi to travel to Tianjin for the SCO summit in early September. The discussions there yielded few tangible outcomes, but the two leaders did arrive at a consensus that India and China were 'development partners and not rivals, and that their differences should not turn into disputes.'[8] Alas, turning this consensus into material reality is going to prove extremely difficult. Fundamental differences persist in terms of how the two sides approach trade, the issue of terrorism, regional balance of power, governance of emerging technologies and, in particular, the boundary issue.

For instance, the Indian side continues to contend that peace and tranquillity at the border remain central to building a stable relationship. In his December 2024 statement before Parliament on the negotiations with China, External Affairs Minister S. Jaishankar essentially acknowledged that India had accepted the altered status quo in eastern Ladakh as part of the disengagement deal. Nevertheless, he reiterated that the 'maintenance of peace and tranquillity in border areas is a pre-requisite for the development' of the bilateral relationship.[9]

The Chinese leadership, meanwhile, insists that the two sides 'should never allow bilateral relations to be defined by the boundary question, or let specific differences affect the overall picture of bilateral ties.'[10] In other words, Beijing would like to de-link economic, political and people-to-people ties from the

[8]Ministry of External Affairs, 'Prime Minister's bilateral meeting with Chinese President Xi Jinping', 31 August 2025, https://tinyurl.com/3fn5cw99. Accessed on 10 November 2025.

[9]Ministry of External Affairs, 'Statement by External Affairs Minister, Dr S. Jaishankar in Lok Sabha', 3 December 2024, https://tinyurl.com/5n7n54xz. Accessed on 10 November 2025.

[10]Ministry of Foreign Affairs of People's Republic of China, 'Member of the Political Bureau of the CPC Central Committee and Foreign Minister Wang Yi Meets the Press', 7 March 2025, https://tinyurl.com/3a97zjhn. Accessed on 10 November 2025.

developments along the boundary. Such compartmentalization, however, is inimical to ensuring stability and predictability in the relationship. It is simply untenable for any Indian government to maintain a normal relationship with China or follow a business-as-usual approach if the boundary remains live and volatile. Chinese diplomats clearly grasp this notion well, considering that this is precisely the argument that they have proffered to their American counterparts over the past few years. For instance, in March 2025, Chinese Foreign Minister Wang Yi lashed out at what he argued were 'two-faced acts' of American policy towards China. 'No country should fantasize that it can suppress China and maintain good relations with China at the same time,' declared Wang.[11]

The difference in perception with regard to the treatment of the issue of peace and tranquillity on the boundary is a critical fault line in the India-China relationship. However, this fault line is a symptom of a deeper problem, i.e., of Beijing's perception of the balance of power between the two countries and New Delhi's anxieties regarding a two-front threat undermining India's rise.

In this context, describing the post-Kazan trajectory of the relationship as a process of normalization is perhaps a misnomer. It implies the possibility of returning to a previous status quo. Such an assumption is not only misplaced but potentially dangerous. For analysts, this risks clouding judgment. For policymakers, lawmakers, businesses and civil society in India, clinging to such an illusion could prove to be a costly miscalculation. What must be arrived at is a new *modus vivendi*.

---

[11]Ministry of Foreign Affairs People's Republic of China, 'Wang Yi: China and the United States Must Seek Peaceful Co-Existence on This Planet', 7 March 2025, https://tinyurl.com/ynft9x34. Accessed on 10 November 2025.

Tender yet Tethered Threads

Historically, the relationship between the modern Indian and Chinese states has been characterized by strands of cooperation, competition and even conflict. These continue to coexist, although increasingly both countries seem to be viewing each other through the threat rather than opportunity prism. Consequently, competition and volatility have become the defining characteristics of the relationship. This situation is likely to persist for the foreseeable future, owing to three structural factors. Each of these deserves deeper consideration.

First, both India and China are rising powers and major economies. Over the past 35 years, the two countries have witnessed simultaneous expansion in their respective geopolitical footprints and national capacities. The fall of the Soviet Union and the end of the Cold War presented both countries with new geopolitical realities. The emergence of American unipolarity posed significant challenges but also fresh opportunities. This moment also came at a time when India and China were embarking on a historic process of re-engagement, which was launched by Prime Minister Rajiv Gandhi's 1988 visit to Beijing. Despite this, in the decades that followed, suspicion of each other coexisted with a desire to cooperate. The former was evident in Prime Minister Atal Bihari Vajpayee's letter to President Bill Clinton after the 1998 Indian nuclear test, which referenced the threat that India faced from a nuclear China.[12] The latter was reflected in the euphoria around the idea of *Chindia*, coined by Jairam Ramesh in the early years of the 21st century.[13] However, towards the end of

---

[12]Vajpayee, Atal Bihari. 'Text of a Letter Sent Monday to President Clinton from Indian Prime Minister Atal Bihari Vajpayee', *Nuclear Weapons Archive, n.d.*, https://tinyurl.com/mudd648m. Accessed on 10 November 2025.

[13]Ramesh, Jairam, *Making Sense of Chindia: Reflections on China and India*. India Research Press, New Delhi, 2005, https://tinyurl.com/cvp2bmkj. Accessed on 10 November 2025.

the first decade of the 2000s, it was evident that greater discord was brewing. This was not simply a product of the lack of trust or divergent perceptions of each other. The expansion of interest and capabilities were driving factors.

Since then, on legacy issues, such as the disputed land boundary between the two countries, enhanced capabilities have resulted in greater friction and jockeying for advantage. For instance, on more than one occasion, Chinese officials have cited India's border infrastructure development as being among the reasons for the standoff in eastern Ladakh. Likewise, assessments by Indian security officials and former diplomats have made the point that infrastructure improvements are leading to more frequent engagements between the two forces as well as rapid mobilization capacities.

India and China's simultaneous rise has also meant that both now have expanding and intersecting circles of interests, which are leading to new sources of contention. This has been evident in New Delhi's frustration with Beijing's deepening engagement in the Indian subcontinent and the Indian Ocean Region. China is among the leading trade and investment partners for India's neighbours. The advancement of the China-Pakistan Economic Corridor, regardless of New Delhi's protests that it violates Indian sovereignty, along with Chinese investments and arms sales in the Indian subcontinent, are further examples of this phenomenon. Likewise, India today has deeper stakes in China's periphery. Almost 55 per cent of India's trade with the Indo-Pacific region passes through the South China Sea.[14] Recent years have seen a significant deepening of India's trade and technology ties with Taiwan, and defence ties with Vietnam and the Philippines. Concurrently, New Delhi has intensified efforts to engage Central

[14]Pant, Harsh V., 'The strategic signal of an Indian presence in the South China Sea', *Observer Research Foundation*, 2 September 2021, https://tinyurl.com/2fr5crka. Accessed on 10 November 2025.

Asia through high-level diplomatic initiatives. India's increasing public rebuking of Chinese policies in the South China Sea and criticism of the opacity of economically unviable BRI projects[15] that result in unsustainable debt burdens underscore fundamental clashes of interests with China.

Second, while both countries have experienced a simultaneous rise, the pace of this growth has been sharply uneven, favouring China. This divergence stems from a combination of domestic political factors, differing approaches to economic policy, and contrasting abilities to adapt to a changing global environment. China launched market-oriented reforms under Deng Xiaoping in the late 1970s, more than a decade ahead of India. Despite significant internal debates on the direction of economic and foreign policy through the 1980s and 1990s, the Chinese party-state system endured with the logic of prioritizing growth. The leadership, therefore, capitalized on the opportunities of economic globalization by easing access to land, labour, water and electricity, attracting global capital and technology, and investing heavily in infrastructure and connectivity. Over the decades, these choices enabled China to emerge as a central node in global industrial supply chains. In contrast, India's reforms moved more cautiously and unevenly, constrained by the pressures of electoral politics, limited state capacity, the complexities of federalism, and local political economy dynamics. The policy differences were reflected in GDP growth rates, with the Chinese economy's expansion significantly outpacing that of the Indian economy. This difference grew even starker after China joined the World Trade Organization in 2001.

Consequently, structurally, there now exists a deep power asymmetry between the two countries. From a state of near-parity

---

[15]Ministry of External Affairs, 'Official Spokesperson's response to a query on participation of India in OBOR/BRI Forum', Government of India, 13 May 2017, https://tinyurl.com/m4cm2hfu. Accessed on 10 November 2025.

in the early 1990s, the Chinese economy has grown to be more than five times the size of the Indian economy. In addition, over the years, China has been far more effective than India in channelizing the gains from rapid GDP growth towards the development of human capital and hard power capabilities. For instance, at present, the UNDP Human Development Index ranks China at 78, faring far better than India, ranked 130, on key social indicators regarding health and education.[16] Improvements along these parameters are significant factors in sustaining the gains made in alleviating poverty, which is again an area in which China's record has been far stronger than India's. In addition, rapid GDP growth has permitted China's defence spending to expand significantly in absolute terms, while officially hovering at around roughly 1.5 per cent of GDP.[17] China's official defence budget for 2025 was estimated at around $246 billion.[18] This, however, is an understatement. The United States Department of Defense estimates that China's official military budget omits several major categories of expenditures, which could account for 40–90 per cent more than the announced budget.[19] Even if one takes the official $246 billion at face value, China spends more on defence than any country in the world except the US, and over three times India's defence allocation. Despite the recent slowdown in China's growth, this gap is unlikely to be bridged anytime soon.

---

[16]UNDP, 'Human Development Insights', 6 May 2025, https://tinyurl.com/5cmty5zv. Accessed on 10 November 2025.

[17]Kumar, Atul, 'Chinese Defence Budget 2025: Lower Allocation, Bigger Impact', *Observer Research Foundation*, 29 March 2025, https://tinyurl.com/yj9yzvub. Accessed on 10 November 2025.

[18]Chen, Laurie and Greg Torode, 'China maintains defence spending increase at 7.2% amid roiling geopolitical tensions', *Reuters*, 5 March 2025, https://tinyurl.com/5n7y72wj. Accessed on 10 November 2025.

[19]US Department of Defense, 'Military and Security Developments Involving the People's Republic of China 2024', 2024, https://tinyurl.com/yzfbz755. Accessed on 10 November 2025.

Beyond its material implications, the strategic predicament generated by such asymmetry lies in the shifting perceptions of the self, the other, and the relative balance of power. In other words, Beijing views itself as a major or great power, and it believes that the essence of power lies in its exercise. Policy, therefore, flows from this self-perception. After all, what value does power hold if it cannot be exercised? And can a state truly be considered a great power if it cannot shape favourable political outcomes through the capabilities it has cultivated? This mindset is reflected in China's active and assertive global diplomacy—articulated through the framework of building a community of shared future for humankind—and increasing use of force along its periphery.

Conceptually, this is captured in Xi's May 2023 call for China's security apparatus to emphasise 'extreme-case thinking' as part of its planning efforts.[20] Chinese discourse describes extreme-case thinking as a method of thinking that pushes problems or phenomena under study to their extreme states for consideration. In other words, it is about figuring out what one should do and what can be done in extreme situations. Chinese analysts contend that extreme-case thinking allows one to distil the 'essence of a problem' and think about what is and what isn't within one's capabilities, permitting 'one to see farther and take further action than others.'[21] In other words, extreme-case thinking is not just about preparing for the worst from a defensive position. It is also a useful tool to think through the outcomes of proactive or assertive actions that China might take. Chinese writers note that extreme-case thinking not only addresses the question of

---

[20]'Xi Jinping presided over the first meeting of the 20th Central National Security Commission and stressed accelerate the modernization of national security system and capabilities to safeguard the new development pattern with a new security pattern', *People's Daily*, 31 May 2023, http://paper.people.com.cn/rmrb/html/2023-05/31/nw.D110000renmrb_20230531_1-01.htm. Accessed on 10 November 2025.

[21]Ibid.

'what should I do', it also answers the question 'what will the other do.'[22] In that sense, it is about playing out scenarios of reactions to Chinese moves, functioning as a type of crisis and conflict simulation. Xi's reference to this is indicative of the desire to proactively use coercive tools like the military instrument to deter and achieve favourable outcomes or to 'create opportunities and seize chances.'[23] That said, it is worth highlighting that since the 1980s, Chinese leaders have demonstrated what analysts have called 'strategic discipline' when it comes to matters of war and peace.[24] In other words, they have eschewed formal alliances and costly wars in favour of focusing on amassing national power. Even under Xi Jinping, China's use of force has generally been calibrated to leverage its military advantage in order to test the adversary's red lines and alter the ground situation while avoiding escalation into all-out conflict.

Consequently, it is imperative for Indian policymakers, defence planners and strategic affairs thinkers to identify comprehensive approaches aimed at narrowing the prevailing asymmetry with China. Importantly, even in the event of a substantive slowdown in China's growth, this asymmetry is likely to endure in the decades ahead. Hence, the objective should not be parity in every domain, but rather identifying key areas where the gap must be narrowed. Bridging asymmetry does not mean matching capabilities across the board; rather, it entails building sufficient capacity in specific domains to alter the adversary's strategic calculus. Achieving this is not a matter of a single policy intervention. It requires

[22]Shuhui, Zhou, 'Let's talk about bottom-line thinking and extreme-case thinking', *Xinxiang Review Issue 15 2023*, 5 August 2023, https://tinyurl.com/2ryn269h. Accessed on 10 November 2025.

[23]Sicong, Yang, 'Dialectically apply bottom-line thinking & extreme-case thinking', *PLA Daily*, 13 July 2023, https://tinyurl.com/3kzadxmf. Accessed on 10 November 2025.

[24]Wuthnow, Joel, and Phillip C. Saunders, *China's Quest for Military Supremacy*, Polity Books, Cambridge, 2025.

a holistic, multidimensional approach. This includes sustained investment in economic growth, the development of indigenous defence capabilities, and a robust external balancing strategy, as evidenced by India's partnerships with countries such as the US, France, Russia, Australia and Japan.

The Story's Three-Way

Third, the shifting balance of power between the United States and China, the changing nature of their bilateral engagement and the churn in the global order towards greater chaos and conflict are impinging on Sino-Indian ties.[25] The past decade has witnessed the gradual re-emergence of great power competition, with the United States and China being the chief protagonists. While significant disparities exist, assessed on broad metrics of power, the two countries are today *the* dominant global actors. Competition across all domains—ideology, geopolitics, security, economics, and science and technology—is increasingly becoming the dominant prism in both Beijing and Washington. That said, nearly three decades of economic globalization has built deep linkages between Chinese and American economic and science and technology ecosystems. It has also resulted in the creation of an unprecedented web of interconnected supply chains, powering the global economy. The Chinese economy is central to these networks and the health of the world economy. Shattering these bonds, therefore, will be a lengthy process and will come at significant costs. This has been evident in the tussle between the two countries since Donald Trump's return to the White House in January 2025.

Both China and the United States also have their own

[25]Pai, Nitin, and Lt General Prakash Menon, 'India's Path to Power: Strategy in a World Adrift', *Takshashila Institution*, 2 October 2021, https://tinyurl.com/y6xn5k8p. Accessed on 10 November 2025.

grievances with the existing international institutional architecture and are engaging in a certain degree of revisionism. However, neither appears to be driven by a revolutionary zeal to upend the UN-centred system. Beijing has talked a good game when it comes to multilateralism and supporting the UN-centred international order. For all the comparisons to Mao Zedong, Xi Jinping's global vision is unlike the revolution that Mao sought. On the contrary, it is rooted in a certain pragmatism. Xi has repeatedly talked about the need to adhere to the sovereign equality of states, pursue greater democracy in international relations, adhere to respect for diversity in international relations, resolve disputes peacefully, and oppose concepts like hegemonism and bloc mentality. China's actions, however, have often run contrary to the spirit of this rhetoric. This has been evident in the frothy waters of the South China Sea, as it is along the treacherous terrain of the LAC with India or with regards to the prickly issues of terrorism, trade and reform of global institutions. Even when it comes to the much-vaunted principle of sovereign equality, China's actions in Ukraine fall short of its words. For all the high-sounding language, Beijing's actions indicate that it views power as the fundamental currency in international relations. And the pathway to maximize its power is through dominating its periphery and leveraging partnerships to reform the institutional architecture of global governance to suit its interests.

US policy, on the other hand, appears to be riddled with ideological confusion. Is the Trumpian worldview one that seeks isolationism through scaling back America's global commitments or one of reconsidering priorities and pursuing greater burden sharing with allies and partners as pathways to maintaining American primacy? Does Make America Great Again (MAGA) desire jettisoning the idea of America as defined by the classical liberal ideals of its founding texts in favour of a narrow ethno-religious definition of American civilization? And by extension, is its vision for the world one that is carved into geographical and civilizational spheres of influence among great powers or one of the universality of certain values, even if not liberal values, realized through the international institutional order? One can identify elements of each of these impulses in American policy since Trump's return to power.

Therefore, it appears that revisionism rather than revolution is what both are pursuing. More importantly, even if revolution were an ambition, as some sections of Trump's MAGA coalition seem to indicate, both countries are evidently inhibited by the constraints of their resources, capacities, domestic politics and global appeal. Consequently, as part of this competition, both sides are seeking to tilt the balance of power in their favour, while stymieing the other's progress. This is creating threats but also opportunities for other actors, who are eyeing capability enhancement, autonomy of action and greater bargaining power. In this context, India is a key pivot state, with both Washington and Beijing adopting very different approaches to influence policy in New Delhi.

Beijing has repeatedly publicly stated that it wants both India and China to 'view their bilateral relations in the context of the once-in-a-century changes in the world.'[26] This simply implies that the Chinese side wants New Delhi to accommodate Chinese interests, given the altered global balance of power and the asymmetry between India and China. To achieve this, China has largely sought to use tools of coercion to shape and constrain India's choices. In doing so, it has also demonstrated increased risk-tolerance and willingness to use force. Over the past decade, Chinese policies have shifted from being unaccommodating of India's interests and rise to being hostile and adversarial. This has been evident in several domains. For starters, there has been a steady escalation of tensions along the disputed land boundary. Despite disengagement in eastern Ladakh, an estimated

[26]Xinhua, 'China, India promise to improve bilateral relations', *XinhuaNet*, 3 March 2023, https://tinyurl.com/y7j4jba2. Accessed on 10 November 2025.

50,000–60,000 troops on either side remain forward-deployed.[27]

Over the years, China has leveraged Pakistan as a strategic asset by bolstering its nuclear and conventional defence capabilities, while shielding it from criticism and consequences in international forums. In essence, it has sought to exacerbate India's security anxieties and constrain its strategic reach to the subcontinent. The intense conflict between India and Pakistan in May 2025 reflected some of these themes rather clearly. At the same time, China has consistently opposed India's entry into key international forums, including the Nuclear Suppliers Group and a permanent seat on the UN Security Council. This has been the case despite repeated high-level diplomatic attempts at a thaw in the past decade, capped off by the two informal summits in Wuhan in 2018 and Mamallapuram in 2019. Beijing has also been rather dismissive of Indian concerns around cross-border terrorism, as evident by its episodic stalling of listing of Pakistan-based terrorists in the UN Security Council's ISIL (Da'esh) & Al-Qaida Sanctions List. Chinese coercion has been evident in the economic domain. In the past few years, the Chinese government has blocked the exports of tunnel-boring machines and fertilizers bound for India, only to later ease this as part of a political process. It has also moved extremely slowly on issuing licences to Indian firms under its new rare-earths export control regime. Meanwhile, a range of non-tariff barriers that it places continue to deny key Indian exports, such as pharmaceuticals, services, digital and entertainment products, access to the Chinese market. Consequently, any future India-China engagement is likely to be encumbered by low levels of political trust, tensions along what are likely to remain live borders in India's north, east and west, and Beijing's anxieties regarding a rising India and its deepening

---

[27]Dutta, Amrita Nayak, 'India, China agree to maintain stability along LAC, continue existing border mechanisms', *The Indian Express*, 30 October 2025, https://tinyurl.com/487pdkyc. Accessed on 10 November 2025.

ties with the US. Any cooperation, even at multilateral forums, is likely to be difficult and transactional.

The United States, on the other hand, has sought to build a deeper strategic partnership with India. This has been driven by a convergence of interests and shared values. Over the past two decades, the India-US relationship has grown by leaps and bounds. The United States is among India's biggest trading partners. Security ties have also strengthened, particularly picking up pace after the signing of foundational defence agreements. For instance, the US designated India as a Major Defense Partner in 2016. As per the US Department of State, defence trade with India has expanded from near-zero in 2008 to over $20 billion in 2020.[28] This is expected to further expand and deepen. The two countries are now cooperating more deeply in the exchange and development of critical and emerging technologies.[29] There has also been greater diplomatic and intelligence engagement between the two sides, across a range of issues. In particular, the US has played a key role in augmenting India's capabilities to counter threats, particularly through intelligence and defence cooperation. It is also noteworthy that the official US Indo-Pacific Strategy[30] under the Joe Biden administration expressly supported India's rise and regional leadership. This approach, however, appears to be shifting since the re-election of Donald Trump as President.

Although the early months of 2025 seemed to indicate continuity in US policy with regard to India, the relationship

---

[28]Bureau of Political-Military Affairs, 'U.S. Security Cooperation With India', US Department of State, 20 January 2025, https://tinyurl.com/38henmae. Accessed on 10 November 2025.

[29]The White House Briefing Room, 'FACT SHEET: United States and India Elevate Strategic Partnership with the initiative on Critical and Emerging Technology (iCET)', 31 January 2023, https://tinyurl.com/ybvpvdvr. Accessed on 10 November 2025.

[30]The White House, 'Indo-Pacific Strategy of the United States', February 2022, https://tinyurl.com/43zzux3e. Accessed on 10 November 2025.

appeared to crater through summer and fall. The administration's imposition of 50 per cent tariffs on select Indian exports in August, Trump's repeated claims of having brokered a ceasefire between India and Pakistan in May, US officials' intemperate comments about the Indian economy and society, increasing incidents of racism targeting Indian immigrants in the US and America's courting of Pakistan have severely strained political trust. Meanwhile, Trump's alienation of partners of allies along with his preference of dealing with China bilaterally has further undermined the strategic logic of the relationship. That said, the two sides remain in dialogue on a trade deal; the security pillar of the relationship has remained largely unimpeded by the broader turbulence; and the tug-o-war between Washington and Beijing on issues of economic security are unlikely to be resolved easily. Therefore, while the political relationship is tense and trust is fractured, structural factors still point to a congruence of interests between India and the US.

That said, New Delhi is observing the shifting dynamic of cooperation and contention in Sino-US relations. Indian policymakers and strategic affairs thinkers do not tend to view the US-China relationship as a zero-sum game. Rather, they believe that it exhibits strands of cooperation—albeit deeply strained—and contention. India's engagement with both, therefore, has been primarily rooted in pragmatism, prioritizing strategic interests, while being mindful of factors like geography, values and legacy. Issue-based tents rather than ideological camps are what India prefers. This has necessitated maintaining a certain degree of strategic autonomy.

Consequently, in responding to the fluidity in Sino-US ties, New Delhi has worked to deepen its relationship with Washington while adjusting to a new, factious equation with Beijing. In addition, it has sought to diversify its outreach with a broader set of partners through new mini-lateral arrangements, or issue-based coalitions. Jaishankar's contention that 'we are now entering a world of greater plurilateralism' underscores this dynamic.[31] The key aspect of this new world, he believes, would be the emergence of 'greater localization and arrangements of pragmatism.'[32]

To summarize, it is important to underline that beyond history, geography, political mistrust and trade imbalances, there are structural dynamics that are driving Sino-Indian competition. At the heart of all of this is a deeper, strategic contestation for the future direction of order in Asia. New Delhi believes that the Asian Century—implying a 'greater weight for Asia in the overall global calculus'—necessitates 'a modus vivendi among its key players,' resulting in a new form of multipolarity.[33] In addition, it stands against what it says is a vision of 'narrow Asian chauvinism.' China, on the other hand, views the future of the Asian order from the perspective of its geopolitical rivalry with the United States.[34] In this context, it has frequently argued for building an Asia for Asians. In practice, its approach, however, has essentially stripped other actors of their agency and engendered a desire for unipolarity.

Future Is in Our Hands

Given the above, how should India deal with the challenges and opportunities that China's rise presents? To this end, the past can often shine a light for future action.

---

[31]Ministry of External Affairs, 'Keynote address by the External Affairs Minister at the 5th Indian Ocean Conference 2021', Government of India, 4 December 2021, https://tinyurl.com/yc46wbzb. Accessed on 10 November 2025.

[32]Ibid.

[33]Ministry of External Affairs, 'Remarks by External Affairs Minister, Dr. S. Jaishankar at the launch of Asia Society Policy Institute,' Government of India, 29 August 2022, https://tinyurl.com/3kxmp3ak. Accessed on 10 November 2025.

[34]Ministry of Foreign Affairs of the People's Republic of China, 'Foreign Minister Qin Gang Meets the Press', 7 March 2023, https://tinyurl.com/4ze9kmsc. Accessed on 10 November 2025.

Despite the tense standoff in Sumdorong Chu in the eastern sector along the McMahon Line, PM Rajiv Gandhi's visit to Beijing in 1988 provided the basis for the two countries to embark on a new path. The visit yielded a broad political understanding that the two sides would engage in more purposeful negotiations on the boundary issue while endeavouring to maintain peace and tranquillity in the interim. In addition, they would focus on developmental issues, seek to better manage conflicts of interest where their peripheries overlapped, and cooperate where broader interests coincided. In the years that followed, sustained engagement by both sides led to the inking of key agreements that helped keep the peace along the land boundary. It is worth bearing in mind that through much of the early phase of this process, soldiers from both sides continued to hold their positions in Sumdorong Chu. Disengagement from eyeball-to-eyeball confrontation only took place in 1995.

History seldom repeats itself; it does, however, tend to rhyme. The world today is far different from that of 1988 or even 1995. Decades of economic globalization have created new dynamics of dependencies. Technological advancements have aided the transformation of business, politics and social interactions. And the international balance of power is undergoing a transition towards a form of uneven multipolarity. These shifts are leading states to redefine terms of engagement. Perceptions of risk and conceptualization of security have expanded. A cascade of conflicts appears to be unfolding amid the major powers' inability to impose their will or act in concert through the UN-centred international system. States are also increasingly looking inward, while seeking more fluid political alignments with international partners. In this background, great power competition between China and the US is shaping a new order and influencing the policy environment of countries like India. Amid this, neither extreme, i.e., a Cold War-style rivalry between China and the US or a coexistence that results in American acceptance of Chinese primacy in Asia, serves Indian interests. A Cold War-like scenario narrows India's options and potentially places it on a volatile frontline. US accommodation of China fundamentally alters Asia's balance of power adversely for India.

Beijing appears to desire New Delhi's acquiescence to its primacy in Asia. The Chinese leadership is well aware that no great power has risen globally without first commanding its neighbourhood. Consequently, China desires that India limit the nature of its engagement with the US, maintain economic openness to China and be accommodative of Chinese interests in the Indian subcontinent. In contrast, what New Delhi seems to want from Beijing is accommodation of its interests and aspirations as a rising power. This would require China to take into account Indian concerns across a wide range of domains, from land boundary and trade to ties with India's neighbours and even at multilateral forums. In essence, it would entail China accepting multipolarity in Asia, despite the power differential with India. On the surface, these two propositions appear irreconcilable. Intense contestation, perhaps even confrontation or conflict, therefore seems inevitable. Such an outcome is not necessarily in India's strategic interest, and calls for deeper thought on how a new balance can be arrived at in the relationship with China.

Good strategy is not about reconciling the irreconcilable. Instead, it involves maximizing the resources and options at one's disposal to shape favourable outcomes. In other words, rather than worry about the irreconcilable nature of the end states desired by each, the focus of Indian strategy and diplomacy should be on cultivating strength and creating new pathways that can enhance stability and predictability in ties. In the aftermath of Operation Sindoor in May 2025, Prime Minister Modi articulated this notion when he said that 'the path of peace also goes through power. Humanity should move towards peace and prosperity. Every Indian should be able to live in peace, and can fulfill the dream of Viksit Bharat (Developed India). For this, it is very necessary for India to be powerful.'[35]

Building on this principle, Indian policymakers must grasp that bridging the power differential with China is key to negotiating a new modus vivendi. This is evidently already the case in some quarters. For instance, speaking at a public lecture in January 2025, External Affairs Minister S. Jaishankar was categorial in assessing that 'India has to prepare for expressions of China's growing capabilities, particularly those that impinge directly on our interests. To hold up its own end, a more rapid development of India's comprehensive national power is necessary.'[36]

However, in order to achieve this expansion of national power, ensuring sustained economic growth and internal social stability are necessary conditions. These will allow India to invest in sources of strength that enhance its negotiating position. At a fundamental level this means avoiding unforced errors. Shifting the domestic political paradigm away from economic growth towards redistribution or enhanced state control over the economy will be deeply detrimental. Rather, policy must focus on better provision of better public goods, boosting economic freedom and being open to foreign capital, talent and technologies, development of infrastructure, military strength and science and technology capabilities along with improvements in education, employment and social security. This is a foundational premise that underpins the strategic outlook advocated in this book.

---

[35]Prime Minister's Office, 'English Rendering of PM's Address to the Nation', *Press Information Bureau,* 12 May 2025, https://tinyurl.com/2s4enbtz. Accessed on 10 November 2025.

[36]Ministry of External Affairs, 'Remarks by External Affairs Minister, Dr. S. Jaishankar at Nani Palkhivala Memorial Lecture "India and the World"',18 January 2025, https://tinyurl.com/2wcvjf8f. Accessed on 10 November 2025.

Planning, Possibilities, Policies

With this context, we offer the following set of concrete policy recommendations. These are examined in greater detail in the chapters that follow.

First, on the specific issue of the standoff in eastern Ladakh, disengagement should not imply the acceptance of the altered status quo. India should continue to insist on restoration of all patrolling rights and new confidence-building measures. That said, considering the current circumstances, any meaningful movement to resolve the boundary issue is highly unlikely. There is little evidence that the Chinese leadership is interested in a resolution. In fact, given the nature of negotiations during the standoff in eastern Ladakh, it is clear that Beijing is likely to continue to leverage the boundary dispute to pressurize New Delhi. In addition, China today boasts of the world's largest navy, which is rapidly developing blue-water capabilities. Although basing will remain a long-term challenge for China, it is only a matter of time that a Chinese carrier group sails through the Indian Ocean. Indian policymakers and military leaders must, therefore, be prepared for a certain degree of volatility in the years ahead. Consequently, it is imperative to strengthen deterrence capabilities, and be prepared to escalate when faced with aggression in order to deter and/or achieve de-escalation. This calls for significant enhancements in India's defence budget, and better rationalization of expenditures to facilitate greater firepower development. Simultaneously, efforts to enhance border infrastructure must continue, and support for border populations must be intensified, and cyberspace defences in the critical infrastructure space must be strengthened. With regard to the specific boundary and confidence building agreements that India and China have inked over the years, there needs to be sustained diplomatic engagement to upgrade these to take into account changes in both sides' infrastructure build-up, deployment capacities, technological capabilities, etc.

For guarantees on paper to be adhered to, they need to be backed by force and modalities for dialogue between military commanders at different levels to prevent accidental escalation.

Second, both sides need to demonstrate greater imagination to restore a broader dialogue process. Such a process need not immediately be a high-profile leader-level affair. However, eventually, having periodic meetings between the Chinese President and the Indian Prime Minister are critical. Given the extreme concentration of power by Xi Jinping, head-of-state diplomacy, as the Chinese term it, will be essential as the fulcrum for a broader process. It is important to note that for all the sabre-rattling, keeping the peace with India is also in China's interest, given its increasingly adverse external environment and economic uncertainty at home. From India's perspective, the objective of engagement with China must be rooted in the goal of placing the relationship within a broader strategic context, deepen understanding of each other's interests and policies, clarify red lines along with negotiating modalities of adherence to them by each side, be it along the disputed boundary or within each other's peripheries, and cooperating where interests coincide. This will take time and patience. Leaders can give directions but the interpretation and implementation have to happen at the levels of ministries and lower bureaucracies, with a particular focus on establishing mechanisms for exchanges on strategic and economic issues and on climate change adaptation and mitigation. In addition, India must seek an annual dialogue of the Special Representatives of India and China on the Boundary Question. While a resolution of the boundary issue may be a long way away, New Delhi must insist on clarity with regard to Chinese territorial claims, including exchanges of maps. This process appears to be on the right track for the moment.

Third, India needs to experiment with new approaches to address the development versus security dilemma in its relationship with China. China having greater stakes in the Indian economy is strategically beneficial. The key is to ensure that the stake does not translate to greater ability to coerce. The framework of policy, therefore, should be one of de-risking rather than decoupling. In terms of trade, this entails diversifying partnerships with other actors, being open to Chinese intermediate goods that support technological advancement and exports, and taking restrictive measures to blunt Chinese subsidies in sectors related to emerging technologies and those that are critical to national security. At the same time, India must remain open to Chinese capital and talent, particularly those that aid the development of India's manufacturing sector and deepen linkages with global value chains. This is not to argue that there isn't any need for scrutiny. In fact, a more robust scrutiny mechanism is needed rather than the current ad hoc process. This book proposes the establishment of a new investment review mechanism with clear guidelines, conditions and timelines. This will engender greater predictability for industry, and ensure adequate democratic oversight. As part of this process, it is necessary to delineate a narrow set of sub-sectors as critical from a national security perspective and therefore walled off from Chinese entities. Likewise, it is important to approve a set of sectors and sub-sectors where capital can flow through the automatic route.

Fourth, India must remain open to deepening engagement with the Chinese people. Deeper people-to-people exchanges are an asset for both sides. There is, in fact, an urgent need to cultivate a uniquely Indian perspective on Chinese polity, economy and society. This will not happen if channels of engagement, including digital access to open-source information, are blocked. Furthermore, lack of engagement is likely to accentuate the threat of misperception and misinterpretation of interests and actions. Indian policy should support exchanges among students, scholars, universities, think tanks, tourists and the entertainment and media sectors. The answer to concerns around espionage, and information and influence operations is not to wall off our societies.

Finally, India must continue to deepen and diversify its partnerships with the US and other international actors. In doing so, it must stress to Chinese interlocutors that ties with other actors are driven by Indian interests and not directed at any third party. It is highly unlikely that Beijing will accept any assurances from New Delhi in this regard. Assuaging Beijing's anxieties, however, should not be the goal of Indian policy. That would be tantamount to lending a veto to China on the nature and extent of India's external partnerships. Instead, Indian policy should focus on leveraging external partnerships to build strength across domains. This can help shift the calculus of relative balance of power vis-à-vis China.

Historically, the PRC has viewed India as an inferior regional actor. Hollow rhetoric that is not backed by capability will not remedy this. Only cultivating greater national power through internal and external balancing and dealing with Beijing from a position of strength on bilateral and international issues can remedy this perception. In other words, India does not merely need to enhance its comprehensive national power; it also needs to emerge as a major power in the Chinese mind. This approach could likely lead to some testy exchanges. But, on the whole, it is likely to be a far more effective method to facilitate more meaningful engagement between the two countries.

1

Suspicious Minds: How China and India Think about Each Other

MANOJ KEWALRAMANI

Nation-states are neither abstract nor mechanistic entities. They emerge owing to the collective desire and activity of a human society to organize and govern themselves by a shared set of values, laws, rules and structures. In other words, they emerge owing to the political expression of national will, and are social creations. Be they primitive societies, such as small tribes, or complex multinational ones, the primary impulse to constitute a state is often a shared sense of identity. In large societies, this identity, as Benedict Anderson argued, is largely imagined, cultivated through deliberate efforts to reproduce a sense of commonality and shared experience.[1]

Every nation-state, in that sense, is rooted in and sustained by national stories and myths. In the modern Indian case, some of them deal with the country's colonial past, non-violent struggle, its sacred geography and moral leadership in the world. For the People's Republic of China, an enduring narrative is the one around the Century of Humiliation[2] and the pursuit of wealth

[1]Anderson, Benedict, *Imagined Communities: Reflections on the Origin and Spread of Nationalism. Revised edition*, Verso, London, 2006.

[2]The Century of Humiliation refers to the period in China from the First Opium War (1839) to the founding of the People's Republic of China (1949). This era was marked by military defeats, foreign intervention, and loss of territory to

and power. Some aspects of these myths manifest through tangible symbols, such as the national flag, anthem and emblem. Others tend to be reaffirmed through the rituals of political life, such as elections, parliamentary procedures and norms of governance. And then there are those that seem somewhat incorporeal but omnipresent. These are the narratives a nation-state constructs about itself and its place in the world. They comprise stories of origin, struggle and destiny and often what differentiates one from the other. These are the realities that nation-states construct about themselves, the world around them and the actors that inhabit it. In the process, they give form to what has come to be understood as *national interests*.

These stories, however, are not static or frozen in time. They evolve in their retelling, reshaped by changing historical circumstances, shifting internal ideological balances, evolving perceptions of threat, and the churn of political, social and material conditions. Leadership plays a role, as do interactions with others in the international system, all of which influence how a nation interprets its past, imagines its future, and defines its place in the world. In other words, as stories evolve, so does the narrative on identity and the conceptualization of interests.

For scholars and policymakers, understanding such narratives offers a window into the psyche of an actor—their capabilities and motivations, fears and anxieties and perceptions of others. These are critical given the informational constraints that characterize international politics, where misperceptions are often the rule rather than the exception. Another crucial purpose that narratives serve is that of cultivating strategic empathy.[3] In the modern

---

Western powers and Japan, leading to a narrative of national shame and weakness that continues to influence China's modern foreign policy.

[3]Bohm, Ingela, 'Cultural Sustainability: A Hidden Curriculum in Swedish Home Economics?', *Food, Culture & Society*, Vol. 26, No. 3, 2023, pp. 742–758, https://tinyurl.com/mu38ap33. Accessed on 11 November 2025.

world of social media bombast and hyper-nationalism, this is an underappreciated yet essential trait of diplomacy. It can often spell the difference between effective engagements and costly miscalculations.

From the perspective of the India-China equation, this is an urgent task. Seldom in history have two major powers, who are geographic neighbours, risen together peacefully. Both command large populations, have tremendous military capabilities, including nuclear capabilities, and are among the fastest growing economies in the world. Significantly, both are civilizational states that share a multi-layered history. On one hand, this featured benign and mutually beneficial exchanges between scholars, travellers and merchants, cross-pollination of knowledge and ideas and extensive religious and cultural interactions.[4] The modern echoes of this are evident through the expanding trade and people-to-people relationship between the two sides, along with a desire to collaborate on issues ranging from climate change mitigation to urban governance. On the other hand, the process of creation of the modern Republic of India and People's Republic of China along with the experiences of their early interactions resulted in political, ideological and territorial cleavages that have fostered lasting mistrust. Today, this manifests in debates around economic dependencies, military coercion, perceived disregard for the other's interests, and each one's relationships with other actors within the international system.

For the present and future, India has articulated its vision for the bilateral relationship through the *three-mutuals*: mutual respect, mutual sensitivity, and mutual interests.[5] This framework

---

[4]For a deeper understanding of the early and multi-faceted interactions between the two countries, see Sen, Tansen, *India, China, and the World: A Connected History,* Rowman & Littlefield Pub Inc, 2017.

[5]PTI, '"Three Mutuals" Will Guide India-China Ties: Jaishankar Tells Wang', *Deccan Herald*, 4 July 2024, https://tinyurl.com/mvapdh77. Accessed on 11 November 2025.

reflects a pragmatic approach to the evolving dynamics between the two countries. New Delhi believes that adherence to these principles by both sides can foster a new balance marked by stability and predictability. Notably, the emphasis is not on deeper collaboration or strategic partnership, suggesting a realistic outlook and measured expectations. In contrast, the Chinese framework of the *five-mutuals* is much more ambitious. The five points include: mutual respect, mutual understanding, mutual trust, mutual accommodation and mutual accomplishment.[6] At first glance, while this might seem like petty one-upmanship or merely symbolic and rhetorical flourishes, there is a substantive political message in this framework. Together, the *five-mutuals* signal a desire for a new type of relationship between India and China. Taken on face value, concepts like *mutual accommodation* and *mutual accomplishment* may appear benign or even positive. However, they cannot be interpreted in isolation from the underlying power asymmetry between the two countries, the everyday realities of Chinese policies concerning India's core interests, and the broader geopolitical environment.

It is, therefore, imperative to scratch below the surface and engage with the internal discourses within India and China to unpack the underlying imperatives that shape policy choices. To put it another way, it is important to understand the narratives that India and China tell their own people and the world about each other. Examining these conversations offers valuable insights into each side's ambitions and anxieties, as well as the conceptual frameworks through which they view one another and the world. Such an exercise also permits an understanding of relative strengths and leverage points. This chapter undertakes precisely that task in the following two sections, by exploring recent policy

---

[6]Embassy of the People's Republic of China in the Republic of India, 'H.E. Mr. Xu Feihong, China's ambassador to India publishes an article in The Hindu', 2 August 2024, https://tinyurl.com/4sb746y3. Accessed on 11 November, 2025.

debates within India and China about each other. It concludes with a summary assessment.

The Indian Debate on China

At the highest levels of government, External Affairs Minister S. Jaishankar, who assumed office in March 2019, has emerged as the face of India's China policy, despite the overarching presence of Prime Minister Narendra Modi. This is likely the outcome of a political assessment made after Modi invested significant personal capital in the relationship with China, with little to show for it. Modi's ascent to power in New Delhi in 2014 was accompanied by a sense of optimism about the future of the India-China relationship. As chief minister of Gujarat, he had visited China on several occasions, courting substantial investment.[7] Indian analysts anticipated the new prime minister to adopt a business-minded approach to Beijing, while being tough on territorial and security issues.[8] Chinese analysts were far more upbeat, anticipating Modi to be 'India's "Nixon" who will further propel the China-India relationship.'[9]

Soon after he was sworn in, Modi hosted Xi Jinping in Ahmedabad in September 2014. A year later, the Chinese side reciprocated this effort at hometown diplomacy. This early dialogue resulted in massive commitments on trade and investment. However, these didn't eventually materialize. In early engagements, the Indian side sought reciprocity, calling on Beijing

---

[7]Chowdhury, Debashish Roy, 'Modi and China: Old Friends, New Challenges', *South China Morning Post*, 17 May 2014, https://tinyurl.com/ya8heuba. Accessed on 11 November 2025.

[8]Mohan, Archis, 'China Builds on 'old Ties' with Modi', *Business Standard*, 29 May 2014, https://tinyurl.com/3zkftd7z. Accessed on 11 November 2025.

[9]Dasgupta, Saibal, 'Chinese thinktank hails Narendra Modi as "India's Nixon"', *The Times of India*, 21 May 2014, https://tinyurl.com/5n6czv2b. Accessed on 14 November 2025.

to respect the One-India Policy if it desired India to acknowledge the One-China Policy.[10] Over time, friction between the two sides over border incidents, the Dalai Lama and the Belt and Road Initiative deepened. Ties subsequently hit a low during the 72-day standoff in Doklam in 2017. Chinese media and officials were particularly brusque through this period, with threats and accusations being hurled on a near-daily basis. The Modi-Xi informal summits of 2018 and 2019 were devised as an effort to break through this cycle of mistrust and bureaucratic inertia. However, the People's Liberation Army's (PLA) encroachment at several points across the LAC in eastern Ladakh in May 2020, and the subsequent killing of Indian soldiers in the Galwan Valley resulted in that effort being aborted. With the BJP's reduced parliamentary majority after the 2024 Lok Sabha elections, one assumes that for the party, the political risks of engagement with China have likely heightened.

Following the Galwan Valley clash, in large part, China policy has since been shaped through Jaishankar's formulation that peace and tranquillity on the borders and respect for LAC are essential for normalcy in bilateral relations. The increased use of the Working Mechanism for Consultation and Coordination (WMCC) as part of the dialogue process with regard to the standoff in eastern Ladakh was indicative of the MEA taking the lead in defining the terms of overall engagement with China. In fact, officials from the MEA were even involved in talks at the Corps Commander level. The break in ties after Galwan did not, however, impact India-China dialogue at multilateral platforms or hurt bilateral trade, which has continued to expand. China is one of India's biggest trading partners, enjoying a trade surplus of around $100 billion; this

[10]Tiezzi, Shannon, 'Why China Embraces Narendra Modi', *The Diplomat*, 30 May 2014, https://tinyurl.com/5crk6r8x. Accessed on 11 November 2025.

accounts for nearly 10 per cent of China's total trade surplus[11].

Nevertheless, Jaishankar's dictum generally seems to have found resonance within the foreign service community and armed forces. For instance, while advocating for a strategic dialogue between New Delhi and Beijing, Ashok Kantha, former Indian ambassador to China, has stressed that improvement in bilateral ties should be 'predicated on the restoration of peace, tranquillity and stability in the border areas without compromising India's traditional patrolling and grazing rights along the LAC.'[12] Former Foreign Secretary Vijay Gokhale concurred that Chinese actions in 2020 had brought the boundary issue 'to the front and centre' of the relationship, which cannot be kept aside while one deals with other issues.[13]

Likewise, the public statements of India's military leaders have highlighted the need for greater preparedness and focus on Chinese activities along the land boundary and in the Indian Ocean Region. For instance, former Army Chief General M.M. Naravane has argued that the PLA's aggression in eastern Ladakh was 'not a bad thing', as it forced India from 'shying away from calling out China as the No. 1 threat.'[14] His successor General Manoj Pande

---

[11]The inference is based on the data. China's trade surplus in 2024 was 1 trillion dollars. Its trade surplus with India is around 100 billion. So that's 10 per cent. Macauley, Richard, 'China Trade Surplus Soars to $1 Trillion Ahead of Trump Return', *Bloomberg*, 13 January 2025, https://tinyurl.com/yuxeebfa. Accessed on 14 November 2025.

Jayaswal, Rajeev, and Rezaul H Laskar, 'Beijing moves to soothe India over $100 billion trade deficit', *Hindustan Times*, 12 April 2025, https://tinyurl.com/59u6vdd7. Accessed on 14 November 2025.

[12]Kantha, Ashok K., 'Resetting India-China ties in an era of tensions: Beyond the 'New Normal' at the Border', *Hindustan Times*, 04 May 2024, https://tinyurl.com/3wemezz4. Accessed on 11 November 2025.

[13]*StatNewsGlobal*, 'Need Fresh Start With China: Former Foreign Secretary Vijay Gokhale', *Youtube*, 18 August 2024, https://tinyurl.com/3c2fwjaj. Accessed on 11 November 2025.

[14]The Print Team, 'Chinese Aggression at LAC in 2020 was "Not a Bad Thing",

was emphatic while in office, stating that the northern borders were the 'primary front' going forward.[15] The current Chief of Army Staff General Upendra Dwivedi believes that a 'two-front war threat' for India 'is a reality'.[16] Former Chief of Naval Staff Chief Admiral Hari Kumar, meanwhile, highlighted the threat of 'salami slicing', expressed concerns about tensions in the South China Sea and indicated that maritime dialogue with China was at a standstill since ties were not normal.[17] His successor Dinesh K. Tripathi has pointed to naval cooperation between China and Pakistan, along with the PLA Navy's presence in the Indian Ocean Region as challenges for India.[18] In addition, increasingly, across India's defence academies and think tanks, there have been greater deliberations on dealing with the challenges presented by China's rise.

Tricks of Trade

At a policy level, placing stability at the border at the heart of the relationship has meant that friction has bled into all dimensions of the relationship. After Galwan, the Indian government took

Says Former Army Chief Gen Naravane', *The Print*, 11 February 2024, https://tinyurl.com/258e7pea. Accessed on 11 November 2025.

[15]Baruah, Sanjib Kr, 'Exclusive: 'China Our Primary Front Now', Says Army Chief Gen Manoj Pande', *The Week*, 27 August 2023, https://tinyurl.com/4625xxea. Accessed on 11 November 2025.

[16]Ahuja, Nakul, 'We Must Accept High Degree of Collusion between Pakistan, China: Army Chief', *India Today*, 8 March 2025, https://tinyurl.com/3ba6bfzp. Accessed on 11 November 2025.

[17]Singh, Dalip, 'India Is Not in Dialogue With China on Maritime Challenges, Says Indian Navy Chief', *The Hindu Business Line*, 1 December 2023, https://tinyurl.com/2cz57bpf. Accessed on 11 November 2025.

[18]Tiwary, Deeptiman, 'No Change in Chinese Approach in Indo-Pacific since Ladakh Negotiations: Navy Chief Dinesh Tripathi', *The Indian Express*, 3 December 2024, https://tinyurl.com/fey32jze. Accessed on 11 November 2025.

a series of actions targeting Chinese interests across economic and technology domains, while seeking to partner more closely with the US and its allies. For instance, in late June 2020, the Indian government banned 59 Chinese mobile apps, citing national security concerns.[19] By 2022, that number expanded to 321.[20] Chinese companies operating in India have also faced increasing political and law-enforcement pressure since 2020. The Enforcement Directorate, Income Tax Department and other agencies launched probes into alleged money-laundering, illegal remittances, tax evasion and other financial misconduct by Chinese companies.[21] At one point, reports indicated that there were nearly 700 cases against companies with Chinese nationals as promoters and directors.[22] Even large Chinese entities like Huawei, Xiaomi and Vivo were caught in this maelstrom. Several have also been denied market access. The Indian debate and policy excluding Chinese vendors from key segments of the country's 5G ecosystem and the ban on TikTok are examples of this. In addition, even before the standoff in eastern Ladakh, the Indian government issued Press Note No. 3 in April 2020, adding a level of scrutiny to Chinese investments. The stated goal of this was 'curbing opportunistic takeovers/acquisitions of Indian companies

---

[19]Ministry of Electronics & IT, 'Government Bans 59 mobile apps which are prejudicial to sovereignty and integrity of India, defence of India, security of India, security of state and public order', *PIB*, 29 June 2020, https://tinyurl.com/4a6d4hb8. Accessed on 11 November 2025.

[20]Reuters, 'India adds 54 more Chinese apps to ban list; Sea says it complies with laws', 15 February 2022, https://tinyurl.com/dsdh65hs. Accessed on 11 November 2025.

[21]Bhardwaj, Ananya, 'Chinese giants committing fraud in India? Why Xiaomi, Vivo, Oppo, Huawei are under fire', *The Print*, 1 August 2022, https://tinyurl.com/8872b87a. Accessed on 11 November 2025.

[22]Rajput, Rashmi, '700 cases against Chinese firms suspected of economic disruption', *The Times of India*, 27 April 2022, https://tinyurl.com/zac97fpk. Accessed on 11 November 2025.

due to the current Covid-19 pandemic.'[23] Although the pandemic is now behind us, the restrictions remain in place. In July 2020, the Indian government also essentially blocked Chinese companies from participating in tenders for government procurement by imposing new levels of scrutiny.[24]

In addition, people-to-people relations, which had been impeded by the pandemic, have only deteriorated further, with flight connectivity and travel between the two countries becoming highly restricted. All of this did dampen the mood for others from China who saw India as a potential investment destination.[25] This sentiment was captured by Lu Yang, a research fellow at Tsinghua University's Institute of the Belt and Road Initiative, who surmised that political tensions had resulted in the 'hype of investing in India' waning among Chinese investors.[26] However, this feeling isn't likely to be sticky, particularly as Chinese firms face increasing restrictions across the developed world. In fact, given the geopolitical churn, Chinese officials remain rather keen to ink some sort of a bilateral free trade agreement and investment protection agreement with India.

---

[23]Ministry of Commerce and Industry, 'Review of Foreign Direct Investment (FDI) policy for curbing opportunistic takeovers/acquisitions of Indian companies due to the current COVID-19 pandemic', Government of India, 17 April 2020, https://tinyurl.com/4xxv7sp7. Accessed on 14 November 2025.

[24]Mishra, Asit Ranjan, 'India restricts Chinese companies from participating in public procurement bids', *Livemint*, 24 July 2020, https://tinyurl.com/3rutr583. Accessed on 11 November 2025.

[25]Reuters, 'Xiaomi says India's scrutiny of Chinese firms unnerves suppliers', *India Today*, 12 February 2024, https://tinyurl.com/bdz826cx. Accessed on 11 November 2025.

'Chinese firms adjust strategy, agree to minority stakes in India amid geopolitical tensions', *MoneyControl*, 17 April 2025, https://tinyurl.com/56dh96af. Accessed on 11 November 2025.

Bhaya, Abhishek G., 'Chinese investors 'cautious' about India's likely move to ease restrictions', *CGTN*, 18 February 2021, https://tinyurl.com/ymehfpu7. Accessed on 11 November 2025.

[26]Ibid.

In his statement in Parliament in December 2024, although Jaishankar argued that the 'conclusion of the disengagement phase now allows us to consider other aspects of our bilateral engagement', he added that this must be done 'in a calibrated manner, keeping our national security interests first and foremost.'[27] In doing so, India has also sought to intensify efforts at internal and external balancing. The stated objective of this approach is to arrive at a new modus vivendi with China, premised on the *three-mutuals*.

It is, however, clear that there are differences of opinion between and within different departments and ministries, when it comes to China policy. For instance, there are deep concerns among and within the political and business communities about the imbalanced nature of bilateral trade and the impact of heavily subsidized and cheap Chinese goods on India's manufacturing sector and job growth.[28] Several studies have detailed the deleterious impact of cheap Chinese imports on India's medium, small and micro enterprises.[29] Consequently, the Indian MSME sector has consistently sought greater government protection, which has often taken the form of anti-dumping measures.[30] In fact, concerns around a massive influx of cheap Chinese goods hurting small enterprises was a critical factor in the Indian government's decision to walk away from the Regional

---

[27]Ministry of External Affairs, 'Statement by External Affairs Minister, Dr. S. Jaishankar in Lok Sabha', 3 December, 2024, https://tinyurl.com/2tenp5ey. Accessed on 14 November 2025.

[28]Patnaik, Ila, and Ajay Shah, 'The Case for Trade Barriers against Chinese Imports', *Business Standard*, 24 June 2024, https://tinyurl.com/2fuky47n. Accessed on 14 November 2025.

[29]TOI Business Desk, 'India MSMEs affected because of rising imports from China: GTRI', *The Times of India*, 2 September 2024, https://tinyurl.com/mr2rr9yz. Accessed on 14 November 2025.

[30]Mishra, Ravi Dutta, 'MSMEs raise alarm over steel import duty hikes amid calls for more protection', *The Indian Express*, 6 September 2024, https://tinyurl.com/mupme55b. Accessed on 14 November 2025.

Comprehensive Economic Partnership agreement.[31] These worries have only been amplified amid the deepening of the China-US trade war. Manufacturing overcapacity is a design feature of China's development model. As Western markets close to Chinese products, it is likely that developing countries will experience greater dumping.

Nevertheless, the Indian Commerce Ministry has, on occasion, highlighted the importance of intermediate and capital goods imports from China, which support Indian exports and enable it to rise up the technology value chain.[32] This is an underappreciated aspect of the India-China trade story. Reports over the past year have indicated that key business groups, particularly those with stakes in consumer electronics, automobiles, telecommunications, new energy, and railways are keen on deepening trade and enterprise linkages and removal of barriers from both sides.[33]

At the same time, Commerce Minister Piyush Goyal has periodically baulked at any suggestion that the government is rethinking its restrictive approach vis-à-vis Chinese investments.[34] The most prominent of such comments came after the government's 2024 economic survey called for openness to Chinese capital.[35]

---

[31]'"My Conscience Won't Permit": Why PM Modi Decided to Keep India Away From the RCEP Trade Deal', *News18*, 4 November 2019, https://tinyurl.com/yhfx2ymy. Accessed on 14 November 2025.

[32]PTI, 'India Has Highest Trade Deficit With China but Gap Narrowing: Goyal', *The Economic Times*, 26 July 2024, https://tinyurl.com/2edszpw3. Accessed on 14 November 2025.

[33]Kay, Chris, and John Reed, 'Can India's economy thrive without China's help?', *Financial Times*, 7 August 2024, https://tinyurl.com/3yrxx72r. Accessed on 14 November 2025.

[34]PTI, 'No Rethinking on Supporting Chinese Investments in India: Goyal', *The Hindu*, 30 July 2024, https://tinyurl.com/3yyee4sk. Accessed on 14 November 2025.

[35]Business Today Desk, 'Hindi-Chini, Buy-buy? Economic Survey Makes a Case for FDI From China Despite Ban', *Business Today*, 22 July 2024, https://tinyurl.com/3k8e4e2b. Accessed on 14 November 2025.

In her post-budget press briefing in 2024, Finance Minister Nirmala Sitharaman did not distance herself from that suggestion.[36] Later in the year, it was reported that a new inter-ministerial panel had been established to deliberate on Chinese investments, indicating that a rethinking of approach is underway.[37] Reports over the past 18 months have indicated that the Indian government is open to select investments in the auto, electronics and technology sectors.[38] In mid-2025, NITI Aayog, the government's apex public policy think tank, called for easing of investment scrutiny that was placed on Chinese entities via Press Note No. 3. It recommended that Chinese companies should be allowed to take a stake of up to 24 per cent in an Indian firm without any approval being required.[39]

This debate is far from settled, as is evident from the writings of the country's strategic affairs analysts. Those viewing China from a primarily security and threat-prism contend that arguments for opening up to Chinese FDI are a product of 'poor thought-craft'.[40]

---

[36]Singh, Sarita, and Nikunj Ohri, 'India's Finance Minister backs increasing Chinese direct investment', *Reuters*, 23 July 2024, https://tinyurl.com/5e8ms8ru. Accessed on 14 November 2025.

[37]Rathee, Kiran, 'Forbidden No More: India Begins OKing Chinese Proposals', *The Economic Times*, 22 August 2024, https://tinyurl.com/mvmh2nbh. Accessed on 14 November 2025.

[38]Patra, Shuddhanta, 'India weighs 20-50% Chinese investment in select sectors as Modi-Xi meet in Tianjin', *Financial Express*, 30 August 2025, https://tinyurl.com/2mr3sau4. Accessed on 16 November 2025.

Singh, Rimjhim, 'India may permit Chinese electronic firms to invest on a select basis', *Business Standard*, 2 May 2024, https://tinyurl.com/bdfpkuk3. Accessed on 16 November 2025.

[39]TOI Business Desk, 'FDI landscape: Niti Aayog suggests easing regulations for Chinese investments; 24% stake may be allowed without clearance', *The Times of India*, 19 July 2025, https://tinyurl.com/yswnc56a. Accessed on 14 November 2025.

[40]Chikermane, Gautam, and Kalpit A. Mankikar, 'India's Thought-Craft Needs to Be in Tune with Its Statecraft', *Observer Research Foundation*, 1 August 2024, https://tinyurl.com/3rtf9kpj. Accessed on 14 November 2025.

Others have argued that a selective, sector-specific approach to accepting Chinese FDI and talent, particularly keeping in mind the needs of the electronics and technology sectors, can be beneficial to boost Indian manufacturing and link to global value chains.[41]

Beyond the investment issue, when it comes to trading with China, there are also serious concerns with regard to the single-source concentration risk across several product categories, which can render Indian industry vulnerable. This was evident in the restrictions that Beijing placed on export of fertilizers and tunnel-boring machines to India, before eventually easing them in late 2025 as part of the broader normalization effort. The impact of China's restrictions on rare-earth supplies in April 2025 on India's electric vehicle manufacturers, however, underscores that single-source concentration is likely to remain a serious challenge.[42] Likewise, China's sweeping new export controls across a range of products—including rare-earth elements and their production technologies along with lithium battery materials, technologies

---

Sridharan, Srinath, 'Chinese FDI: A Strategic Gamble for India's Economic Future', *Businessworld*, 27 July 2024, https://tinyurl.com/435rznjm. Accessed on 15 November 2025.

[41]Das, Shouvik, 'FDI from China can help India increase value addition, exports', *Livemint,* 22 July 2024, https://tinyurl.com/4thjnfhu. Accessed on 15 November 2025.

Dhar, Biswajit, 'Is India Ready to Welcome Chinese Capital Again?', *The New Indian Express*, 9 August 2024, https://tinyurl.com/yruju6u6. Accessed on 15 November 2025.

Krishnan, Anand P., 'With or Without Chinese Companies Is the Question', *The Hindu*, 9 September 2024, https://tinyurl.com/5e7bhaca. Accessed on 15 November 2025.

Kotasthane, Pranay, 'Confronting Trade-offs for India's Electronics Manufacturing Success', *Lee Kuan Yew School of Public Policy*, 27 July 2023, https://tinyurl.com/mthtfe7x. Accessed on 15 November 2025.

[42]Kartik, Ayaan, and Nehal Chaliawala, 'EV industry, government struggle to find alternative as China throttles rare earth magnets supply', *Livemint*, 20 May 2025, https://tinyurl.com/jb8zfkb4. Accessed on 15 November 2025.

and equipment—announced in October 2025 will hinder the advancement of Indian industry across several sectors, such as energy, electronics, machinery, new energy, automobile, etc.

While some might argue that because Chinese controls are targeted at the US, India need not be too concerned. It can negotiate licences and exemptions bilaterally. However, this is a myopic view. Firstly, once a system of controls has been operationalized, it will impact entities from all geographies. Secondly, Beijing is likely to use the logic of geopolitical competition to not only coerce New Delhi but also constrain India-US business-to-business and defence collaboration. The Indian government and particularly businesses must, therefore, actively invest in supply chain resilience. Consequently, some in the Indian bureaucracy have been arguing that restricting Chinese goods, capital and talent is necessary to shape the incentives of domestic industry. They believe such limits will push Indian businesses to invest more in manufacturing, R&D and innovation instead of relying on cheap sourcing from China.

Balancing the Politics, Inside-Out

In essence, in its broader relationship with China, India appears to be grappling to balance the competing objectives of security, autonomy and development.[43] Given this, China policy is increasingly acquiring far greater salience in India's domestic

[43]Note comments by Sanjeev Sanyal, member of the Economic Advisory Council to the Prime Minister, in October, calling for India to be open to Chinese capital and talents while defining a 'sensible balance' when it comes to security concerns. In Kewalramani, Manoj, 'Contours of a New Modus Vivendi with China', *Takshashila Institution*, October 2025, https://tinyurl.com/3sdua9f7. Accessed on 18 November 2025.

Also see, Seshadri, V.S., 'Policy Brief: The China Factor in India's Economic Security', *Delhi Policy Group*, Vol. IX, Issue 24., Delhi, 26 September 2024, https://tinyurl.com/3mtbc6uj. Accessed on 15 November 2025.

political discourse. The Indian Parliament has unfortunately not had a substantive debate on ties with China, despite calls for such a discussion over the past few years. However, if one were to use the periodic questions raised in Parliament and the April 2022 debate on the Russia-Ukraine war as proxies, then there is ample evidence that there is growing concern around the impact of Chinese economic and security policies on India. Parliamentarians from parties like the Indian National Congress (INC), the Biju Janata Dal (BJD), the Bahujan Samaj Party (BSP) and the Dravida Munnetra Kazhagam (DMK) have expressed concerns about an adversarial China.[44]

In fact, while antagonism towards China might not excite the voter-base, given that the relationship does not seem to have the visceral, emotional appeal that frictions with Pakistan command, it is clear today that there is little upside for Indian politicians to appear dovish on China. This dynamic is likely to intensify, especially in light of public discourse surrounding China's support for Pakistan following the brief India-Pakistan conflict in May 2025. Therefore, it seems highly unlikely that India's China policy can be de-politicized as some have called for.[45]

In March 2023, the INC issued a lengthy International Affairs Resolution. Unsurprisingly, the document was very critical of the NDA government's handling of Indian foreign policy. The resolution contained a paragraph on China policy, which criticized the government's 'unstructured' handling of the relationship, but it was thin on policy solutions. The resolution called to 'urgently enhance capabilities to deter China from attempting any military coercion along the LAC', 'aggressively step up' efforts to attract

---

[44]Kewalramani, Manoj, 'Special Post: Indian Parliament's Discussion on China', *Tracking People's Daily,* 6 April 2022, https://tinyurl.com/4w2nj5mz. Accessed on 15 November 2025.

[45]Baru, Sanjaya, 'Time to Restore Balance in India-China Relations', *Deccan Chronicle*, 2 September 2024, https://tinyurl.com/pkk92f2w. Accessed on 15 November 2025.

manufacturing and assembly into India, and also referenced the importance of freedom of navigation in the South China Sea.[46] In its manifesto prior to the 2024 elections, the INC mentioned as a goal to 'restore the status quo ante on our borders with China and to ensure that areas where both armies patrolled in the past are again accessible to our soldiers.'[47]

Rashtriya Swayamsevak Sangh (RSS) Chief Mohan Bhagwat's comments on China over the years have also demonstrated a recognition of the national security challenges that the country poses. In his *Vijay Dashmi* speech in October 2020, he lashed out at China's 'expansionist nature', while calling on the Indian government to move ahead with 'caution and strategic preparation'.[48] 'We need to surpass China strategically, economically, and diplomatically. We must keep doing this, only then will we be able to stop China,' he added.[49] At a public event discussing global affairs in December 2020, Bhagwat went further, claiming that expansionism was in China's 'basic nature'.[50] He contended that China's policy was aimed at expanding its influence. In subsequent engagements, making a pitch for self-reliance, the RSS chief has argued for addressing trade dependencies, particularly with China. 'If dependence on China increases, we will have to bow down to it,' he told a gathering marking India's 75th Independence Day.[51]

---

[46]Congress Sandesh, 'International Affairs Resolution', *Indian National Congress*, 15 March 2023, https://tinyurl.com/4h68bysx. Accessed on 15 November 2025.

[47]Congress Manifesto 2024, 'Introduction', *Indian National Congress*, https://tinyurl.com/4y76uszu. Accessed on 15 November 2025.

[48]'Bhagwat patter PM Modi's back on China, saying that the 'dragon' has been frightened by the push given by India this time', *Navbharat Times*, 25 October 2020, https://tinyurl.com/bdhm6h8a. Accessed on 15 November 2025.

[49]Ibid.

[50]Tiwary, Deeptiman, 'China Has Now Risen, Doesn't Care What World Thinks of It: RSS Chief', *The Indian Express*, 3 December 2020, https://tinyurl.com/4yrtfaf5. Accessed on 15 November 2025.

[51]PTI, 'Will Have to Bow before China If Dependence on It Increases, Says

Similar views on China have been articulated by RSS National Executive Member Ram Madhav, who also heads a prominent think tank called the India Foundation. He has argued that Beijing is pursuing a policy of expanding its global reach, seeking to anoint itself at the top of the global hierarchy. Madhav has postulated that the world has entered a phase akin to the Cold War, wherein China is working to 'displace the US as the hegemon.'[52] In this context, it is seeking to export its model to other countries, thereby negatively impinging on the 'democratic, free and liberal world order.' In this context, he has supported the Indian government's assertions with regard to tensions in the South China Sea.[53] When it comes to China's growing influence in the Indian subcontinent, Madhav has argued that New Delhi must not view ties with neighbours simply from a China prism.[54]

Vijay Chauthaiwale, who heads the Foreign Affairs Department of the BJP, has generally been reticent about a detailed exchange on the India-China relationship. His views have largely supported the Narendra Modi-led government's policies, while targeting the opposition for its past engagements with the Communist Party of China. On occasion, he has expressed concerns on the proximity between China and Russia[55] and even indicated that 'isolated skirmishes' between India and China on the boundary

---

RSS Chief Mohan Bhagwat', *The Hindu*, 15 August 2021, https://tinyurl.com/2pcekzae. Accessed on 15 November 2025.

[52]Madhav, Ram, 'China as Broker of Peace: How Cold War 2.0 Is Heating Up', *The Indian Express*, 27 July 2024, https://tinyurl.com/y4v2w5wb. Accessed on 15 November 2025.

[53]Madhav, Ram, 'India's message to China: Respect the rules you expect everyone else to follow', *The Indian Express*, 6 April 2024, https://tinyurl.com/ytyrmymp. Accessed on 15 November 2025.

[54]India Today Global, 'Ram Madhav on India's China Challenge', *YouTube*, 11 June 2024, https://tinyurl.com/mrumb37r. Accessed on 15 November 2025.

[55]India Global Forum, 'Shaping a Global Order in Flux with Dr Vijay Chauthaiwale, In Charge, Foreign Affairs Department BJP', *YouTube*, 30 March 2023, https://tinyurl.com/3d2k7ejd. Accessed on 15 November 2025.

are likely to continue in the future.[56] Swaminathan Gurumurthy, another prominent thinker associated with the RSS, has argued that India and China are 'spiritual cousins but political rivals'.[57] He has contended that the 'Chinese are empire builders' and 'China is targeting India because it knows that India is not its enemy but an impediment to its global ambition.'[58] Gurumurthy has been particularly scathing in his criticism of US policy of engagement with China over the decades, arguing that it is American policies that have created a 'Frankenstein's Monster'.[59]

Historically, the Indian public has not had a very positive view of the Communist Party-led state in China. This is part of the legacy of the 1962 war. Both countries dealt with the memory of that conflict very differently. In China, until very recently, the war barely figured in public or popular discourse.[60] In India, it left a deep scar on the nation's psyche. This was reflected in popular books, movies and songs. Indians felt deeply betrayed by a fellow Asian power, whose international socialization Prime Minister Jawaharlal Nehru had supported. The war, in many ways, also deeply challenged the sense of idealism and Asian romanticism that was once a feature of Indian foreign policy.

The normalization of ties in the late 1970s started the process of repairing the relationship. By the first decade of the 2000s, one

---

[56]*News18*, 'BJP's foreign affairs in charge Dr Vijay Chauthaiwale (@vijai63) says 'Pakistan uses anti-India tactics for their survival' on Bilawal Bhutto's derogatory remark against PM Modi', *Facebook*, 16 December 2022, https://tinyurl.com/mwysk9js. Accessed on 15 November 2025.

[57]@sgurumurthy, *X* (formerly *Twitter*), 28 February 2022, 6.29 a.m., https://tinyurl.com/2h782ztu. Accessed on 15 November 2025.

[58]Gurumurthy, S., 'India and the Changing World Order', *Vivekananda International Foundation Podcast*, 21 October 2022, https://tinyurl.com/45b8ufmm. Accessed on 15 November 2025.

[59]Ibid.

[60]Dang, Yuanyue, 'New Chinese textbooks play up national security, Xi Jinping Thought and Vietnam, India wars', *South China Morning Post*, 28 August 2024, https://tinyurl.com/yc6a5wb8. Accessed on 15 November 2025.

could argue that popular perception of China in India was truly shifting. This was partly due to the economic optimism around India and China being emerging economies and partly a product of the demonstration effect of China's phenomenal growth. For many Indians, China's remarkable growth story was a matter of inspiration. This was evident in Prime Minister Manmohan Singh, referencing Shanghai's development as a model when talking about Mumbai's future in 2004.[61] In the following years, trade, tourism and educational and cultural exchanges grew.

However, escalating friction and political discord over the past decade, particularly since 2017, have dealt a severe blow to public perception. At its height, towards the end of the first decade of the 2000s, China's favourability rating among Indians was around 40 per cent.[62] The most recent Pew survey found that Indians' perceptions of China had turned sharply negative since then. Negative opinions about China in India rose from 46 per cent in 2019 to 67 per cent in 2023.[63] Surveys conducted by Indian think tanks have also reflected the worsening of public and elite opinion in India.[64] Most of these have indicated weakened trust

---

[61]Archive PMO, 'PM's Speech at the Inauguration of the Platinum Jubilee Celebrations of the Utkal University', 16 October 2004, https://tinyurl.com/5n8a5ak9. Accessed on 12 December 2025.

[62]Silver, Laura, Kat Devlin, and Christine Huang, 'China's Economic Growth Mostly Welcomed in Emerging Markets, but Neighbors Wary of Its Influence', *Pew Research Center*, 5 December 2019, https://tinyurl.com/c3ppa842. Accessed on 15 November 2025.

[63]Huang, Christine, Moira Fagan, and Sneha Gubbala, 'Indians' Views of Other Countries', *Pew Research Center*, 29 August 2023, https://tinyurl.com/bdcrrkd4. Accessed on 15 November 2025.

[64]Pant, Harsh, Aditya Gowdara Shivamurthy, Shivam Shekhawat, and Sahil Deo, 'The ORF Foreign Policy Survey 2023: Young India and the Multilateral World Order', *Observer Research Foundation*, 5 February 2024, https://tinyurl.com/3t4kkm4a. Accessed on 15 November 2025.

Kewalramani, Manoj, Shrey Khanna, Ruturaj Gowaikar, and Aneesh Jaganath, 'How Indians View the World: Findings of India's Global Outlook

but a willingness to continue economic engagement.

Unsurprisingly, with heightened tensions along the boundary, particularly since May 2020, Indian media coverage of China has overwhelmingly been through the threat prism rather than an opportunity prism. The May 2025 conflict between India and Pakistan, following the terror attack in Pahalgam in Jammu and Kashmir, has evidently added new dimensions to and strengthened this perception. Former Foreign Secretary Nirupama Menon Rao put it succinctly, contending that 'Beijing is not merely a diplomatic shield for Pakistan but a material enabler.'[65] Social media and television discourse about China in India has been extremely shrill. This is reflected in the raucous civil society conversations around boycotting Chinese products or purported Chinese information and influence operations.[66] It is also evident in discussions around India's Tibet[67] and Taiwan[68] policies, calling for greater assertiveness by New Delhi. In a manner of speaking, Beijing's actions have meant that it has lost the trust of at least a generation of Indians, particularly amid the

---

Survey', *Takshashila Institution*, 22 February 2022, https://tinyurl.com/dd3z9kyp. Accessed on 18 November 2025.

[65]Rao, Nirupama, 'What makes this face-off with Pak structurally different is China's embedded role', *The Indian Express*, 21 May 2025, https://tinyurl.com/5726x6se. Accessed on 15 November 2025.

[66]Law and Society Alliance, 'Mapping Chinese Footprints and Influence Operations in India', 2021, https://tinyurl.com/8c8yu8mt. Accessed on 15 November 2025.

[67]Kranti, Vijay, 'Xi's China Deserves a Diplomatic Surgical Strike by India on Tibet', *Organiser*, 24 March 2024, https://tinyurl.com/ymfskbfb. Accessed on 15 November 2025.

[68]Dogra, A., 'Should India Review Its One China Policy?', *United Service Institution of India*, 10 February 2023, https://tinyurl.com/muyten5f. Accessed on 15 November 2025.

Pant, Harsh V., and Shashank Mattoo, 'India's Taiwan Moment', *Foreign Policy*, 19 August 2022, https://tinyurl.com/mrx63pk2. Accessed on 15 November 2025.

rising tide of nationalism in India. This is not to say that there isn't a strand of Asian Century optimism[69], suspicion about America gaining from discord between India and China[70], and civilizational romanticism[71] that persists. That said, the mainstream, dominant view appears to recognize the realities of geography, power and the economic significance of China, resulting in a certain amount of pessimism about the relationship[72] along with pragmatism with regard to available policy options.[73]

---

[69]The Editorial Board, 'Broad Vision: Editorial on India and China Working Together to Realise the Asian Century', *The Telegraph*, 11 October 2022, https://tinyurl.com/3jrx96kz. Accessed on 15 November 2025.

PTI, 'India, China Should Cooperate Closely for Realisation of Asian Century: Think-Tanks Forum', *The Economic Times*, 30 November 2019, https://tinyurl.com/nhj5u9ka. Accessed on 15 November 2025.

[70]Bhadrakumar, M.K., 'Opinion: Why US Wants India-China Conflict to Simmer', *Rediff*, 8 July 2020, https://tinyurl.com/3wczheee. Accessed on 15 November 2025.

[71]Deepak, B.R., 'India-China: Clash or dialogue between civilisations?', *Sunday Guardian*, 1 June 2019, https://tinyurl.com/yp3t9m9j. Accessed on 15 November 2025.

Kulkarni, Sudheendra, 'On China, BJP and Congress Must End Blame Game', *The Indian Express*, 23 November 2023, https://tinyurl.com/a4a6h876. Accessed on 15 November 2025.

[72]Chellaney, Brahma, 'Tread Carefully', *Open Magazine*, 14 October 2022, https://tinyurl.com/4d7tz7ms. Accessed on 15 November 2025.

The Hindu Bureau, 'Next 15 Years Will Be a Tough Period in India-China Ties, Says Ex-Foreign Secretary', *The Hindu*, 11 September 2024, https://tinyurl.com/5f9raehs. Accessed on 15 November 2025.

[73]BS Reporter, 'BS Manthan: India Should Chart Own Path to Shed West's 'China-plus' Tag', *Business Standard*, 28 March 2024, https://tinyurl.com/59edvjx5. Accessed on 15 November 2025.

Joshi, Manoj, 'India needs a two-track policy to handle China', *The Tribune,* 10 September 2024, https://tinyurl.com/hebf2dhb. Accessed on 15 November 2025.

Kantha, Ashok K., 'Weighing in on 'Business as Usual' with China', *The Hindu*, 24 September 2024, https://tinyurl.com/2ham2epe. Accessed on 15 November 2025.

The Duality in Dragon's Discourse

There exist several versions of India in the Chinese imagination. Historically, Chinese writers, scholars and policymakers have viewed India through many different lenses. Ancient India was often considered a centre for spirituality and learning.[74] In fact, there was a time during the Han dynasty that India was described as *Tianzhu,* or Heavenly Jewel. But as the centuries wore on, this view faded into the background.

The writings of Kang Youwei, who visited India twice in the first decade of the 20th century, have perhaps had the most significant impact on modern Chinese thought on India. In his writings, Kang held up India's example as a warning for a China that was undergoing deep political churn. This approach of using India as an object to project Chinese political anxieties has been a constant motif in Chinese discourse about India. This process often entails the denigration of the other, while reinforcing one's own sense of superiority. In India, Kang saw the decline of a great, ancient civilization into colonial enslavement owing to deep disunity, a reluctance to change, and fundamental social inequalities.[75] Several other prominent Chinese intellectuals also lamented the state of Indians as 'slaves of a conquered nation.'[76] Kang's warning was that China must be wary of such an outcome. This view was shared by many

---

[74]Saran, Shyam, *How China Sees India and the World*, Juggernaut, New Delhi, 2022.

[75]Scobell, Andrew, 'China's Real Strategic Culture: A Great Wall of the Imagination', *Contemporary Security Policy*, Vol. 35, No. 2, 2014, pp. 211–226, https://tinyurl.com/fy44aasv. Accessed on 15 November 2025.

Idier, Nicolas, 'Kang Youwei (1858-1927) and India: The Indian Travels of a Cosmopolitan Utopian', *India-China: Intersecting Universalities*, Anne Cheng and Sachit Kumar (eds.), Open Edition Books, Paris: Collège de France, 2020.

[76]Thakur, Ravi, and Tan Chung, 'Enchantment and Disenchantment: A Sino-Indian Introspection', Indira Gandhi National Centre for the Arts, https://tinyurl.com/49uw975a. Accessed on 15 November 2025.

philosophers and reformers, like Liang Qichao, Lu Xun and Liang Shumin.

For many others at the time, encounters with Indian soldiers shaped their perspectives of India as a 'sub-imperial power'.[77] These soldiers were part of the British forces that launched campaigns in China through the mid- and late-1800s. Along with this, the involvement of Indian communities in the opium trade played an important role in shaping negative perceptions. In addition, leaders like Chiang Kai-shek saw the Indian freedom movement as lacking revolutionary zeal, determining this to be the product of an inherently weak and submissive Indian attitude.[78] This, of course, was distinguished from Chiang's aggressive and militaristic self-perception. Early leaders of the Communist Party of China imbibed some of these perspectives.[79] In addition, they saw independent India as an inheritor of and collaborator with Western imperialism. From their viewpoint, the modern Indian state was an expansionist entity that sought to hold on to vestiges of British imperial power. This was in sharp contrast to the People's Republic of China's policy of undoing the legacies of colonialism, particularly agreements that were termed unequal. India's adoption of the Westminster-style parliamentary system of democracy was also viewed as a 'transfer of power' rather than a choice by a modern Republic of India.

In the first few years since India's Independence and the formation of the People's Republic of China, such antagonistic strands of thought coexisted with significant friendly exchanges, both in the cultural or political domains.[80] India was among the

---

[77]Menon, Shivshankar, *India and Asian Geopolitics: The Past, Present*, Penguin Allen Lane, 2021.

[78]Saran, Shyam, *How China Sees India and the World*, Juggernaut, New Delhi, 2022.

[79]Saran, Shyam, 'China's India Complex', *Open Magazine*, 3 June 2022, https://tinyurl.com/2xb6dauw. Accessed on 15 November 2025.

[80]Quanyu, Shang, 'Sino-Indian Friendship in the Nehru Era: A Chinese

first countries to recognize the PRC, with formal diplomatic relations being established in April 1950. In the subsequent years, there was steady engagement across domains, which was driven by the personal relationship between Indian Prime Minister Jawaharlal Nehru and Chinese Premier Zhou Enlai. The early 1950s were an era characterized by intense top-level engagement between the leadership in both countries and efforts to build on shared interests, while adopting a cautious approach towards the more difficult issues like the boundary dispute. What drove this was the narrative around a shared historical experience of colonialism and pan-Asianism, along with the imperatives of nation-building and the challenges posed by the emerging bipolar world order.

These ideas continue to resonate in modern-day Chinese discourse on India. Reportage of India in Chinese media tends to be limited but is frequently negative. Kang's depiction of India as a fragmented polity and backward society are reflected in Chinese media's coverage of the country, through constant stories of crime, corruption and chaos. Dismissiveness, hostility and condescension are common in the tone of coverage with regard to India.[81] In fact, over the past decade, Chinese media outlets have adopted a far more acerbic, and sometimes even racist, tone with regard to India.[82] Indian democracy is often derided as an unsuitable system 'grafted from the West'[83] and an

---

Perspective', *China Report*, Vol. 41, No.3, 2005, https://tinyurl.com/xez88k94. Accessed on 15 November 2025.

[81]For a detailed assessment, see Shen, Simon, and Debasish Roy Chowdhury, 'The Alien Next Door: Media Images in China and India', *Routledge Handbook of China–India Relations*, Kanti Bajpai, Selina Ho, Manjari Chatterjee Miller (eds.), Routledge, England, 2022.

[82]Hu, Tracy, 'Chinese State News Agency Slammed over 'Racist' India Border Row Video', *South China Morning Post*, 17 August 2017, https://tinyurl.com/3xrmfjc3. Accessed on 15 November 2025.

[83]GT Staff Reporter, 'China's 'dual carbon' goals not to affect economic growth:

impediment to the country's rise.[84] For instance, after the 2024 Lok Sabha elections resulted in the BJP needing coalition partners to form government, Chinese analysts assessed that 'continuous internal strife' was a 'typical characteristic of Indian politics.'[85] This is, of course, inevitability juxtaposed with the apparent efficiency and representative nature of 'whole-process democracy' under the Communist Party of China.[86] This contrast has become more prominent as the Communist Party has sought to intensify the projection of systemic influence globally.[87] While the underlying tone with regard to Indian democracy is derisive, it masks a certain sense of competition. This opens up the possibility that there is a deeper anxiety about what a politically plural, socially diverse and economically thriving democracy of a comparable size at the doorstep means for the legitimacy of the Communist Party's rule.[88]

From a geopolitical perspective, the image of India as not simply a regional irritant but rather an adversary is taking shape within China. This is evident in the public rise to prominence

---

expert', *The Global Times*, 30 August 2021, https://tinyurl.com/3zt225m6. Accessed on 15 November 2025.

[84]Jiadong, Zhang, 'India Loses Its Way with Major-Power Ambitions', *The Global Times*, 1 September 2020, https://tinyurl.com/3ku32npf. Accessed on 15 November 2025.

[85]Juecheng, Zhao, Bai Yunyi, and Zhang Yuying, 'The results of the Indian election are out, why do you say that Modi "wins but still loses"', *The Global Times*, 5 June 2024, https://tinyurl.com/4dr4dnf4. Accessed on 15 November 2025.

[86]'China: Democracy That Works', *The State Council Information Office of the People's Republic of China*, 4 December 2021, https://tinyurl.com/2cwancub. Accessed on 18 November 2025.

[87]Bo, Zhou, 'China and India Should Be Global South Anchors, Not Power Competitors', *South China Morning Post*, 2 February 2024, https://tinyurl.com/5ffcxc9v. Accessed on 15 November 2025.

[88]Joshi, Devin K., and Yizhe Xu, 'What do Chinese Really Think about Democracy and India?', *Journal of Contemporary China*, Vol. 26, No. 105, pp. 385–402. https://doi.org/10.1080/10670564.2016.1245897. Accessed on 18 November 2025.

of PLA regiment commander Qi Fabao, who was involved in the Galwan Valley clash.[89] The Chinese government's decision to include discussions about the 1962 war in new textbooks also reflects this trend.[90] Increasingly, public opinion surveys are also shedding light on the Chinese citizenry's negative perceptions of India. Recent surveys conducted by Tsinghua University have consistently indicated very poor favourability for India among the Chinese public, although India fares better than the US and Japan.[91] Meanwhile, an April 2025 opinion survey by researchers from The Carter Center and Emory University found that 79.7 per cent of Chinese people would prefer a military conflict to maintain sovereignty over China's claimed territorial borders with India over negotiation and compromise.[92] This reflects the broader trend of nationalism within China and the enduring impact of sustained negative propaganda over the past decade, portraying India as a collaborator with the US in efforts to contain China. Beijing also appears to be concerned about Indian assertion on territorial issues. This is particularly the case with India's advancing border infrastructure and military drills with what it calls extra-regional actors. A key aspect of this anxiety is around China's own two-front problem.[93] There

[89]'Galwan Valley border clash hero Qi Fabao honoured for outstanding performance as CPPCC member', *Global Times,* 3 March 2025, https://tinyurl.com/3tx43re2. Accessed on 25 November 2025.

[90]Dang, Yuanyue, 'New Chinese textbooks play up national security, Xi Jinping Thought and Vietnam, India wars', *South China Morning Post,* 28 August 2024, https://tinyurl.com/yc6a5wb8. Accessed on 18 November 2025.

[91]Center for International Security and Strategy, Tsinghua University, 'Chinese Outlook on International Security, 2024', https://tinyurl.com/2695se7r. Accessed on 15 November 2025.

[92]Zeller, Nick, Renard Sexton, Michael Cerny, and Yawei Liu, 'Sovereignty, Security, & U.S.–China Relations: Chinese Public Opinion. U.S.–China Perception Monitor', *The Carter Center*, April 2025, https://tinyurl.com/4jtrzmma. Accessed on 15 November 2025.

[93]Kumar, Amit, 'China's Two-Front Conundrum: A Perspective on the India-

is, of course, historical precedent to this concern.

Likewise, there is increasingly a competitive edge in official and analytical discourse around economic issues. Chinese scholars and analysts tend to discuss India's economic expansion and future potential with a unique blend of condescension and competition. The former is evident in comments highlighting how China's economic growth has outpaced India's over the past four decades. The latter is seen in writings that view India's economic policy and diplomacy primarily from the perspective of strategic competition with the United States and the worsening of bilateral ties.[94] Chinese analysts tend to assess India's economic strategy as one premised on taking advantage of the West's anxieties with regard to China's dominance in key supply chains to present itself as an alternative. In their writings, they push back against any suggestion that India can be an attractive alternative investment destination for Western firms and a market that can rival the Chinese consumer market. In making this case, they tend to highlight challenges related to policy, regulatory and business environments in India; infrastructure limitations and inadequate supply chain development; and issues related to labour rights and socio-political and cultural factors.

Some, like Hu Shisheng from the China Institutes of Contemporary International Relations, have explicitly argued for a restrictive policy when it comes to industrial chain transfers to India, so as to avoid contributing to the country's development at the cost of China's development.[95] Others like Hu's colleague

China Border Situation', Observer Research Foundation, 7 May 2023, https://tinyurl.com/yzv5257k. Accessed on 15 November 2025.

[94]For a detailed discussion on this, see Kewalramani, Manoj, 'Supply Chain and Market Scale: India as the Next China?', Institut Montaigne, April 2024, https://tinyurl.com/364dy525. Accessed on 15 November 2025.

[95]Shisheng, Hu, 'India's Policy Practices and Underlying Logic Regarding Industrial Substitution with China', *China US Focus*, 8 January 2024, https://tinyurl.com/bdua8y9s. Accessed on 15 November 2025.

Wang Shida believe that India's development of manufacturing industries creates a significant demand for, and even dependence on, upstream and midstream sectors in China, which can help strengthen Sino-Indian economic and trade relations.[96] Such perspectives raise concerns about how open the Chinese government will likely be to facilitate manufacturing investments into India. That said, this is not simply an India-centric view among the analytical community in China. For instance, Peking University researcher Wei Xin has expressed concerns about China's transfer of low-end manufacturing capacities to other countries under the Belt and Road Initiative potentially leading to a hollowing out of the Chinese manufacturing base.[97] These arguments co-exist with persistent anger and frustration with regard to the treatment of Chinese enterprises in India and policies that are seen as denying Chinese capital access to the Indian market. In that sense, Chinese analysts want the Indian market to be open to Chinese goods and capital, but are also incredibly weary of the consequences of open economic cooperation with India. On one hand, there are a fair few voices within the system that desire a new free trade agreement and a bilateral investment protection treaty with India. The lure of India's growing affluent class, estimated to reach 100 million by 2027, is rather powerful.[98] Moreover, several Chinese analysts believe that given intensifying

---

Adlakha, Hemant, 'Expert Explains: Why Anti-India Business Sentiment Is Growing in China', *The Indian Express*, 1 October 2024, https://tinyurl.com/2tekwtrt. Accessed on 15 November 2025.

[96]Shida, Wang, 'Where Will China–India Relations Go After the Indian Election?' *The Global Times*, 5 June 2024, https://tinyurl.com/yts5xc55. Accessed on 15 November 2025.

[97]Xin, Wei, 'Economic Security Risks in Belt and Road Implementation and Their Control Methods', *Center for Strategic and International Studies*, 20 September 2022, https://tinyurl.com/y73swyzc. Accessed on 15 November 2025.

[98]'India's affluent population is likely to hit 100 million by 2027', *Goldman Sachs*, 16 February 2024, https://tinyurl.com/bcjuzcbb. Accessed on 16 November 2025.

India-US tensions owing to the Trump administration's coercive policies, there is greater opportunity today to lock in access to the Indian market for the long term. Political trust, however, is far too low on both sides to achieve such expansive outcomes.

Double-Speak

This duality is also present in Chinese discussions on Indian foreign policy. On one hand, Chinese scholars cast India's strategy of multi-alignment as opportunistic hedging to seek advantageous positions. There is some grudging praise of this approach too. But in general, India is deemed to be an expansionist power—particularly with the rise of Hindu nationalism—that has hegemonic designs in the Indian Ocean Region.[99] At the same time, India is also viewed as a status-seeking power that is trying to rid itself of the tag of a 'poor and backward developing country' by aligning closely with the West and projecting itself as a 'leading power'.[100] The undercurrent in this line of thinking, of course, is that India is a power unequal to China. This is also underscored by the hierarchical diplomatic structuring of the world in Chinese official discourse. Under this framework, Russia, the US and the EU are categorized as major powers, while India is viewed from the lens of peripheral diplomacy.

Contestation with India, therefore, is largely discussed from a regional lens or from the perspective of China's strategic competition with the US. Liu Zongyi, a researcher at the Shanghai Institutes for International Studies, contends that India's strategic affairs elite 'will never accept China becoming the dominant force

---

[99]Shisheng, Hu, 'Will the Modi Government's "high-tension" diplomacy continue?', *CRI Online*, 18 June 2024, https://tinyurl.com/sscw2sd8. Accessed on 15 November 2025.

[100]Jianxue, Lan, 'India's calculations behind the "US-India-Israel-UAE quadrilateral mechanism"', *World Affairs, China Institute of International Studies*, No. 7, 2023, https://tinyurl.com/bdhxsr5t. Accessed on 16 November 2025.

in Asia.'[101] Consequently, over the next decade, Indian policy will continue to be pro-US and confrontational with China. Liu and Lan Jianxue, who works with the Chinese Ministry of Foreign Affairs' think tank, both place the onus of the 2020 boundary clash on India, with Lan blaming India's 'highly speculative and risky' foreign policy.[102] Others like Fudan University's Zhang Jiadong have not gone as far as apportioning blame. Zhang contends that Indian policy has shifted towards 'a great power strategy', which entails diversified major power relations or balancing among major powers and a more 'assertive' foreign policy.[103] This viewpoint appreciates New Delhi's insistence on strategic autonomy, pointing out that India tends to act in its interests rather than simply following the US.

In general, however, Chinese scholars and analysts have a tendency to deny India agency, viewing the country as an instrument of American containment.[104] Discussions around India

---

[101]Zongyi, Liu, 'India's Indo-Pacific Strategy and China–India Relations in the Next Decade', 2023 Spring Forum of the Chongyang Institute for Financial Studies at Renmin University of China, 9 January 2023, http://rdcy.ruc.edu.cn/zw/jszy/lzy/lzygrzl/6d6959a338224dedafbbb971e3d51c40.htm. Accessed on 16 November 2025.

[102]Jianxue, Lan, 'Transformation of China-India Relations and the Way Forward', *Aisixiang*, 30 August 2023, https://tinyurl.com/rrz8m56p. Accessed on 18 November 2025.

Zongyi, Liu, 'India's "Indo-Pacific Strategy"', *Cfisnet*, 29 February 2024, https://tinyurl.com/27ry8zcd. Accessed on 15 November 2025.

[103]Jiadong, Zhang, 'What I feel about the 'Bharat narrative' in India', *Institute of International Studies Fudan University*, 2 January 2024, https://iis.fudan.edu.cn/en/d4/85/c38332a644229/page.htm. Accessed on 15 November 2025.

[104]See, Li Li, and Jiang, Tianjiao, 'From conceptual idea to strategic reality: 'Indo-Pacific Strategy' from the perspective of Chinese Scholars', *Asian Perspectives*, Vol. 47, No. 1, 2023, pp. 101–119.

Fengling, Wang (ed.), '[Zhongtong Forum] G20 Foreign Ministers' Meeting Will Once Again Focus on the Russia–Ukraine Issue; Scholars Say the Meeting is Unlikely to Succeed', *China News Service*, 3 March 2023, https://tinyurl.com/2h86sb3a. Accessed on 15 November 2025.

seeking to undermine the Shanghai Cooperation Organisation (SCO) essentially at the behest of the US are a case in point.[105] This view clearly has some cache with the Chinese leadership, considering that Indian Foreign Secretary Vikram Misri was vehement in underscoring India's support for the SCO after the Modi-Xi meeting in Kazan. Another example was the *Global Times* article in 2024 attacking External Affairs Minister S. Jaishankar, accusing him of scuttling a thaw with China for the purpose of 'pleasing the US'.[106] This antipathy towards the minister has been fairly evident in Chinese discourse for some time,[107] although never expressed so directly, particularly in English-language media.

Personalities aside, there is an undercurrent of acknowledgement among Chinese analysts that India and the US share a convergence of interests. In other words, the US is seeking to draw India into its orbit to contain China, and India is engaging with the US to further its own rise. Rong Ying, Vice President of the China Institute of International Studies, succinctly captures this viewpoint, stating that despite practical limitations, both India and the US 'are getting what they need' from the relationship.[108] This line of thought tends to coexist with the argument that the

---

Kewalramani, Manoj, 'Quad through Chinese Lens', *MoneyControl*, 26 September 2024, https://tinyurl.com/ybkbyhu3. Accessed on 15 November 2025.

[105]Zhuge, 'India deliberately 'snubbing' China and turning to attend the G7 summit and visit Russia and China?', *Baidu Baijiahao*, 12 July 2024, https://tinyurl.com/bdezct95. Accessed on 11 November 2025.

[106]Daming, Wang, 'India's diplomacy has a 'S. Jaishankar problem', *Global Times*, 9 September 2024, https://tinyurl.com/3k4hc6y9. Accessed on 11 November 2025.

[107]GT Staff Reporters, 'With Jaishankar's reappointment, 'no major change in India's China policy anticipated', *Global Times*, 12 June 2024, https://tinyurl.com/58w3ye28. Accessed on 11 November 2025.

[108]Zhuoying, Yang, and Yin Meimei, 'Experts believe that the advancement of trade, economic, and military cooperation between India and the United States is mutually beneficial, and that both countries are getting what they need', *China Radio International,* 24 June 2023, https://tinyurl.com/3c5b4s43. Accessed on 15 November 2025.

India-US partnership faces significant challenges, with New Delhi trying to maintain autonomy while Washington uses a vast array of tools, including interference in Indian domestic politics, to coerce it into obedience.[109]

A more recent strand of thought in this regard has been around the US's involvement in the ceasefire between India and Pakistan following the May 2025 conflict. Chinese analysts have sought to highlight the different narratives on the ceasefire that have emerged from New Delhi and Washington, arguing that the relationship faces significant strain. Some have even contended that the Indian government was likely left very disappointed by the Trump administration's approach to the conflict.[110] This view has been further strengthened after Trump's announcement of 50 per cent tariffs on select Indian exports in August 2025. Chinese officials have since openly sought to make common cause with New Delhi in pushing back against the American 'bully'.[111] In private conversations, there has been a notable sense of schadenfreude, with Chinese interlocutors urging their Indian counterparts to recognize the true nature of American imperialism and to embrace deeper cooperation with China, along with its regional primacy.

Unlike scholars and analysts, official statements from Chinese leaders and diplomats have been much more circumspect. In general, Chinese officials have been extremely cautious in not

---

[109]Jianxue, Lan, 'Russia-Ukraine tensions an occasion for India to reassess ties with US', *China Institute of International Studies*, 17 March 2022, https://tinyurl.com/bdykk3y6. Accessed on 15 November 2025.

Zongyi, Liu, 'Why is India "discarding its usefulness after it has served its purpose" at this time?', *Guancha*, 25 June 2023, https://tinyurl.com/4vk6r3fs. Accessed on 15 November 2025.

[110]Minwang, Lin, 'Why did India and Pakistan suddenly reach a ceasefire agreement?', *Global Times*, 12 May 2025, https://tinyurl.com/3c9z8hzf. Accessed on 15 November 2025.

[111]Mollan, Cherylann, 'Beijing opposes 'bully' US for 50% tariffs on India', *BBC*, 22 August 2025, https://tinyurl.com/4kkknpmc. Accessed on 11 November 2025.

stressing discord with India over the past year or so. In fact, there appears to have been a concerted effort at avoiding what came to be termed as wolf warrior diplomacy, which had become commonplace in the aftermath of the Galwan clash.

For instance, Beijing was rather measured in response to critical statements from New Delhi with regard to Chinese actions in the South China Sea in June 2024. Likewise, it lashed out at the US and not India for remarks by members of a US Congressional delegation to Dharamshala in the same month. Similarly, following the Quad leaders' summit in Delaware in late September 2024, the Chinese foreign ministry criticized the US but was rather measured in its remarks when it came to a specific question on India.[112] At the same time, since his appointment in May 2024, Ambassador Xu Feihong has been engaged in quiet diplomacy, meeting with key stakeholders, and adopting softer public outreach through social media. In particular, the Chinese ambassador has been keen to highlight cultural linkages and China's openness to Indian travellers.

A close reading of Chinese statements, however, does not indicate a shift in established positions. For instance, while speaking to Indian media in September 2024, Ambassador Xu called for greater 'dialogue and communication at all levels in various fields.' He added that the two sides need to 'view bilateral relations from a strategic perspective, form the right perception of each other, view each other's strategic intentions objectively, and stick to the right vision—that China and India are partners and development opportunities to each other instead of being rivals or threats.'[113] On the boundary issue, meanwhile, he was rather clear

---

[112]'Foreign Ministry Spokesperson Lin Jian's Regular Press Conference on September 23, 2024', Ministry of Foreign Affairs of the People's Republic of China, 23 September 2024, https://tinyurl.com/aearchph. Accessed on 11 November 2025.

[113]'The Five Guidelines to A Dragon-Elephant Tango', Embassy of the People's Republic of China in India, 2 August 2024, https://tinyurl.com/bdcsms2b.

that 'the key is to form a correct perception of differences and handle them in a proper manner...our relationship is all-round and cannot be defined by certain differences, and our cooperation cannot be disrupted by a single incident.' Likewise, Wang Yi's remarks in March 2025 about seeking a 'cooperative pas de deux of the dragon and the elephant' and the need for India and China to 'support each other rather than undercut each other, work with each other rather than guard against each other' do not reflect in Chinese actions.[114] Reports indicate that Beijing has cautioned its companies from investing in India.

For instance, a report in June 2024 claimed that the Chinese Ministry of Commerce had asked Chinese EV companies to avoid investing in countries like India and Türkiye, owing to concerns around political tensions, boycotts and technology theft.[115] More significantly, it is also actively impeding foreign enterprises with a significant base in China from engaging with Indian officials or considering capacity development in India. In addition, Beijing has also actively blocked the transfer of equipment, machinery and technical personnel to India in recent times. These actions are essentially a product of anxieties around export of production capacity along with a desire to retard the expansion of electronics, automobile and solar energy sectors in India, unless Delhi aligns with Beijing's priorities.

Therefore, it would be strategically imprudent for New Delhi to read too much into stylistic or rhetorical adjustments by Chinese officials. Instead, the focus should be on tangible changes in Chinese policy to accommodate India's interests and aspirations

---

Accessed on 11 November 2025.

[114]Padmanabhan, Keshav, 'Dance of elephant, dragon is the only right choice for India and China, says Chinese FM Wang Yi', *The Print*, 7 March 2025, https://tinyurl.com/3ttfwfe5. Accessed on 11 November 2025.

[115]Ren, Daniel, 'Beijing urges Chinese EV makers to avoid investments in countries like India and Turkey', *South China Morning Post*, 12 September 2024, https://tinyurl.com/4ss5yum7. Accessed on 11 November 2025.

and engender stability and predictability in the relationship, which is critical for both countries' strategic ambitions.

Conclusion

To summarize, this chapter has argued that India and China have very distinct narratives and perceptions of each other. These are rooted in their historical experiences, legacy of territorial and ideological differences and geopolitical aspirations. Importantly, at present, both sides view the other from a threat-prism, with mutual trust being extremely low. There also exists a distinct absence of strategic empathy on both sides. From an Indian perspective, the core challenge lies in balancing the opportunities presented by China's rise with the need to mitigate the associated risks. This calls for a strategic recalibration of both defence and economic policies, as well as a careful navigation of the development-versus-security dilemma. For China, India presents a significant obstacle. Despite being a regional power, India has the potential to inhibit Beijing's broader global ambitions. Yet, a policy of coercion, thus far, has proven rather counterproductive. The real challenge for Beijing is to find a way to leverage and manage India's ascent without turning it into an adversary. Neither of these are easy tasks, but these are necessities, as both remain bound by the inescapable realities of geography.

2

Keeping the Powder Dry: A New Security Outlook for India's China Policy

ANUSHKA SAXENA

China is India's main security challenge. Said challenge manifests in conventional forms, such as eyeball-to-eyeball contestation along the Line of Actual Control (LAC), or the threat of expanding Chinese naval presence in the Indian Ocean Region. But it also spans new and emerging realms of contestation, such as in the form of cyberattacks conducted by Chinese threat actors, or in the form of cognitive warfare impacting policies and people. Chinese media posturing on the weaknesses in India's military standing at the border,[116] or attacks by malignant Chinese cyber actors on India's power grids, are examples.[117] Naturally, India needs a renewed vision of security against the China Challenge, inclusive of a doctrine to achieve military modernization, and a policy approach to defend its continental territory, waters, infrastructure and cyberspace.

In this regard, this chapter discusses five broad domains.

---

[116]Xingchun, Long, 'India flexing its muscles at the border shows its loser mentality', *Global Times*, 14 November 2021, https://tinyurl.com/3fspsjjr. Accessed on 15 November 2025.

[117]'Continued Targeting of Indian Power Grid Assets by Chinese State-Sponsored Activity Group', *Recorded Future, Insikt Group*, 6 April 2024, https://tinyurl.com/362z73a2. Accessed on 15 November 2025.

First, it begins by fleshing out the primary conventional military challenges posed by the Chinese People's Liberation Army (PLA) to India, and the preparedness tactics of its Western Theater Command (WTC). This section summarizes India's response and deployment capabilities, specifically in terms of Electromagnetic Warfare (EW),[118] border infrastructure development, and drone systems capabilities. The second section assesses the key maritime challenges India faces from China, while recommending an approach covering both Chinese civilian scientific and military vessels operating in waters near India. The third focus is on the cyber threat posed by Chinese state-sponsored and territory-based threat actors. In this context, this chapter addresses how India can tackle the cybersecurity question, through offensive, defensive and multilateral means. The fourth section articulates the need to create integrated forces, and budget for a modern, multi-domain and holistic defence strategy. For these purposes, there is a discussion on the trajectory to theaterization, including through Higher Defence Organisation Reforms (HDOR). Finally, the chapter analyses budgetary allocations for defence and shortcomings in capital outlay and defence acquisition processes, with an emphasis on enhancing indigenization. What is not covered is a discussion on nuclear capabilities and doctrine, given the relative inertness of nuclear posture on both sides.

Facing Down the Continental Threat

As a result of the military skirmishes in eastern Ladakh in 2020, India and China continue to sustain tensions in bilateral ties. Despite disengagement, both sides still have as many as

[118]Electronic warfare (EW), or electromagnetic warfare, is a military action involving the use of electromagnetic energy and directed energy to control the electromagnetic spectrum (EMS). Its purpose is to attack an adversary, impede their operations, and ensure friendly, unimpeded access to and use of the EMS.

50,000–60,000 troops deployed in the region.[119] Given that de-escalation and de-induction processes are yet to be undertaken, the troop and weapons systems deployment are likely to remain. In this regard, it becomes important to assess the power differential prevalent between the Indian armed forces and the PLA. The purpose of this exercise is to grasp which systems, technologies and skills can enable India to gain an advantage over the PLA.

Operations pertaining to India fall under the remit of the PLA's Western Theater Command (WTC). Understanding the achievements and challenges of its Multi-Domain Integrated Joint Operations (MDIJO) endeavours is therefore consequential to Indian decision-making. The *Science of Military Strategy* documents,[120] published by the Military Strategy Studies Department of the PLA Academy of Military Sciences in 2013 and 2020, lucidly explain the pillars of MDIJO.[121] The primary goal of the PLA is to become a force that can win 'localised wars under conditions of informatization.'[122] To be able to do that, the requirement is two-fold. First, it calls on the services and support arms of the PLA to fuse their operational expertise and

[119]Roy, Shubhajit, 'India and China have agreed on disengagement, patrolling arrangements along LAC: Foreign Secretary Vikram Misri', *The Indian Express*, 21 October 2024, https://tinyurl.com/59375aar. Accessed on 15 November 2025.

[120]'Science of Military Strategy (2013)', *In Their Own Words: Foreign Military Thought (Science of Military Strategy 2013)*, China Aerospace Studies Institute, April 2021, https://tinyurl.com/yve8hctu. Accessed on 15 November 2025.

[121]'Multi-Domain Integrated Joint Operations' (or MDIJO) refer to campaigns where multi-service combat and non-combat units are 'fused' via a networked information system to conduct unified operations across all domains, including, but not limited to, land, sea, air, outer space and cyberspace. The goal is to achieve systemic effects, such as paralysing an adversary's military tactical and operational systems, rather than simply winning isolated force-on-force or platform-on-platform confrontations.

[122]The State Council Information Office of the People's Republic of China, 'China's Military Strategy (full text)', *Xinhua*, 27 May 2015, https://tinyurl.com/5azmm7bv. Accessed on 15 November 2025.

platforms to the highest possible degree (i.e., preparing a 'joint combat force'). Second, it requires them to do so via a 'seamlessly linked up networked military information system.'[123] The former constitutes the material basis on which operational strengths can be complemented and the boundaries and hierarchies of services and arms can be transcended. The latter constitutes the safe and reliable supporting link so that all operational elements have a common awareness of battlefield postures.

Why MDIJO is vital in evolving battle is because there is increasing network dependence in war. Interlinkages between ground, air and naval weapons systems and personnel can determine how effective a military response can be. Further, because warfare today is fought in multiple domains (cyber, space, conventional and non-conventional), integrated operations must focus on multi-pronged defence and offence to be effective. This is evident from both international conflicts between Russia and Ukraine and Israel and Palestine, as well as in the India-Pakistan hostilities in May 2025.

The WTC is unique as compared to its counterpart theatres in that it also boasts two Group Army (GA)/sub-theatre-level Military Districts (MDs) in Tibet and Xinjiang. The two MDs further comprise various infantry battalions, border defence regiments, and mountain infantry brigades. An example of an infantry battalion with a special assignment for border defence is the Gyantse County 1st Independent Battalion (Military Unit Cover Designator 77655).[124] Placed under the ambit of the Tibet MD, this battalion is designated to be deployed for operations on China's borders with India and Bhutan.

---

[123]China Aerospace Studies Institute, 'In Their Own Words: Science of Military Strategy 2020', January 2022, p. 93, https://tinyurl.com/yve8hctu.

[124]O'Donnell, Frank, and Alex Bollfrass, 'China-India Ground Posturing', *Google Maps*, October 2023, https://tinyurl.com/yurkfmnw. Accessed on 15 November 2025.

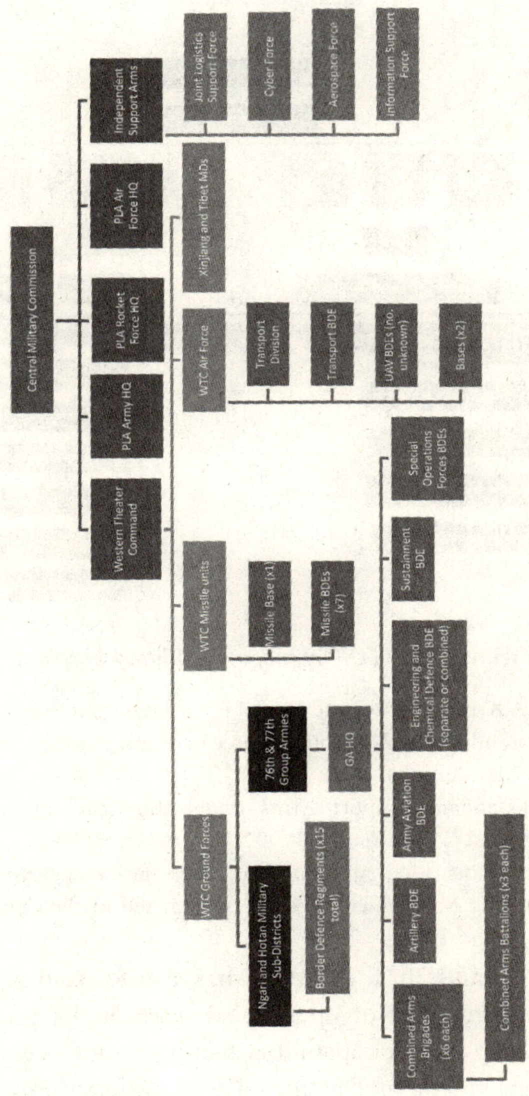

Figure 2.1: WTC Organogram-Services[125]

[125]Saxena, Anushka, 'Assessing Operations and 'Jointness' in the PLA Western Theater Command', *Takshashila Institution*, 16 May 2024, https://tinyurl.com/5a238cx3. Accessed on 16 November 2025.

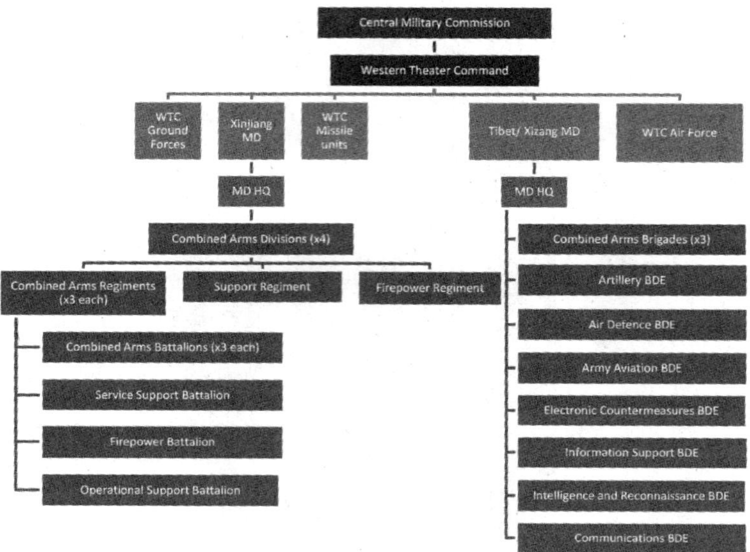

Figure 2.2: WTC Organogram-Military Districts[126]

Note: The PLA Army, Airforce and Rocket Force HQs exercise administrative (organizing, training and equipping-related) control over the WTC Army, Airforce and Missile units.

The Independent Support Arms under the CMC provide tactical support to the WTC.

There may exist other specialized brigades and/or departments under the Tibet/Xinjiang MD, which may not be depicted in the Organogram.

Between 2022 and 2024, the WTC has also focused on building an increasing number of operational bases in its geographical domain to keep diverse capabilities handy. As of December 2024, the US Department of Defense's *China Military Power Report* (CMPR)[127] informed that major PLA units in the WTC include

[126]Ibid.

[127]'Military And Security Developments Involving The People's Republic Of China 2024', US Department of Defense, 18 December 2024, https://tinyurl.

the 76th and 77th GAs, Xinjiang Military District (84th GA), and Xizang Military District (85th GA) comprised of 16 combined arms brigades and three infantry brigades; three air bases, eight fighter/ground attack brigades, one transportation division and brigade each, and one UAV unit; and eight PLA Rocket Force (PLARF) missile brigades and two PLARF combat missile bases.

As evident from the data points collated in the CMPR, between 2021 and 2024, the number of combat missile brigades has gone up from about 6 to 8, even as the 8 border defence regiments deployed in both 2021[128] and 2022[129] have been withdrawn, possibly owing to disengagement-related deliberations. There are now two missile bases instead of the single one in 2023.[130] The number of combined arms brigades has also gone up to about 17, from about 12 in 2022 (many of them have replaced infantry divisions). The new introduction includes bases of the now disbanded Strategic Support Force, specifically the three new emerging warfare arms of the PLA—the information support, cyber and military aerospace forces. As of December 2024, five Cyber/SIGINT units, three ASF space warfare units, and one EW unit (close to Arunachal Pradesh) have been positioned in the WTC.[131]

What is also particularly special about the WTC's training

---

com/yzfbz755. Accessed on 16 November 2025.

[128]'Military And Security Developments Involving The People's Republic Of China 2021', US Department of Defense, 3 November 2021, https://tinyurl.com/4a944fz3. Accessed on 16 November 2025.

[129]'Military and Security Developments Involving the People's Republic Of China 2022', US Department of Defense, 2022, https://tinyurl.com/4crr8v3d. Accessed on 16 November 2025.

[130]'Military and Security Developments Involving the People's Republic Of China 2023', US Department of Defense, 19 October 2023, https://tinyurl.com/bdzzf8ns. Accessed on 16 November 2025.

[131]'Military And Security Developments Involving The People's Republic Of China 2024', US Department of Defense, 18 December 2024, https://tinyurl.com/yzfbz755. Accessed on 16 November 2025.

is that it experiments with terrains. This is important since the WTC is the largest theatre command by area, covering both the arid northwestern deserts of Xinjiang and the high-altitude areas of Tibet, along the border with India. Public information suggests terrain training can be achieved through both combat and non-combat tasks. For example, in February 2023, it was reported[132] that personnel deployed at the radar station of an Air Force brigade in the WTC managed to connect its dormitories to a tap water pipeline. The radar station was described as being situated in a snow-covered plateau at a height of about 4,000 metres, indicating that this could be a station located in Tibet, since the PLA uses the term plateau to denote the Tibetan Plateau. This development, among others, depicts emphasis on resource constraints and the subsequent importance of terrain acquaintance work in the WTC.

Combat tasks, too, are formulated to prepare for the terrain and altitude conditions. Earlier in 2023, for example, an Army Brigade of the WTC was conducting snowfield training to enhance combat preparedness under cold (high altitude) and hypoxic (low oxygen) conditions.[133] This is essential to meet the criteria of 'effective training' in the PLA, wherein combat situations are simulated as accurately as possible, and tasks are assigned to test multiple components of a joint operation.

Further, when pitted against India, an assessment of the Orders of Battle (ORBATs)[134] formulated by US-based Belfer Centre, a

---

[132]Zhang, Leifeng, Deng Zongzhi, and Zheng Lei, 'A radar station at an altitude of 4,000 metres now has running water', *PLA Daily*, 7 February 2024, https://tinyurl.com/484xht8p. Accessed on 16 November 2025.

[133]'Spring Festival Visit to Grassroots Levels: Braving the Winds - Border Guards' Patrol Route in Level 10 Gale-force Winds', *CCTV*, 26 January 2023, https://tinyurl.com/yp9ez3f4. Accessed on 16 November 2025.

[134]An ORBAT is a detailed organogram showing the composition, structure, positioning and disposition of a military force. It typically includes: the hierarchy of command (e.g., 'x' regiment belongs to a brigade which reports to 'y' Group

research institute affiliated with the Harvard Kennedy School, indicated that, as of 2020, the ground forces deployed on both sides of the border were similar in numbers (over 205,000 troops). Indian fighter jets, meanwhile, outnumber Chinese jets available in the WTC–250 to 157.[135] Additionally, to enable air-based ground defence, China has deployed over 50 precision strike, ground attack and reconnaissance Unmanned Aerial Vehicles (UAVs) in the WTC. India, meanwhile, has reportedly deployed four Heron Mark-II drones (since 2021) and 68 ground attack aircraft across the Eastern, Central and Western Air Commands.

In terms of ground-based air defence, four Air Defence Brigades are each attached with the Xinjiang and Tibet MDs and the WTC 76th and 77th Group Armies. At the same time, the WTC-PLAAF has its own long-range surface-to-air missile installations. Further, WTC is enabling PLAA and PLAAF to conjoin air defence systems, as air defence battalions affiliated with an Army Air Defence Brigade have now started to integrate into the chain of command of an Air Force Base.[136] The goal behind this is for the PLAAF to lend its long-range expertise to the more mechanized ground forces, and in handling low-level targets. Another report from 2021 suggests cross-service air defence integration in the WTC is geared towards achieving successes in early warning and network system's jointness, so that there is no delay in battlefield data transmission.[137]

Army stationed in the mountains of Tibet); the strength of the units (how many personnel); the major equipment they operate; and even their peacetime location.

[135]O'Donnell, Frank, and Alex Bollfrass, 'The Strategic Postures of China and India: A Visual Guide', Belfer Center, Harvard Kennedy School, March 2020, https://tinyurl.com/mr26brxw. Accessed on 18 November 2025.

[136]Xuanzun, Liu, 'China's western airspace more secure with PLA Army, Air Force integration', *Global Times*, 26 January 2021, https://tinyurl.com/ywvdh96t. Accessed on 16 November 2025.

[137]Jin, Yang, and Yang Songsong, 'Army air defense forces integrated into the air force command', *81.cn*, April 2021, https://tinyurl.com/69kwv29p. Accessed

India is investing in its own indigenous Very Short-Range Air Defence Systems (VSHORADS) and Man-Portable Air Defence Systems (MANPADS) to expand Army Air Defence (AAD) capabilities. Clearly, in regard to aerial superiority, there exists a tough capacity competition between China and the WTC's principal operational target, India. At the same time, there is a gap in the Indian Air Force's standing and required squadron force numbers—the actual-to-required ratio stands at about 32:42.[138] The shortfall is partially a result of the phasing out of Mig-21s and 27s, as well as the relatively slower induction of the Tejas Mk-II and the Rafales. This may mean India is not in a ready position to engage in a two-front conflict with China and Pakistan. Similarly, while troop numbers may currently be matched on both sides, the fact is that India raised 50,000–60,000 troops along the LAC by repositioning personnel from the Pakistan front.[139]

Moreover, the future battlefield is expected to be a systems warfare scenario.[140] This essentially refers to combat between two systems or two sides with integrated systems, with one emerging decisively victorious. The key element in this is coordination between command and communication, reconnaissance and intelligence, firepower, EW and cyberwarfare, engineering and battlefield management. Achieving such coordination requires top-notch aerial reconnaissance to provide information on enemy positions, heavy rocket artillery to overwhelm enemy Command & Control (C2) and air defence positions, and supplementary EW

---

on 16 November 2025.

[138]Shukla, Ajai, 'At least 42 fighter squadrons essential, says Indian Air Force chief', *Broadsword*, 5 October 2022, https://tinyurl.com/msxz9mrs. Accessed on 16 November 2025.

[139]ANI, 'From Ladakh to Northeast, 6 Indian Army Divisions shifted from Pak front, anti-terrorist roles to tackle China threat', *The Print*, 15 May 2022, https://tinyurl.com/3zb9zew7. Accessed on 16 November 2025.

[140]'Chinese Tactics', Headquarters, Department of the Army, August 2021, https://tinyurl.com/yavuh6kx. Accessed on 16 November 2025.

and cyber capabilities as countermeasures. This is also why, over the years, anti-aircraft artillery units, together with ground-to-air missile units, have become part of the backbone of the WTC's integrated capabilities.

In this light, in May 2021, the Xinjiang MD engaged in six rounds of weapons acquisition from the State-Owned Enterprise (SOE), China North Industries Group Corporation Limited (or NORINCO).[141] At the time, India and China were still only recovering from deadly clashes in the Galwan Valley region of June 2020. The fifth and sixth rounds of this acquisition focused solely on aerial superiority through the induction of the PHL-11 122-mm-calibre self-propelled multiple rocket launcher system and the HQ-17A field air defence missile system.

Similarly, electromagnetic warfare training is becoming increasingly significant to the PLA in general and the WTC in specific. China's security planners realize that the PLA is likely to face a 'complex electromagnetic environment' (CEME) during battle.[142] Consequently, there will be a need to deploy counter-EW measures to ensure systems security. To this end, in July 2022, the PLA inducted a new variant of the FH-95 series of drones developed by Aerospace Times Feihong Technology.[143] These drones are capable of performing electromagnetic jamming and armed reconnaissance, especially in border patrol scenarios. In fact, this latest variant is being first put to the test by the

---

[141]Xianzun, Liu, 'PLA Xinjiang Military Command gets new anti-aircraft missile, rocket artillery', *Global Times*, May 2021, https://tinyurl.com/4jh7anss. Accessed on 16 November 2025.

[142]Dahm, J. Michael, 'Electronic Warfare and Signals Intelligence', *South China Sea Military Capability Series: A Survey of Technologies and Capabilities on China's Military Outposts in the South China Sea*. Johns Hopkins Applied Physics Laboratory, 2020, https://tinyurl.com/yc3ak5mt. Accessed on 16 November 2025.

[143]Xuanzun, Liu. 'China's FH-95 electronic warfare drone passes performance test', *Global Times*, July 2022, https://tinyurl.com/mr47txnv. Accessed on 16 November 2025.

Xinjiang MD. Further, to practise 'effective concealment' in combat training, Air Force Brigades in the WTC have also been deploying measures to 'clear the electromagnetic fog' in a battlefield scenario.[144] This refers to a situation in which radar systems experience interference, leading to the loss of the 'enemy aircraft signal.' Together, the abovementioned efforts are indicative of a 'whole-of-systems' approach to achieving joint operational capacity with air superiority at the core in the WTC.

What Does India Need?

Throughout the period of the standoff in eastern Ladakh since 2020, the Indian defence leadership has expressed great certainty in the armed forces' capabilities to deal with the PLA. Source-based reporting has carried claims like the deployment is 'more than enough.'[145] However, given the rapid advancement of the PLA, deeper thinking is needed. In particular, India must focus on the development of certain asymmetric capabilities that require investment in the form of joint planning and military acquisition.

The first is network security and centricity, which are slowly becoming central to the future of warfare. From access to satellite imagery to the existence of an Integrated Battlefield Management System (IBMS), enabling command, control and coordination in surveillance, recce through the use of drones, and digitization of special vehicles, India must match China's network warfare efforts.

There is little publicly revealed information on the successes of

---

[144]Pei, Zechao, and Hu Yonghua, 'A brigade of the Western Theater Command Air Force has encountered numerous special situations, honing its combat skills', *PLA Daily*, June 2023, https://tinyurl.com/2fk7h8eb. Accessed on 16 November 2025.
[145]Pandit, Rajat, '"More Than Enough" Troops deployed along LAC: Officials', *The Times of India*, 14 August 2023, https://tinyurl.com/378bakkf. Accessed on 16 November 2025.

India's IBMS programme, the IAF Vayulink.[146] This purportedly is an ad-hoc data link communication system, which, when installed on an aircraft, can provide encrypted data on nearby aerial threats. It may serve as a basis for the development of a joint jamming- and spoofing-proof battlefield network link. The strength of the Vayulink can well be complemented by the Software Defined Radios (SDRs) to be procured by the IAF from Bharat Electronics Limited (BEL). In the meantime, the BEL-produced Samyukta Electromagnetic Warfare Systems, two of which were procured[147] by the Indian military in 2023, must be tested for battle-readiness at the earliest. While India does not necessarily have to match troop deployment strength-to-strength against the Chinese, it does require a pathway to acquire asymmetric communications and systems capabilities to be able to deal with the nature of the challenge, without compromising on deployment along the Line of Control with Pakistan.

Secondly, the PLA WTC is making significant strides in bridging any gap that may have existed between its troops and India's experienced mountain divisions. In this regard, it is crucial to ramp up border infrastructure development to ensure all-weather access for troops.

The Border Roads Organisation (BRO) is the key body responsible for constructing and maintaining roads, tunnels and railways at high altitudes near the LAC. It was created in 1960, and was placed under the ambit of the Defence Ministry in 2015. However, it is only since 2017 that it has enhanced financial and administrative powers. Near the end of the 72-day-long Doklam standoff, on 20 August 2017, the BRO chief engineer

---

[146]PTI, 'IAF develops indigenous 'Vayulink' platform for jammer proof communication with base station', *The Times of India*, 17 February 2023, https://tinyurl.com/2tr8jntw. Accessed on 16 November 2025.

[147]Bisht, Inder Singh, 'India Procures Indigenous Electronic Warfare Systems for $364M', *The Defense Post*, 27 March 2023, https://tinyurl.com/3ct4cvm6. Accessed on 16 November 2025.

and the Director General and Additional Director General of Border Roads (DGBR & ADGBR) were given additional monetary spending and longer-term hiring powers by the MoD.[148] As the importance of building connectivity in tense terrains was realized, this move was meant to enable the BRO to quickly complete ongoing projects and undertake new ones.

Further, since 2017, budgetary allocation for the BRO has increased as well. And especially since the Galwan Valley clash, BRO funding has seen massive spikes—a 9.9 per cent increase of BE-stage allocation from ₹6,500 crore (~US$783 million) in FY 2025, to ₹7,146 crore (~US$861 million) in the latest budget for FY 2026.[149] As compared with the FY 2021–22 allocations, the BE-stage allocation has increased by over 160 per cent. Correspondingly, there's also been an uptick in project completion. For instance, in FY 2021–22, the BRO finished a total of 102 infrastructure projects—87 bridges and 15 roads—in border areas.[150]

The key border development projects the BRO has undertaken in the past few years include constructing the world's highest motorable road in Umling La, tunnelling the Se-La, Zoji-La and Shinku-La tunnels, building two new helipads in eastern Ladakh by 2022, and developing crucial airfields, such as the Nyoma, as close as 30 kilometres from the LAC. This is in addition to planning out long rail projects such as the '200 km broad gauge

---

[148]Ministry of Defence, 'Ministry of Defence approves delegation of Powers to Border Roads Organisation', *Press Information Bureau*, Government of India, 20 August 2017, https://tinyurl.com/4yc4utu4. Accessed on 16 November 2025.

[149]Sharma, Shivani, 'Budget 2025: Rs 7,146 crore allocated for boosting border infrastructure', *India Today*, 1 February 2025, https://tinyurl.com/bp8ycyfd. Accessed on 16 November 2025.

[150]Ministry of Defence, 'Enhance capability through latest technology for faster infrastructure development in border areas: Raksha Mantri tells BRO on its 63rd Raising Day', *Press Information Bureau*, Government of India, 7 May 2022, https://tinyurl.com/3v9f76nx. Accessed on 16 November 2025.

line between Bhalukpong to Tawang (Arunachal Pradesh), 87 km line between Silapathar (Assam) to Along via Bame (Arunachal Pradesh) and 217 km line between Rupai (Assam) to Pasighat (Arunachal Pradesh).'[151]

In an interview in June 2023, DGBR Lt Gen. Rajeev Chaudhry pointed out that 70 per cent of the BRO's construction work near the border was above 14,000 feet, which is significant from a preparedness perspective.[152] The extensive rail-road-tunnel networks would also enable armed forces to access key areas of contention in Arunachal Pradesh and Ladakh with relative ease across weathers, from relatively inside the territory in Himachal and Uttarakhand.

However, challenges remain. For example, even though the project progress is rapid, landslides, low temperatures, mountainous terrain, lack of cover from enemy firepower, and bureaucratic hurdles still need to be dealt with. For example:

- May to October is considered to be the only appropriate construction season for Ladakh. Therefore, projects may be delayed due to snow accumulation. The Nyoma Airfield, the highest airfield in Ladakh, put Indian troops and weaponry at the forefront, as it is constructed nearly 30 kilometres away from the LAC. However, as of 2023, it is likely to take two working seasons[153] to build the airbase, and protect it against direct firepower from China. The fact that de-escalation is not yet complete means there is an urgent need to complete the airbase and put

---

[151]Gupta, Moushumi Das, and Snehesh Alex Philip, 'India's NE strategic rail link to LAC with China gathers pace, plans to connect 8 capitals too', *The Print*, 26 December 2022, https://tinyurl.com/4ms3pr59. Accessed on 16 November 2025.
[152]*Hindustan Times*, '"Galwan Changed India's Border Infra Blitz Vs China" | Lt Gen Rajeev Chaudhry | HT Podcast', *Youtube*, 13 June 2023, https://tinyurl.com/2t4w6pbp. Accessed on 16 November 2025.
[153]Ibid.

security protocol and training requirements in place to make forces acquainted with the base's protection.

- While the Indian land warfare doctrine of 2018[154] specifically instructs strike formations deployed on northern borders to acclimatize themselves to the conditions in which they would be required to fight, there is little information on the challenges soldiers face and how they are being circumvented.
- Since the Galwan Valley clash, BRO projects are receiving quicker approvals. With the granting of greater powers to BRO leaders, slow MoD approvals, too, are mitigated. However, because a lot of the road and rail construction may involve protected forested areas, the Ministry of Environment, Forest, and Climate Change needs to be engaged in construction plans. Quick forest clearance and subsequent rehabilitation efforts may be crucial in the interest of national security.
- The BRO is experimenting with rock-bolt technology to ensure that vulnerable rock formations are stabilized and projects are not delayed by landslides.[155] This has proven effective in the case of the Sela tunnel, which connects Tezpur with Tawang. The use of the tech must be expanded. There must also be provisions for snow clearance and road washaways due to melting, to ensure cross-season access. Again, the Sela tunnel is an excellent example of how a bi-lane tunnel with an emergency escape tube can be designed to circumvent snow and landslide damage.
- Ensuring access to high-altitude regions is of strategic

---

[154]Indian Army, 'Land Warfare Doctrine – 2018', https://tinyurl.com/njtksmz7. Accessed on 16 November 2025.

[155]Sethi, Narendra, 'Border Roads Organisation turns to rock-bolt tech to tackle landslips', *The New Indian Express*, 7 December 2024, https://tinyurl.com/jbd2f77v. Accessed on 16 November 2025.

importance. In this regard, the success of the BRO's Vijayak and Beacon frontline projects, which enabled the Zoji-La pass to remain accessible beyond 31 December for the first time in January 2022,[156] must be replicated.

- Undertaking railway projects is time-consuming and requires multiple clearances. Railway networks are also vulnerable to attack by enemy fire. Nonetheless, proposed networks are essential for troop and cargo movement.[157] In this regard, materialization of the Bhalukpong gauge line is essential, given that helicopter service to areas like Tawang is susceptible to extreme wind conditions.[158]

Third, and finally, the vitality of Unmanned Combat Aerial Vehicles (UCAVs)/drones is increasingly becoming evident. China itself is one of the largest producers and exporters of military drones. In this regard, India is preparing to deploy its own drones in battle for a host of purposes. India's primary arsenal includes DRDO's self-developed drones, such as Netra, Rustom II, Ulka, Fluffy, and Ghatak, HAL's self-developed RUAV 200 and CATS Warrior, BEL's Trinetra, and the Israeli Heron, Harpy and Harop drones. These drones perform a range of functions. The Heron and Netra perform ISR, while Harpy and Harop act as loitering munition/kamikaze drones. CATS Warrior engages with manned aircraft as 'loyal wingman', while the Trinetra has a thermal camera to identify targets hiding under a canopy.[159] Ulka and Fluffy are

---

[156]'Border Roads Organisation breaks record at Zoji La battling extreme weather conditions', *Press Information Bureau,* Government of India, 4 January 2022, https://tinyurl.com/yf3u8bke. Accessed on 16 November 2025.

[157]Swartz, John, 'Tracking India's Infrastructure Development Near the Line of Actual Control', Observer Research Foundation, 17 October 2023, https://tinyurl.com/szt7wjx5. Accessed on 16 November 2025.

[158]Karmakar, Rahul, 'Train to Tawang near China border in Arunachal closer to reality', *Hindustan Times*, 4 April 2017, https://tinyurl.com/22k3dmpw. Accessed on 16 November 2025.

[159]Philip, Snehesh Alex, 'Army inducts drones in use with Ukrainian military.

air-launched expendable target drones. Some of these drones, like the RUAV and the Rustom, are still in development and have yet to be tested. Infamously, in April 2025, HAL failed to meet operational expectations with the RUAV-200.[160] In October 2024, India also signed a contract with the US to import 31 MQ-9B 'Reaper' drones and their components.[161]

Swarming and stacking must be experimented with for military purposes. This is because drones—not Medium-/High-Altitude Long Endurance (MALE/ HALE) UCAVs—but cheaper kamikazes, quadcopters, or the Khargas (Kharga Kamikaze Drone) provide strengths in the form of penetrating ISR and air suppression in large numbers. The capability of the main adversary here is demonstrable by the fact that China holds the world record in both fixed-wing and quadcopter drone swarming. Because of China's civil-military fusion strategy, its biggest drone manufacturers, such as the CETC and EHang, are readily providing for the PLA's needs.[162] Perhaps similarly, India must leverage the capabilities of its private sector for effective procurement of new and emerging technologies, such as drones, at cheaper costs.

In March 2023, India inducted its first batch of NIMBUS and BELUGA swarm drones, developed by NewSpace Research and Technologies. NRT was given the contract under the

---

Trinetra to boost surveillance', *The Print*, 27 September 2024, https://tinyurl.com/3hwv8e4d. Accessed on 16 November 2025.

[160]'CAG slams HAL for RUAV-200 Program Failures: Calls for Market-Driven Reforms in UAV Development', *IRDW*, 15 April 2025, https://tinyurl.com/yrbzjxpe. Accessed on 16 November 2025.

[161]'India, US to finalise INR 34,500 crore deal for MQ-9B drones', Ministry of External Affairs, Government of India, 15 October 2024, https://tinyurl.com/564xmuwh. Accessed on 16 November 2025.

[162]Saxena, Anushka, 'Takshashila SlideDoc - China's Approach to Military Unmanned Aerial Vehicles and Drone Autonomy', *Takshashila Institution*, 28 September 2023, https://tinyurl.com/ywv4v2hz. Accessed on 18 November 2025.

Indian Army's post-Galwan emergency procurement powers of up to ₹500 crore (~US$60 million), which eventually put the swarm drones under the Army's Fast-track Procurement (FTP) mechanism.[163] Although there is no publicly available information on the testing and deployment of the NIMBUS or BELUGA swarms, in January 2021, on Army Day, a live demonstration of 75 kamikaze drones was conducted, demonstrating some degree of swarming capability. Further, in 2022 and 2023, respectively, the Indian Army put out Request For Proposals (RFP) for 363 non-combat multi-domain drones for operational missions in high-altitude areas along the LAC, and 850 indigenously-produced nano-drones for ISR.[164] It remains to be seen how these capabilities are being tested, and whether they will deliver in conflict. As for neutralizing drone swarms, India's Bhargavastra counter-drone system was reportedly test-fired after the hostilities with Pakistan between 7 and 10 May 2025.[165] It uses micro-missiles in hard-kill mode to decimate drone swarms, although there is no official confirmation on its efficacy and kill rate.

Churn in the IOR

From the Chinese perspective, sea power is essential for the PLA to become a 'world-class fighting force.' Consequently, it has demonstrated its ability to use joint naval sorties bringing together civilian scientific vessels, the PLA Navy (PLAN), the

---

[163]IMR Reporter, 'Defence Forces Get Emergency Powers Up To Rs 500 Cr Per Acquisition', *Indian Military Review*, 22 June 2020, https://tinyurl.com/3f3xzzuy. Accessed on 16 November 2025.

[164]Simha, Rakesh Krishnan, 'Pack Attack: Swarm Drones are set to Transform Warfare', *Raksha Anirveda*, Vol. 6, No. 1, April-June 2023, p. 32, https://tinyurl.com/3r66v4sh. Accessed on 16 November 2025.

[165]Swarjya Staff, '"Bhargavastra": India's New Low-Cost Drone Swarm Killer Successfully Conducts Salvo, Single-Rocket Trials', *Swarajya*, 14 May 2025, https://tinyurl.com/2uxkdpza, Accessed on 16 November 2025.

Coast Guard (CCG), and the Chinese Maritime Militia (CMM) in nearby waters to project capability and preponderance. China also possesses the world's largest shipbuilding base, which is facilitating the PLAN's efforts to truly become a blue water navy. While India views itself as a major naval power, the Indian Navy's operational focus has been on HADR, anti-piracy and sea lanes protection operations.

Chinese presence in waters around India and its neighbourhood is increasing, and so are its shipbuilding capabilities and fleet numbers. China currently operates about 370 ships and submarines under the PLAN's ambit, while its total active naval fleet, including CCG and CMM vessels, is over 400. This makes it the largest maritime power by quantity. Among these, the PLAN operates nearly 50 destroyers, frigates and corvettes each, around 43 mine warfare vessels,[166] and 60–65 submarines. These include nuclear-powered, diesel-electric and ballistic missile attack submersibles.[167]

The PLAN has also operationalized two aircraft carriers, namely Liaoning and Shandong, while the third carrier, Fujian, has been inducted in late 2025 after undergoing prolonged sea trials. In fact, China is now widely deploying carrier battle groups (CBGs) in contested maritime zones such as the South China Sea. The most recent example is that of a Shandong CBG, with eight warships, simulating its tactical role in a Taiwan Strait conflict as part of the April 2025 Strait Thunder A exercises. Before that, in October 2024, a Liaoning CBG (Carrier Battle Group) conducted drills in the Philippine Sea. With the induction of Fujian, it is likely that above and beyond the Taiwan Strait and the South China Sea, the IOR could become a regular theatre of Chinese CBG sorties.

---

[166]'People's Liberation Army Navy (2025)', World Directory of Modern Military Warships, https://tinyurl.com/m3jy88bn. Accessed on 16 November 2025.

[167]'China Submarine Capabilities', NTI, 13 August 2024, https://tinyurl.com/34dcw8xn. Accessed on 16 November 2025.

Further, China's operational civilian-scientific research vessels number around 64. Many of these are active in the IOR. The Chinese party-state also provides substantial economic support to shipbuilding firms such as COSCO Shipping Holding Ltd, which has reportedly supplied most task-force vessels China deploys for counter-piracy operations in the Gulf of Aden.[168] Many Chinese commercial fleets also engage in Illegal, Unreported and Unregulated (IUU) fishing. CMM vessels constitute a large chunk of China's Distant Water Fishing (DWF for IUU) fleet. As of 2018, 12,000-plus vessels were believed to have been active in international waters.[169] This number would likely have expanded with time.

Further, China is expanding its basing capacity in the IOR, through either investments or partnerships. The Djibouti naval support base, built at a cost of US$590 million, is the PLAN's solitary base in the region so far.[170] It has been utilized for practising live-fire tactics, ensuring logistics supply through nearby maritime trade routes like the Bab-el-Mandeb, and hosting warships and submarines for immediate deployment in areas like the Gulf of Aden.[171]

Apart from the Djibouti base, China has made strategic investments in the Gwadar Port in the Balochistan province of Pakistan. The rights for the operation of and construction on the port were granted to the China Overseas Port Holding Company

---

[168]Palve, Shubhangi, '"Enough To Devastate Every U.S Navy Warship At Norfolk": China's "Shadow Fleet" Raises Alarm In Washington', *EurAsian Times*, 10 January 2025, https://tinyurl.com/3tpkbtas. Accessed on 16 November 2025.

[169]Pedrozo, Raul (Pete), 'China's IUU Fishing Fleet: Pariah of the World's Oceans', *International Law Studies*, Vol. 99 No. 319. 2022, https://tinyurl.com/4tburuj. Accessed on 16 November 2025.

[170]Zhou, Laura, 'How a Chinese investment boom is changing the face of Djibouti', *South China Morning Post*, 17 April 2017, https://tinyurl.com/3b6hkeyk. Accessed on 16 November 2025.

[171]Headley, Tyler, 'China's Djibouti Base: A One Year Update', *The Diplomat*, 4 December 2018, https://tinyurl.com/bky8ed45. Accessed on 16 November 2025.

(COPHC) in 2013. In 2015, COPHC guaranteed an investment of US$1.6 billion to enhance the economic potential of the port and grow it substantially. Progress, however, has been slow.[172] Bangladesh, too, has depended on Chinese naval capabilities. The BNS Sheikh Hasina Submarine Base, now renamed BNS Pekua, is perhaps one of the most vital collaboration projects between the two countries. China has not only assisted in its construction, but the first two submarines to be based there were purchased by Dhaka from Beijing for a price of US$203 million.[173]

In Southeast Asia, Cambodia and Myanmar have proven to be consistent partners for China's naval ambitions. In 2024, for example, the Ream Naval Base in Cambodia provided four months of continued presence for two Chinese warships. Even though the Cambodian government denied terming it 'permanent presence', it has acknowledged that China has assisted in expanding the base and that the PLAN's vessels frequent it.[174] In Myanmar's Rakhine state, situated on the western coast facing India, is the Kyaukphyu Port. The port is a pillar of the China-Myanmar Economic Corridor under the BRI. The Myanmar government has already handed a Concession Agreement to the China International Trust and Investment Corporation Group (CITIC) to handle the port's operations.[175] Some reports suggest that PLA personnel and security systems, such as drones, jammers and mines, have been

---

[172]PTI, 'China, Pak sign deals worth USD 1.6 billion to beef up CPEC', *Business Standard*, 12 August 2015, https://tinyurl.com/6h2xumpz. Accessed on 16 November 2025.

[173]Funaiole, Matthew P., Brian Hart, Aidan Powers-Riggs, and Jennifer Jun, 'Submarine Diplomacy: A Snapshot of China's Influence along the Bay of Bengal', *CSIS*, 17 November 2023, https://tinyurl.com/mr24ta2t. Accessed on 16 November 2025.

[174]Tiwari, Sakshi, 'Days After Official Inauguration, Chinese Troops Drill At Cambodia's 'Controversial' Ream Naval Base; What's Cooking?', *EurAsian Times*, 8 April 2025, https://tinyurl.com/yabk6dnf. Accessed on 16 November 2025.

[175]'Kyaukphyu Deep Sea Port', Myanmar Port Authority, https://tinyurl.com/msxf3yrk. Accessed on 16 November 2025.

deployed at the base.[176] Similarly, there is speculation around the presence of Chinese SIGINT systems and intelligence forces being deployed on the Great Coco Islands in Myanmar, which are situated 55 kilometres from the Andaman and Nicobar Islands.[177]

Sri Lanka and Maldives, India's two closest maritime neighbours, have also assisted China by hosting its civilian scientific research vessels with dual-use capabilities. Sri Lanka has infamously leased the Hambantota Port for 99 years to China Merchants Port Holdings. And even though in 2024 Colombo placed a moratorium on the docking of any foreign research vessels at its ports for a year, with the new Anura Dissanayake government in power, internal support for the extension of the moratorium appears to be dwindling.[178]

Moreover, in early 2025, the Xiang Yang Hong 01 Research Vessel was tracked off the coast of the Andaman and Nicobar Islands. It conducted a 76-day-long voyage with stops in the Bay of Bengal as well. In the past, similar Chinese research vessels have even conducted collaborative operations with Sea Wing Unmanned Underwater Vehicles (UUVs), dispersing over a dozen underwater gliders in the Bay of Bengal region to conduct a continuous assessment of oceanographic data. Sea Wing UUVs were launched both in 2017 and 2019 to conduct 'cooperative observation in a designated sea area.'[179] The value

---

[176]Graceffo, Antonio, 'An analysis of Chinese security forces' activities in Myanmar', *Democratic Voice of Burma*, 4 May 2025, https://tinyurl.com/2x97kw68. Accessed on 16 November 2025.

[177]Ratcliffe, Rebecca, 'Military construction on Myanmar's Great Coco island prompts fears of Chinese involvement', *The Guardian*, 1 May 2023, https://tinyurl.com/4a3htena. Accessed on 16 November 2025.

[178]Saxena, Anushka, 'India's Island Neighbours: Assessing Ties with Maldives and Sri Lanka', *Takshashila Institution*, 23 October 2024, https://tinyurl.com/mr33sdnb. Accessed on 18 November 2025.

[179]Saxena, Anushka, 'India Has Good Reason to Be Concerned About China's Maritime Research Vessels', *The Diplomat*, 2 February 2024, https://tinyurl.com/yh2sdpaz. Accessed on 16 November 2025.

of the large amount of hydrological data collected over time, including temperature, salinity, turbidity and oxygen content, is unprecedented.

It is vital to acknowledge that India possesses a geographical advantage in the IOR. However, China is rapidly catching up by building economic and military partnerships to match India's preponderance. To deal with this, India requires a diverse security toolkit.

Dual Challenge of Dual-Use Ships

Chinese civilian scientific research vessels have continued expanding their presence in the IOR, turning off their Automatic Identification Systems (AIS) and collecting hydrological data. The primary concern lies in the capabilities of such a survey ship, which, while ostensibly engaged in peaceful research and maritime tracking activities, can covertly gather critical data about the ocean's seabed, maritime currents and oceanographic patterns. This information can be repurposed for military applications. These include analyzing optimal seasonal deployment strategies for submarines, acquiring oceanographic insights, such as maximum depths to plan mine warfare scenarios, and studying marine wind data to assess ocean wind resources in coastal areas at specific times. Such data can further be utilized to evaluate the take-off and landing requirements of enemy aircraft, as well as optimize China's own airpower operations within the IOR.

In this regard, it is pertinent for India to maintain a large enough fleet of Kamorta-class corvettes, Khukri-class corvettes and Shivalik-class frigates to track Chinese vessels in the Indian Exclusive Economic Zone, and respond with its own hydrological data-collection mechanisms. India must also deploy diplomatic means, as it did with Sri Lanka in 2023, to prevent Chinese RVs from docking close to the Indian peninsula and turn into listening posts with emitting radars.

India must also be proactive in deploying its own naval countermeasures against expanding Chinese civilian scientific presence in the IOR. This should first centre around enhancing naval ISR capabilities, through either the deployment of the Indian Navy's Searcher drones, or image intelligence using land-, sea-, air-, or space-based sensors.[180] Subsequently, data collected on activities of Chinese vessels can be analysed to position submarines and warships for conducting chase actions, especially in the Indian EEZ. India must also leverage its partnerships with extra-regional naval powers like Australia, especially given that the two sides have concluded a Maritime Domain Awareness (MDA) agreement. Joint MDA drills can not only act as a power projection tool, but also build collaborative practices toward securing the waters against 'dark' Chinese vessels.

Countering Carriers, Surveilling Seas

As discussed above, China has rapidly developed three aircraft carriers, and plans to construct a fourth one. In the near future, PLAN CBGs will have the capability to be deployed in three or four core maritime theatres, including the IOR. While Chinese doctrine currently places the IOR relatively low on the list of priorities for naval deployment, with increasing capabilities, Chinese CBGs may experiment with semi-permanent deployments in the IOR, and India will likely have to respond in kind.

A permanently positioned Chinese CBG in the IOR has several security implications from India's perspective. Firstly, it puts India's geographical advantage and regional preponderance in jeopardy. But beyond that, regular sorties enable a CBG's various vessels to continuously gather hydrological data for

---

[180]Mirwankar, Yashodhan, 'Comparative analysis of the maritime ISR capabilities of India and China in the IOR', *Electronic Journal of Social and Strategic Studies*, Vol. 5, No. 2, August-September 2024, https://tinyurl.com/3w3zrsmk. Accessed on 16 November 2025.

military purposes, and eventually utilize it for stealth warfighting or air-battle formations in the Bay of Bengal. The CBG's vessels could also map Indian naval movements, and easily establish communication links with nearby Chinese naval facilities over which data on such movements can be shared. Carrier decks would also provide Chinese fighter jets an opportunity to practise take-off and landing in the IOR airspace, assessing wind data for future deployments. Increased aerial sorties can subsequently disrupt air traffic and create escalatory tensions in the region. Finally, the CBG could, with enough firepower, disrupt Sea Lines of Communications (SLOCs) based on Chinese whims, impacting India's economic security.

CBGs create many challenges in a hot war. They are susceptible to missile attacks due to their slow movements, and their losses are costly. The diverse coverage of their various vessels' weapons systems can lead to disrupted targeting and waste of ammunition. They have extensive refuelling and replenishment requirements, and need consistent tracking, which ties up resources. But in peacetime, Chinese CBGs can be useful for fulfilling the abovementioned purposes, thus fuelling tensions in the IOR.

While the debate on whether India should build a third aircraft carrier has continued for a long time, with two carriers, the INS *Vikramaditya* and the INS *Vikrant*, deployed on either side of the peninsula, a third carrier, or a fleet of vessels, may be required to conduct regular sorties in the IOR. Currently, the Indian Navy collaborates with littoral states such as Tanzania, Mozambique, Mauritius and Seychelles for military exercises, and plans to build a joint coastal surveillance architecture with them, under the Africa-India Key Maritime Engagement (AIKEYME).[181]

---

[181]'Indian Navy's Maiden Initiatives of Indian Ocean Ship Sagar (IOS SAGAR) and Africa India Key Maritime Engagement (AIKEYME)', *Press Information Bureau*, 24 March 2025, https://tinyurl.com/nhm34dfb. Accessed on 16 November 2025.

Such architecture must include the following:

1. A focus on robust legislative collaboration to track and crack down on IUU. India can build a joint mechanism with littoral states, especially in the western IOR, to use technologies like Automatic Identification Systems (AIS) and Vessel Monitoring Systems (VMS) that use satellite tracking to transmit vessel locations, which can be used to track fishing activity.[182] This is not standard practice in the region.
2. Interoperability between IOR maritime surveillance centres, to bolster maritime surveillance networks. The efforts of the Information Fusion Centre-the Indian Ocean Region (IFC-IOR) in India are enhanced by Regional Maritime Information Fusion Centres (RMIFCs), the Regional Operations Coordination Centre (RCOC), and national centres in the region.[183] There is a need to build interoperability between these centres. Further, Comoros, Djibouti, France, Kenya, Madagascar, Mauritius and Seychelles all have national centres for maritime surveillance, which can be roped into such a networked partnership.
3. The Quad's space-based assets cooperation endeavours can be useful for advanced surveillance of high seas in the IOR, which can not only help WIOR countries to combat IUU, but also enhance MDA and meet disaster mitigation needs.[184]

---

[182]Sharma, Bharat, and Kingshuk Saha, 'The Quad in the Western Indian Ocean Region', *Takshashila Institution*, 10 January 2024, https://tinyurl.com/239w7b33. Accessed on 18 November 2025.

[183]Ibid.

[184]Deshpande, Harshada, 'The Quad's Space Collaboration: Advancing Satellite and Space Security Initiatives', Forum for Integrated National Security (FINS), 14 April 2025, https://tinyurl.com/mr2y8kj3. Accessed on 16 November 2025.

Regularizing such endeavours, and engaging the coast guard in seafaring exercises, may build robust capability and enhance power projection.

Deployments of Tomorrow, Today

The November 2024 Zhuhai Airshow unveiled important naval technologies that shed light on China's priorities in the maritime domain. The J-15T naval fighter made its debut at the show. It is an upgraded version of the original Shenyang J-15, and is equipped with the latest radar and weapons. It is also compatible with catapult launch systems. Given that the PLA Navy's Type 003 Aircraft Carrier, the 'Fujian', is currently undergoing sea trials and is equipped with catapult launchers, the J-15T may pair nicely with it.[185] The 'T' in the J-15T reportedly stands for *tán shè*, literally meaning to launch/to eject.

The PLAN's J-15D carrier-based electronic warfare aircraft also debuted with the J-15D and J-15T carrier-based aircraft, forming a three-aircraft team showcasing naval-specific manoeuvres in their first post-induction performance. But perhaps the most outstanding performers in the Navy-Marine Corps' show were the 'Lynx' all-terrain vehicles (ATVs), in an aerobatic demonstration alongside six shipborne and transport aircraft, three each of the Z-20J and the Z-8C models, respectively.[186] The Z-20J is adopted from the Harbin Z-20, whose anti-submarine variant, the Z-20F/Z-20 ASW, has already been quite popular.[187] The 20J debuted too, and is considered capable of carrying Anti-Tank Guided Missiles (ATGMs), though its main role is likely to be for

---

[185]Saxena, Anushka, 'Pulling out the Big Guns', *Eye on China*, 26 November 2024, https://tinyurl.com/mu3sc3de. Accessed on 16 November 2025.

[186]Ibid.

[187]Cui, Meng, 'Z-20J shipborne helicopter and Z-8C transport helicopter in aerial display training at Airshow China', *Global Times*, 10 November 2024, https://tinyurl.com/22sww4vv. Accessed on 16 November 2025.

shipboard operations—namely, transport, combat and utility.[188]

Unmanned vessels also performed 'water ballets', and the large unmanned combat vessel 'Orca' made an appearance too. 'Orca' went to sea trials in 2022 and debuted this time, but its details grabbed international attention. As official sources highlighted, it is a 58-metre-long, 23-metre-wide, 4-metre-deep, and 500-tonne displacement, high-speed stealth unmanned surface combat vessel.[189] It is equipped with a diesel-electric dual-mode propulsion system, providing it with a maximum speed of 40 knots (74 kilometres per hour), and a range of more than 4,000 nautical miles (7,400 kilometres). As an autonomous combat vessel, it is like a mobile fortress on the sea that is capable of undertaking tasks such as beyond visual range (BVR) fire strike, air and missile defence, and anti-submarine search and strike.

In terms of integrated reconnaissance and strike zones, the display of the Wing Loong-X (hereon, WLX) was noteworthy. When the WLX was first displayed at the 2022 Airshow, it was referred to as Wing Loong-3, but only its potential to perform reconnaissance, ground strikes, and even communication relay tasks was depicted.[190]

In 2024, the WLX was displayed as an operational unit, potentially signalling that the technology is now mature and deployment-ready. The weapons pods and the sonar buoy it featured this time indicate that it can be deployed for anti-submarine warfare (ASW). The weapons pods included anti-submarine torpedoes that the WLX can deploy. Further, commentators suggested that a stack of WLXs can be

---

[188]@RupprechtDeino, *X* (formerly *Twitter)*, 19 July 2022, 11:49 a.m., https://tinyurl.com/3uvbpp56. Accessed on 16 November 2025.

[189]Wei, Liqun, 'China's large unmanned combat vessel "Orca" attracts wide attention', Ministry of National Defence, People's Republic of China, 18 November 2024, https://tinyurl.com/35rj2y29. Accessed on 16 November 2025.

[190]Saxena, Anushka, 'Pulling out the Big Guns', *Eye on China*, 26 November 2024, https://tinyurl.com/mu3sc3de. Accessed on 16 November 2025.

paired with anti-submarine systems like the KQ-200 and the PLAN Air Force's ASW aircraft, to cover a vast area in a 'submarine hunting' scenario.[191]

This rapid expansion by the PLAN will require India to invest in its own asymmetric naval capabilities. These include a combination of stealthy submarines, unmanned aerial vehicles for ISR, and naval airpower to enhance coordination and command and control at sea. Currently, India possesses around 13 destroyers, 18–20 corvettes, and 14 frigates, and operates two aircraft carriers. In total, the Indian Navy operates around 130 medium-to-large vessels, and plans to expand the fleet strength to about 160 by 2030 (as of 2023).[192] The Coast Guard operates around 182 vessels, and plans to grow its strength to 200 by 2030 (as of 2024).[193] India also possesses approximately 20 submarines, of which a majority are of the conventional attack, diesel-electric class.[194] As evident from the comparison with the fleet strength of the PLAN and CCG, India is not a close competitor to China.

While it is also not necessary to match Chinese fleet strength, given the latter's occupation in several maritime theatres, it is uncertain if the current Indian fleet strength is enough to establish regional dominance. Vessels often also halt operations in refuel and repair stages, which means the actual deployed strength is

---

[191]Asia Pacific, 'Wing Loong-X shows off a 'furious' configuration: it can carry air-launched ballistic missiles, anti-radiation missiles, and medium-range air-to-air missiles', *Tencent*, 13 November 2024, https://tinyurl.com/4javkjjd. Accessed on 18 November 2025.

[192]DH Web Desk, 'India planning a 175-ship Navy fleet to counter China in Indian Ocean: Report', *Deccan Herald*, 18 September 2023, https://tinyurl.com/2u2sdn5p. Accessed on 16 November 2025.

[193]ANI, 'Indian Coast Guard poised to achieve its target force levels of 200 surface platforms and 100 aircraft by 2030', *The Economic Times*, 31 January 2025, https://tinyurl.com/4p7c94vt. Accessed on 16 November 2025.

[194]Vyas, 'Naval Warships, submarines and helicopters/aircrafts used by Indian Navy', *DOSPDP Blogs*, 16 May 2023, https://tinyurl.com/2jc8cja8. Accessed on 16 November 2025.

lesser than the total active vessel numbers.

The Indian Navy Maritime Capability Perspective Plan (MCPP) 2023–37[195] is the guiding document for the country's military and civilian maritime power development. One of the MCPP's focal areas is self-reliance in naval development. While DPSU shipyards and the Directorate General of Naval Design have made significant strides in R&D and production efforts, especially for bigger vessels, there is a need to integrate civilian naval development capabilities. In terms of the warfare of tomorrow, MSMEs are best suited to supply the Indian Navy with indigenous Unmanned Underwater/Surface Vehicles (UUVs/ USVs). When deployed, these are useful for tracking hydrological data, and conducting mine countermeasures and ISR.[196] The development of the Navy Technology Development Accelerator Cell (TDAC), specifically its task force to collaborate with MSMEs and start-ups, is a welcome move. It is reported that in the last two years, 13 AoNs have been converted to contracts with MSMEs. Expanding this further is vital.[197]

The MCPP also details the need to induct three aircraft carriers and at least six operational nuclear submarines (SSNs) by 2037. While the timeline seems realistic, it requires support in the form of budgetary allocations for capital outlay, and accelerating the acquisition and/or domestic production capabilities of crucial components. One example of this may be the 26 carrier-borne

---

[195]The Hindu Bureau, 'Navy's Maritime Infrastructure Perspective Plan 2023-37 released', *The Hindu*, 4 September 2023, https://tinyurl.com/muru2dzp. Accessed on 16 November 2025.

[196]Heo, Jinyeong, Junghoon Kim, and Yongjin Kwon, 'Technology Development of Unmanned Underwater Vehicles (UUVs)', *Journal of Computer and Communications*, Vol. 6, No. 7, May 2017, https://tinyurl.com/4f4fwxkr. Accessed on 16 November 2025.

[197]Peri, Dinakar, 'Navy has set up two special task forces for development of niche technologies: Vice Chief', *The Hindu*, 22 October 2024, https://tinyurl.com/4a9jwd89. Accessed on 16 November 2025.

Rafale (M) jets that India has placed an order for in April 2025. Deliveries of this are expected to only be complete by 2030, provided there are no bureaucratic or payment-related hurdles.[198]

It is also important to take stock of previously recognized indigenization requirements for the navy, where there has been excessive dependence on foreign providers, leading to delays. In its 2018 Technology Perspective and Capability Roadmap,[199] HQ Integrated Defence Staff of the MoD identified non-magnetic marine engines and diesel engines of 1–7 MW thrust as two such items. In April 2025, the Navy reportedly struck a deal with Kirloskar Oil Engines Limited for indigenously built 6 MW marine diesel engines.[200] However, to date, it seems there are no domestic alternatives for the former.

India's submarine programmes, Project 75(I) for the acquisition of diesel electric submarines and Project 77 for nuclear-powered submarines, currently face slow development and institutional ad-hocism. In fact, in early 2025, it was reported that the two main contenders who have presented designs for the advanced diesel-electrics to the Indian Navy, Spain's Navantia and Germany's TKMS, have not been able to fulfil the exact requirements of the project.[201] Beyond this, technical adjustments will also require an extended period of time.

In this regard, institutional reform is essential to accelerate

---

[198]International Year of Cooperatives 2025, 'Rafale-Marine: Enhancing India's Naval Strength', *Press Information Bureau,* Government of India, 29 April 2025, https://tinyurl.com/475rkuhp. Accessed on 16 November 2025.

[199]HQ Integrated Defence Staff, Ministry of Defence, 'Technology Perspective and Capability Roadmap', April 2013, https://tinyurl.com/3dc2vb93. Accessed on 16 November 2025.

[200]ANI, 'Indian Navy, Kirloskar sign Rs 270 crore deal for 6MW marine diesel engine', *The Economic Times*, 2 April 2025, https://tinyurl.com/36u635u6. Accessed on 16 November 2025.

[201]Kunde, Raunak, 'Indian Navy faces challenges with AIP Trials for Project-75I Submarines', Indian Research Defence Wing, 16 January 2025, https://tinyurl.com/354jzf7b. Accessed on 18 November 2025.

the timeliness for acquisition, starting from RFPs and AoNs to production and induction. In January 2025, Defence Secretary Rajesh Kumar Singh lauded the 2025 MoD agenda, the 'Year of Reforms', and argued that within 12 months the acquisition and procurement procedures in India would be reformed.[202] Three challenges that he highlighted need focus. In the naval domain, there is a 'gold plating' of General Staff Quality Requirements (GSQR) for domestic procurement. GSQR and RFP parameters detailing the military's requirements are often set too high a bar, leading vendors to make tall claims without demonstrating existing capability. Hence, shortcomings become evident only at the trial stage. Further, parameters may also leave no room for flexibility in requirements. Therefore, it is important to find a balance between rigidity and extreme subjective interpretation.[203]

As discussed above, with the submarine programme in specific, the stealth- and air-independent propulsion (AIP) systems-related requirements laid out by the Navy have been termed as 'unrealistic' in the past.[204] This may especially be so because the Defence Acquisition Plan (DAP) of 2020[205] requires that submarines and other naval platforms be acquired based on the ideas maintained in the Maritime Capability Perspective Plan (MCPP), making the Indian Navy's requirements implicit and vague. Clarifying the exact requirements for procurement

---

[202]Kumar, Bhaswar, 'MoD to reform procurement policy in 6-12 months: Defence Secretary', *Business Standard*, 10 January 2025, https://tinyurl.com/sefse4m3. Accessed on 16 November 2025.

[203]Verma, Sanjay, 'Decoding the GSQR Conundrum, Nuts and Bolts', *DefStrat*, Vol. 15, No. 2, 1 July 2021, https://tinyurl.com/2ra9yuv2. Accessed on 9 December 2025.

[204]Bedi, Rahul, 'Navy's 'Unrealistic' Expectations for Submarine Tender Will Have Operational Ramifications', *The Wire*, 17 August 2022, https://tinyurl.com/2fa34z5p. Accessed on 16 November 2025.

[205]Ministry of Defence, 'Defence Acquisition Procedure 2020', Government of India, https://tinyurl.com/bp5ctkrr. Accessed on 16 November 2025.

and balancing qualitative needs with quantitative necessities are a must going forward.

The Cyber Challenge

Because of the transnational nature of cyberspace, India is also at risk of cyberattacks against critical national security infrastructure by foreign state and non-state actors. An example is the ShadowPad malware attack faced by Indian power grid institutions in April 2022.[206] The hackers responsible, believed to be sponsored by the Chinese state, preyed on already infected IoT devices to navigate through compromised networks and conduct espionage activities in the Ladakh region of India. The Chinese Ministry of State Security and the PLA have been associated with multiple ShadowPad malware attacks in the past, reportedly using a group of hackers that have come to be known as RedEcho.

Before that, in 2021, private cyber-intelligence firm Group-IB attributed a ColunmTK campaign against Air India's IT servers to a Chinese group called Advanced Persistent Threat (APT) 41 (also known as BARIUM and Wicked Spider-Panda).[207] As part of the attack, 4,500,000 data subjects were affected globally, including Air India customers. The severity of the challenge is clear, and has multifaceted implications for data security, internet governance, and a safe and secure IT infrastructure in India.

Moreover, there exists the threat of Intellectual Property (IP) theft, which requires a more vocal call to action from the Indian government. For example, cyber-intelligence firm Cyfirma informed the public in March 2021 that a Chinese APT Stone

---

[206]'Continued Targeting of Indian Power Grid Assets by Chinese State-Sponsored Activity Group', *Recorded Future, Insikt Group*, 6 April 2024, https://tinyurl.com/362z73a2. Accessed on 16 November 2025.

[207]Rostovcev, Nikita, 'Big airline heist', *Group-IB*, 10 June 2021, https://tinyurl.com/vzz3ka49. Accessed on 16 November 2025.

Panda (APT 10) was responsible for leaking vaccine data from the web servers of Bharat Biotech and Serum Institute of India.[208] However, the Indian government has made no confirmations regarding the involvement of a Chinese APT. This is a hurdle in the applicability of punitive measures under multilateral instruments like the Paris Convention for the Protection of Industrial Property. This is because such measures depend on state attribution and good faith interpretation of treaties by member countries.

The nature of the challenge is broader and more complex when looked at from a global lens, given that India is not the only victim of Chinese cyberattacks. In fact, some of the most technologically advanced countries, such as the US, have also been prey to Chinese cyberattacks. Since 2021, for example, US-based firm Microsoft has identified a China-based cyberespionage group, Volt Typhoon, as being responsible for targeting critical American infrastructure. The group has allegedly affected organizations in the communications, manufacturing, utility, transportation, construction, maritime, government, information technology and education sectors. It was also responsible for the attack on Singapore Telecommunications Ltd in 2024. US officials contend that the Singtel cyberattack is a 'test run' for targeting US telecommunications networks.[209] As of 2025, the FBI has said that it has conducted a deep cleanse of US critical infrastructure and managed to eliminate Volt Typhoon's botnets.[210] Nonetheless,

---

[208]Das, Krishna N., 'Chinese hackers target Indian vaccine makers SII, Bharat Biotech, says security firm', *Reuters*, 1 March 2021, https://tinyurl.com/2p9u4due. Accessed on 16 November 2025.

[209]Robertson, Jordan, and Katrina Manson, 'Chinese Group Accused of Hacking Singtel in Telecom Attacks', *Bloomberg*, 5 November 2025, https://tinyurl.com/yc6rwvpx. Accessed on 16 November 2025.

[210]'U.S. Government Disrupts Botnet People's Republic of China Used to Conceal Hacking of Critical Infrastructure', US Department of Justice, 31 January 2024, https://tinyurl.com/nhb292wt. Accessed on 16 November 2025.

there is a lot of information that could have been stolen and substantial infrastructure that was likely compromised since the group reportedly began operations in mid-2021. The Chinese have categorically denied supporting Volt Typhoon, and have referred to the attacks in the US as 'false flag' operations.[211]

Offence as the Best Defence

Given the length and breadth of cyberspace, offence is the best defence. Consequently, there is great value in investing in deterrence mechanisms to protect the Indian ICT infrastructure. India has set up institutional capacity domestically to conduct offensive cyber operations. To enhance the cybersecurity posture of its defence forces, India set up a Defence Cyber Agency (DCA) and three Cyber Groups in each of the three services in 2018.[212] One of the key aims of these efforts is to ensure better preparedness to respond to cyberwarfare. Such efforts may include hacking into networks, mounting surveillance operations, laying honeypots, recovering deleted data from hard drives and cell phones, and infiltrating encrypted communication channels.[213]

The DCA's operations will be incomplete without collaboration from CERT-In and the National Cybersecurity Coordination Centre, which are responsible for tracking and generating real-time information on cybersecurity threats in the country.[214]

---

[211]'Report reveals more conspiracies behind U.S. 'Volt Typhoon' misinformation campaign', *Xinhua*, 14 October 2024, https://tinyurl.com/48cfj2nh. Accessed on 16 November 2025.

[212]Press Information Bureau, 'Cyber Warfare', Government of India, 3 December 2021, https://tinyurl.com/4wzw9wjz. Accessed on 16 November 2025.

[213]'Defence Cyber Command', *SP Naval Forces*, 6 July 2021, https://tinyurl.com/3w9ej648. Accessed on 16 November 2025.

[214]Basu, Arindrajit, 'India's International Cyber Operations: Tracing National Doctrine and Capabilities', United Nations Institute for Disarmament Research, December 2022, https://tinyurl.com/3n3bhwk5. Accessed on 16 November 2025.

But even though it was announced in August 2021 that this agency is now fully operational, assessments of its activities, operations conducted, and even figures on the budget allocated are not publicly available.

However, research conducted by the Manohar Parrikar Institute for Defence Studies and Analyses suggests that if India indeed undertakes offensive cyber operations to 'punish acts of aggression' in cyberspace, the agency in charge shall be the National Technical Research Organisation (NTRO).[215] Such acts of 'aggression' may comprise breaches of sensitive data and upload of critical national security information to the Dark Web; attacks on Critical Information Infrastructure (CII), such as power grids and nuclear, oil and gas facilities; and cyberterrorism. Punitive measures may include diplomatic expulsions, criminal prosecutions, and economic sanctions, with due authorization directly from the Prime Minister's Office (PMO). This is because the NTRO is a secretive agency that reports directly to the PMO, and whose annual budget is classified. Further, its code of conduct guidelines are similar to those established for the Intelligence Bureau (IB) or the Research and Analysis Wing (R&AW), which indicates that there are restrictions on the freedoms of speech and political association for NTRO members.[216]

Domestically, surveillance operations are an important part of the Indian government's policy to address irresponsible cyber behaviour. As per Section 69 of the amended IT Act of 2008, the central and state governments have the authority to 'intercept, monitor or decrypt or cause to be intercepted or monitored or decrypted any information generated, transmitted, received or

---

[215]Samuel, Cherian, and Munish Sharma, 'India's Strategic Options in a Changing Cyberspace', Pentagon Press and Manohar Parrikar Institute for Defence Studies and Analyses, New Delhi, 2019, https://tinyurl.com/yxfjm9d6. Accessed on 16 November 2025.

[216]Singh, Vijaita, 'NTRO now under Intelligence Act', *The Hindu*, 18 May 2017, https://tinyurl.com/2had9zk2. Accessed on 16 November 2025.

stored in any computer resource.'[217] This can be done for the purposes of 'protecting sovereignty, national security, friendly relations with international governments, [and] integrating public order,' which are priorities that relate directly to the government's top-down approach to monitoring cyber and telecommunications networks.

India requires a coordinated approach to offensive cyber practices, involving the technical expertise of CERT-In, the security assessment of the National Cybersecurity Coordinator, and the cyber-military capabilities of DCA. CERT-In requires a mandate that goes beyond monitoring risks, and includes preparing a surveillance and response toolkit for attacks on critical infrastructure. It is also recommended that India develop hacking capabilities to gather information on espionage and terror activities brewing in rival states such as China and Pakistan. This may require robust engagement with start-ups and cyber-intelligence firms, who have been investing in monitoring and understanding APTs of these countries for a long time.

Further, the Corps of Signals of the Indian Army have a crucial role to play in training for cyber offence and defence. Signals Corps are trained at the Military College of Telecommunication Engineering (MCTE) at Mhow[218] to achieve electronic and information security and dominance in battle. They can develop the capability to conduct 'lights-out' cyber operations in rival countries (especially Pakistan), and prepare deception tactics to distort narratives, radio chatter, and intelligence (especially along the LAC). It is reported that since March 2024, the 21 Signals Group has been converted by the Indian Army into the Signals Technology Evaluation

---

[217]'The Information Technology Act, 2000', https://tinyurl.com/pn9mnueh. Accessed on 16 November 2025.

[218]@ARTRAC_ia, *X* (formerly *Twitter*), 14 May 2023, 7:24 p.m., https://tinyurl.com/23me9bwz. Accessed on 16 November 2025.

and Adaptation Group (STEAG).[219] STEAG is responsible for studying how to leverage cutting-edge technologies such as 5G, 6G Quantum and AI for strengthening India's military power. It is vital that this project be encouraged and enhanced in the next few years to prepare for future wars.

High Stakes, Global Takes

India will also benefit from internationalizing the importance of cybersecurity, and working in coordination with global entities to mitigate the threat and gain cyber-intelligence. India's statement at the fifth substantive session of the UN Open-Ended Working Group on Cyberspace, in July 2023, has already delved into detail regarding the threat to national security posed by Quasi-State Actors (QSAs).[220] It has also included state-sponsored cybercriminals in this ambit. Having been at the receiving end of state-sponsored cybercrime, especially emanating from China, India has called on its international partners to develop joint accountability mechanisms on the irresponsible cyber behaviour of QSAs.

However, given the highly privatized nature of Critical Information Infrastructure (CII) and Information and Communications Technology (ICT), the Indian government cannot act alone in building governance and resilience for responsible cyber behaviour. A multi-stakeholder mechanism is essential to support India's diplomatic priorities. So far, because of India's top-down, government-led approach to responsible cyber governance, its stance on engaging the private sector and civil

---

[219] The Hindu Bureau, 'Army repurposes 21 Signal Group to research futuristic communications tech', *The Hindu*, 19 March 2024, https://tinyurl.com/53xutnuy. Accessed on 16 November 2025.

[220] 'India Statement on Quasi-State Actors (QSA): Open Ended Working Group on the Security Of and In The Use Of ICTS 2021-2025 (Fifth Substantive Session)', *UN ODA Library*, 2021, https://tinyurl.com/4pvx3jrm, Accessed on 16 November 2025.

society has been lackadaisical.

To begin with, India, like many other major cyberpowers including Russia, China, and the US, has not signed on to the Paris Call of 12 November 2018 for Trust and Security in Cyberspace.[221] This is considered one of the largest multi-stakeholder repositories of responsible cyber behaviour working groups. This is even though some of the Paris Call's private sector signatories include Indian industry-body leaders such as the Federation of Indian Chambers of Commerce & Industry (FICCI), Confederation of Indian Industry, and Internet and Mobile Association of India.[222]

Since 2021, India has made some progress in building a multi-stakeholder approach. One example is the organization of an annual multi-stakeholder consultative conference called the Internet Governance Forum (IGF). Moreover, in his June 2021 speech, India's then Info-Tech Joint Secretary Atul M. Gotsurve also indicated a significant shift in India's stance by offering to break the deadlock between states on multi-stakeholder participation.[223] He proposed to do so by calling on states to voluntarily declare reasons for their denial of the participation of NGOs/multi-stakeholder entities in cybersecurity-related multilateral deliberations.

Moving forward, as India builds a resilient cyber and ICT security policy, including in the form of the upcoming National Cybersecurity Strategy, engaging private sector firms, NGOs, think tanks and civil society will become pertinent. The existence of

---

[221]'The supporters', *Paris Call*, https://tinyurl.com/5n8ruux3. Accessed on 16 November 2025.

[222]Saxena, Anushka. 'India', *Responsible cyber behaviour in the Indo-Pacific*, January 2025, https://tinyurl.com/2yukxhtf. Accessed on 16 November 2025.

[223]'Opening Statement on 13 December 2021 by Mr. Atul M. Gotsurve, Joint Secretary [EG & IT and CD]: Open Ended Working Group on Security of and in the Use of ICTs 2021-2025 (First Substantive Session)', Permanent Mission of India to the UN, New York, December 2021, https://tinyurl.com/y42tc4f6. Accessed on 16 November 2025.

such a multi-stakeholder dynamic domestically will automatically reflect in India's diplomatic approach.

Higher Defence Organisation Reforms

The contemporary concept of the Revolution in Military Affairs (RMA) emphasises the integrated capabilities of armed forces, which are essential for harmonizing personnel and systems across the army, navy and air force to form a cohesive fighting unit. In India, over the past decade the pursuit of such integration has been evident in the reforms of the Higher Defence Organisation (HDO). This is particularly highlighted by the establishment of the Chief of Defence Staff (CDS) position, discussions surrounding Integrated Theater Commands (ITCs), and the systematic inclusion of jointness within the Indian military doctrine. With the highly interoperable PLA posing a threat to India's national security, these HDO reforms are a significant step toward preparing for future warfare, albeit with inherent challenges.

Chief of Effective Jointness

Launched by Prime Minister Narendra Modi and the Cabinet Committee on Security (CCS) in December 2019, the CDS position represents a pivotal advancement towards achieving jointness within the Indian armed forces. Serving as a first among equals among the Chiefs of Army, Air Force and Navy Staff, the CDS is tasked with several responsibilities.[224] The CDS acts as a central figure for facilitating joint tri-service combat capabilities, serves as the statutory secretary in charge of the Department of Military Affairs (DMA) within the MoD, and holds the position

[224]Press Information Bureau, 'Functions of Chief of Defence Staff (CDS)', Government of India, 3 February 2020, https://tinyurl.com/2hw2rj7v. Accessed on 18 November 2025.

of Permanent Chairman of the Chiefs of Staff Committee (CoSC). Additionally, he provides military advice to the Defence Minister and plays a role in the Defence Acquisition Council, alongside advising on nuclear command matters.

While not an operational commander with authority over wartime mobilization, the CDS's primary responsibility is to cultivate a culture of tri-service integration and interoperability. Wartime decisions remain under the purview of individual Chiefs of Staff from each service. Nevertheless, during peacetime the CDS's role is crucial in developing and implementing a joint doctrine for India's armed forces. Given that the previous Joint Doctrine of 2017[225] was created before the establishment of the CDS post, they are now outdated. Thus, assigning the CDS as Chairman of CoSC is a positive step that enables him to unify tri-service doctrines into a comprehensive new joint doctrine. To effectively prioritize initiatives, the CDS needs to address three strategic questions: what are we preparing for, who are we preparing against, and how will we achieve our objectives?

To answer these questions effectively, it is vital that the DMA, rather than the Department of Defence, becomes the primary agency responsible for Long Term Defence Planning (LTDP). Inputs from both the MoD and the National Security Council—of which the CDS is a member—are necessary to achieve civil-military integration.[226] Prior to establishment of the CDS position, this responsibility was shared between the Integrated Defence Staff Headquarters (HQ IDS) and the MoD. With a CDS in place, HQ IDS can now compile operational directives along with intelligence assessments from both the Defence Minister and service chiefs to

---

[225]'Joint Doctrine: Indian Armed Forces', *BharatShakti.in*, September 2015, https://tinyurl.com/4dzukz9b. Accessed on 16 November 2025.

[226]Saxena, Anushka, 'Higher Defence Organisation Reforms in India', *A Decade of Defence Reforms Under Modi*, Kartik Bommakanti (ed.), Observer Research Foundation, Delhi, July 2024, https://tinyurl.com/8dszkhb2. Accessed on 16 November 2025.

facilitate a contemporary LTDP. Moreover, it falls upon the CDS to prioritize budget proposals from the tri-services while keeping unified objectives in mind.

On 18 June 2024, the current CDS finalized a joint doctrine addressing military aspects of cyber operations during a CoSC meeting. This initiative aims to establish clarity on integrating tri-services to tackle India's complex cybersecurity landscape. A similar approach should be adopted for developing joint doctrines concerning missile operations, space-based operations, electronic warfare, maritime operations—including aerial superiority at sea—and ground-based air defence.

Theatres of Contest and Collaboration

In an interview in May 2024, Defence Minister Rajnath Singh remarked that there cannot be a strict timeline for implementing theatre commands within India's armed forces; some nations have taken over two decades to operationalize ITCs. An open-ended timeline, however, is not beneficial. ITCs represent the essence of jointness—a fact underscored by operational practices observed in American and Chinese military forces.

Drawing lessons from foreign militaries suggests that India's ITC model should aim for four key objectives:[227]

1. **Establishment of Regional ITCs:** India should create at least five regional ITCs with designated operational directions—one each for northeastern and northwestern borders with China and Pakistan respectively—and three additional commands located in eastern (Odisha), western (Maharashtra), and southern (Tamil Nadu/ Kerala) India.
2. **Authority within Each ITC:** Each ITC must include a service headquarters led by a single theatre commander empowered to conduct joint training exercises and wartime mobilization.

[227]Ibid.

3. **Combined Arms Structure:** Each theatre should feature combined arms brigades/battalions structured for interoperability across weapons systems—light CABs focusing on high-mobility operations while medium/heavy CABs integrate armoured systems.
4. **Support Arms Focused on Jointness:** The CDS-ITC structure should incorporate support arms that address logistical needs alongside nuclear force operations, cyberwarfare, information operations, and space-based initiatives.

India's theaterization efforts face obstacles due to the absence of a non-lapsable defence modernization budget that could sustain long-term investments across multiple fiscal years. Currently, provisions for such funding have not been approved as officials argue that defence spending already constitutes a significant portion of central ministries' budgets amid competing priorities. Consequently, critical demands for theaterization may remain unmet for over two decades despite recognizing their importance in enhancing military readiness.

Budgeting for Defence

Allocating money for defence is complex. It doesn't just demand a near-accurate estimation of monetary requirements based on the potential national security situation in the future. It also calls for thorough analyses of committed liabilities, for how much is needed to meet modernization standards for the armed forces, and for a revenue expenditure outlook that keeps defence personnel satisfied. In checking all these boxes, India's defence budget estimate for FY 2025–26 continues to remain under 2 per cent of estimated GDP.[228]

---

[228]India Budget, 'Budget At A Glance: 2025-26', Government of India, February 2025, https://tinyurl.com/4tfz8tjv. Accessed on 16 November 2025.

Money to Modernize

Capital outlay expenditure, estimated at around ₹180,000 crore (~US$22 billion), is the heart and soul of military modernization. This is the money spent on acquiring new and advanced defence equipment and technologies. At a time when Chinese aggression in both continental and maritime theatres continues to escalate, capital expenditure on must-have platforms has the potential to determine the confidence in India's response.

In the Indian Budget, the Budget Estimate (BE) refers to the initial amount the government seeks approval for to spend in the coming financial year. The BE is based on projections and estimates of requirements, market conditions, and asks from concerned agencies. The Revised Estimate (RE), released months later after the BE but before the FY comes to an end, is an adjusted figure of what the budget expenditure should be for the FY. The actual spending is revealed at the end of the FY. With this context in mind, data from the February 2025 budget report shows that the estimated capital outlay for FY 2025–26 has been hiked by a mere 4.6 per cent as compared to the FY 2024–25 BE. As compared to the RE for FY 2024–25, the hike is at 12.8 per cent.[229] However, trends of capital outlay over the past few years indicate that the BE is always higher than the RE, while the RE is always higher than the actuals.

[229]Saxena, Anushka, 'It's Your Everyday Defence Budget', *Takshashila Institution*, 4 February 2025, https://tinyurl.com/ytb66kwe. Accessed on 18 November 2025.

Table 2.1
Defence Budget Capital Outlay: BE vs RE vs Actuals (₹cr)[230]

Year	*BE*	*RE*	*Actuals*
2022–23	152,369.61	150,000	142,940.01
2023–24	162,600	157,228.20	154,256.28
2024–25	172,000	159,500	N/A
2025–26	180,000	N/A	N/A

In this regard, the main concern, as also expressed in the *Demand for Grants* reports prepared by the Parliamentary Standing Committee on Defence in the past few years, is the underutilization of funds and the potential need for a non-lapsable, roll-on fund for defence modernization. A Secretary of the Finance Ministry argued in the Committee's 2023–24 report that there was no need for such a fund to guarantee continued progress in military modernization.[231] This was so because the budget allocation process had now become more consultative, involving representatives from the armed forces.

And yet, in the Committee's report for 2024–25, it was again specified that barring the Army and the Joint Staff, all other defence services and organizations had fully exhausted their capital budget allocation for FY 2023–24 (at RE stage).[232] This sheds light on an interesting double whammy. The exorbitant

[230]Ministry of Finance, 'Union Budget', Government of India, https://tinyurl.com/mfb4wr9x. Accessed on 16 November 2025.

[231]'Demands for Grants (2023–24): Capital Outlay on Defence Services, Procurement Policy and Defence Planning (Demand No. 21), 37th Report of the Standing Committee on Defence (2022–23)', Parliament E-Library, Government of India, March 2023, https://tinyurl.com/578pj6m5. Accessed on 18 November 2025.

[232]'Demands for Grants (2024–25): Capital Outlay on Defence Services, Procurement Policy and Defence Planning (Demand No. 21). 3rd Report of the Standing Committee on Defence (2024–25)', Parliament E-Library, Government of India, December 2024, https://tinyurl.com/mr4468kd. Accessed on 18 November 2025.

funds being allocated to the Army and the Joint Staff are not being utilized optimally. At the same time, the Air Force, Navy and other Defence Services, such as Land, Aircraft and Aeroengines, and the Rashtriya Rifles are being underfunded, as they almost always completely utilize their funds. They are also not being promised additional spending space under a non-lapsable fund.

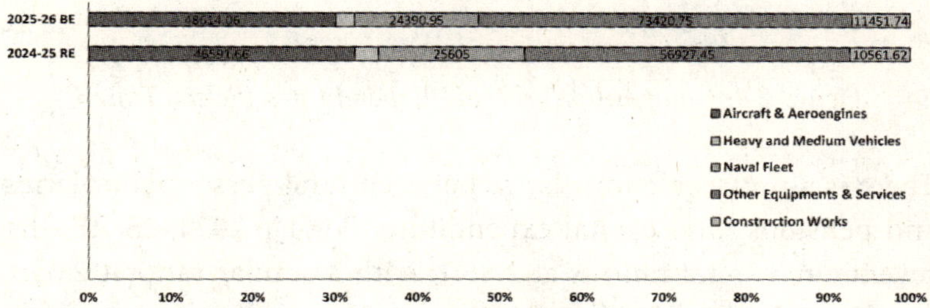

Figure 2.3: Capital Outlay Split between Defence Services under Central Sector Scheme/Projects (excluding Army, Navy, Air Force)[233]

The committee report for FY 2021–22 also recommended creating a separate head for committed liabilities, so that the ability to buy new and additional weaponry remained unhindered. But now, that recommendation has been dropped in favour of a chunk of the capital outlay being allotted to a Capital Acquisition (Modernisation) Budget, which is also used for committed liabilities.

So far, if there is a mismatch between allocated/projected funds and actual requirements, the Finance Ministry is required to seek them at the RE stage. However, trends indicate that the mismatch continues.

Per usual, pensions and salaries continue to constitute the largest chunk of defence budget expenditure.

[233]Ministry of Finance, 'Union Budget', Government of India, https://tinyurl.com/mfb4wr9x. Accessed on 16 November 2025.

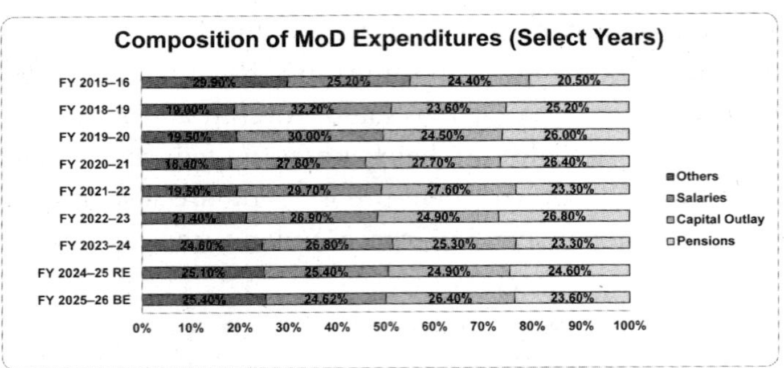

Figure 2.4: Composition of MoD Expenditures (Select Years)[234]

There is a noticeable imbalance between total personnel (salaries and pensions) and capital expenditure. For FY 2024–25 RE, the revenue to capital ratio is at 2.85:1, with a similar ratio at 2.63:1 for FY 2025–26 RE. The Parliament Committee has regularly expressed concern that the higher revenue expenditure may hinder the modernization of the armed forces. However, there is also cognizance of the need to aptly maintain and operate the forces. The hope is that with the introduction of the Agniveer scheme, and the deducted expenditure on pensions, gratuity and other Ex-Servicemen benefits, over the next few years total revenue expenditure will see a decline.

Priorities ahead

Firstly, it is important to acknowledge that there is a consistent expansion in the defence budget of China. Over the past three financial years, the Chinese defence budget has been consistently expanded by 7.2 per cent year-on-year. Between FY 2025 and FY 2026, the targeted expenditure has hence risen from 1.67 trillion yuan (~US$232 billion) to 1.78 trillion yuan (~US $247 billion).[235]

---

[234]Ibid.

[235]*Xinhua*, 'China to increase defense budget by 7.2 percent in 2025, marking

More broadly, India's main challenge is its two-front conundrum. The events in eastern Ladakh since 2020 have shown that the LAC has become a live border. Meanwhile, the May 2025 hostilities with Pakistan and what appears to be an Indian doctrinal shift to punish terrorist attacks with penetrating conventional strikes have raised the stakes on the western front. Hence, today, both the LAC and the LoC are active hotspots. This presents a strategic imperative for Indian defence planners to optimize troop and weapons systems deployment in a way that the capability to respond in neither theatre is compromised.

Given that India is dealing with an extraordinary challenge, it must undertake extraordinary measures. A surge in defence expenditure, especially in the capital outlay domain, is essential to ensure battle-readiness and enhanced firepower. Of course, proposals for a non-lapsable fund or a surge budget can include a sunset clause. But till such a time as India's neighbourhood remains volatile and hostile, the government's endeavour should be to both hike the defence budget and defence expenditure as a percentage of total government spending. For this, the executive must also get Parliament on board. One way this can be achieved is through the inclusion of the Parliamentary Defence Committee's recommendations in its military and security outlook going forward.

Further, the defence budget intends to prioritize military reform and the indigenization of weapons and weapons components production. Of the ₹6.81 lakh crore (~US$82 billion) allotted, ₹148,722.80 crore (~US$17 billion) is intended solely for capital acquisition for the purpose of modernization.[236] In

---

single-digit growth for 10th year', The State Council, People's Republic of China, 5 March 2025, https://tinyurl.com/2s36n5dr. Accessed on 16 November 2025.

[236]Ministry of Defence, 'A record over Rs 6.81 lakh crore allocated in Union Budget 2025–26 for MoD, an increase of 9.53% from current Financial Year', *Press Information Bureau*, Government of India, 1 February 2025, https://tinyurl.com/ysm59fv7. Accessed on 16 November 2025.

this regard, it is first important to assess the challenges and opportunities the Defence Ministry's five Positive Indigenisation Lists (PILs) present. It is vital that MSMEs and start-ups be encouraged to contribute to the PIL initiative, lest the public-private trust and partnership deficit in India's defence sector continue to widen. A few points that create causes of concern are:

1. The Srijan platform shows which products of the 5,012 total are designated under the 'indigenized' category, and what the timeline for indigenization for each of the products/systems is. If one looks at the second PIL launched in May 2021, 100 out of 108 products are designated to be indigenized between December 2021 and December 2024 (the remaining by December 2025).[237] However, the Srijan portal informs us that only 40 of 107 products have been indigenized so far. The delay can be a result of a lot of complex bureaucratic factors, ranging from red tape and delivery delays to a lack of clarity in specifications issued by the services. These need to be addressed, with the enhancement of ease of doing business.
2. If one looks at most contract/bid winners, they are established DPSUs such as Goa Shipyard Limited, Garden Reach S&E Limited, Armoured Vehicles Nigam Limited, HAL, BEL, etc. This means that for so many products, only a few DPSUs are still under the most pressure, and continue to be the most favoured. If the challenge is that private sector firms/MSMEs are unable to meet government requirements, there should be encouragement to collaborate with foreign firms to 'Make in India'.
3. In the past, Swiss firms supplying India's thermal protection soldier kits have even volunteered to help

[237]'2nd Positive Indigenisation List', *Srijan Defence*, 2021, https://tinyurl.com/5d4zeeet. Accessed on 16 November 2025.

domestic production. But for some reason, we still import most kits.[238] It seems to the public eye that there is an inherent inertia in this regard.

4. The Defence Acquisition Procedure (DAP) often leads to vague and unspecific EOIs and RFPs, which hinder business sentiment and willingness to invest in the government's indigenization programmes. A similar problem has been faced by the advanced diesel electric submarine project 75 (I), where the Spanish firm Navantia has withdrawn after its Air Independent Propulsion (AIP) model demonstration, and the remaining contenders (German ThyssenKrupp, in partnership with L&T) have only demonstrated a land-based AIP model. It is only in the post-R&D stage that firms understood what exactly the Indian Navy was looking for.[239] As of February 2025, the ThyssenKrup-designed submarine is assigned to a DPSU, the Mazagaon Dock Shipyard, for total production.[240]
5. In this regard, as discussed above, the armed forces' GSQR process may require balanced flexibility, and can also consider including advice of technical experts, designing and certification entrepreneurs, and commerce groupings and unions such as CII and FICCI.[241] These entities would be best suited to highlight existing capabilities and

---

[238]Think Change India, 'Indian Army approves 'made-in-India' gear for Siachen troops', *YourStory*, 21 August 2018, https://tinyurl.com/5n7kahu5. Accessed on 16 November 2025.

[239]Kunde, Raunak, 'Indian Navy faces challenges with AIP Trials for Project-75I Submarines', *Indian Defence Research Wing*, 16 January 2025, https://tinyurl.com/354jzf7b. Accessed on 18 November 2025.

[240]'Project 75-I: Winner-Takes-It-All will Fail Call for Diversified Submarine Construction', *Indian Defence Research Wing*, 2 February 2025, https://tinyurl.com/3trx26hz. Accessed on 18 November 2025.

[241]Verma, Sanjay, 'Decoding the GSQR Conundrum, Nuts and Bolts', *DefStrat*, Vol. 15, No. 2, 1 July 2021, https://tinyurl.com/2ra9yuv2. Accessed on 9 December 2025.

business models to provide the armed forces the best provider for their RFPs.

6. It also doesn't help to have an import embargo timeline on PIL products. It was extended till December 2028. But at the current rate, it is unlikely all 5,012 products will be taken up for indigenization by then. But foreign vendors would already have been discouraged from placing bids. Hence, options for partnership should remain globally open.

The creation of assets in a self-reliant manner needs to focus on two governmental priorities going forward.

The first is the Buy Indian (IDDM–Indigenously Designed, Developed, and Manufactured) procedure, introduced in 2016, which is integral to the Defence Acquisition Procedure 2020.[242]

The IDDM plan relies on the Defence Ministry's Technology Perspective & Capability Roadmap (TPCR) to inform domestic producers about military modernization needs. Yet, the lengthy process—from issuing a Request for Information (RFI) to contract approvals—can take years. The question remains: are foreign vendors open to trade in defence components till such a time, especially if there are fears of technological obsolescence? As the Parliamentary Committee has also suggested, the progress towards self-reliance cannot compromise transparency, fairness or timely deliveries.

Further, while the first two editions of the TPCR were published with a five-year gap, in 2013 and then 2018, as of 2025, there hasn't been a revised edition expressing the contemporary requirements of India's defence development needs.[243] Proceeding

---

[242]Press Information Bureau, 'Self-Reliance In Defence Manufacturing', Government of India, 4 February 2022, https://tinyurl.com/yt64rmv3. Accessed on 16 November 2025.

[243]Ministry of Defence, 'Technology Perspective and Capability Roadmap', Government of India, https://tinyurl.com/y7kf3tjx. Accessed on 16 November 2025.

forward on the modernization trajectory, a third TPCR is crucial to guide systems acquisition and equipment procurement.

Second are offset procedures, which mandate that foreign vendors procure 30 per cent of their contract value from indigenous manufacturers. While recent changes approved by the Defence Acquisition Council (DAC) aim to make changes in offset obligations more flexible post-contract signing, a robust Indian Offset Providers (IOP) ecosystem is essential for effective partnerships. By the end of 2021, penalties totalling US$43.14 million were imposed on 16 offset contracts for annual shortfalls.[244] A preferable approach would involve re-phasing contracts with minimal penalties rather than imposing strict shortfall penalties that fail to address non-compliance effectively.

Finally, there has to be a broad-based focus on enhancing India's defence manufacturing capabilities. While demand for indigenous products is expansive, there is a lack of an industrial base with the requisite technical skills to produce not just turnkey products but also critical defence components. This requires investing in competitive commercial contracts, and enabling MSMEs to move higher up the value chain through state support. In the naval domain, it can also manifest in the form of privatization of one of the four main shipbuilding DPSUs: Mazagon Dock Shipbuilders Limited, Garden Reach Shipbuilders and Engineers, Goa Shipyard Limited, and Hindustan Shipyard Limited.[245]

---

[244]Press Information Bureau, 'Offset Obligations In Defence Contracts', Government of India, 4 April 2022, https://tinyurl.com/s7d93xje. Accessed on 16 November 2025.

[245]Manoj, P., 'Privatisation of one of the four State-run defence shipyards on government's radar', *The Economic Times*, 3 June 2022, https://infra.economictimes.indiatimes.com/news/ports-shipping/privatisation-of-one-of-the-four-state-run-defence-shipyards-on-governments-radar/91987107. Accessed on 15 November 2025.

Conclusion

India's evolving security outlook towards China reflects a pragmatic recognition of the multifaceted nature of the challenge, spanning conventional military threats, maritime contestation, and the rapidly growing domains of cyber and cognitive warfare. The chapter demonstrates that while India has made significant strides in border infrastructure, force deployment, and the indigenization and modernization of its military capabilities, the challenge posed by the PLA's integrated multi-domain operations and China's overall technological advancements remains formidable. India's efforts to match troop numbers and enhance air and ground defences, especially along the LAC, are crucial steps. Yet the persistent gaps in maritime and air power and accelerated acquisition need attention.

The chapter underscores that the future of India-China competition will be increasingly defined by the ability to operate seamlessly across multiple domains. India's push for integrated theatre commands, reforms in higher defence organization, and leveraging private sector expertise in both conventional and cyber domains are essential to building a resilient and adaptive security architecture. At the same time, the necessity of rapid infrastructure development, terrain-specific training, and the adoption of advanced technologies such as drones and electronic warfare systems cannot be overstated. These measures, coupled with a focus on offensive cyber capabilities and robust diplomatic engagement, will be central to countering China's expanding influence and maintaining strategic stability in the region.

As India's two-front dilemma comes to light, its approach must be holistic, combining military modernization with institutional reforms, inter-service integration and international partnerships. Bridging the gap between policy ambition and implementation, particularly in defence budgeting, procurement processes and operational readiness, will determine India's ability to deter and, if necessary, respond effectively to Chinese provocations. By keeping its 'powder dry' through sustained investment, innovation and strategic foresight, India can safeguard its sovereignty and interests in the face of an assertive and technologically advanced neighbour.

3

The Intractable Dilemma: A Vision for De-Risking Trade with China

AMIT KUMAR

Speaking to a leading Indian daily in early November 2024, a spokesperson for Herrenknecht, a German company that's a leading global player in the design and manufacturing of tunnel-boring machines (TBMs), confirmed that the Chinese customs authorities were blocking their supplies meant for India.[246] He said, 'For several months now, we have been observing extraordinary circumstances in the customs clearance processes for machines to be delivered from China to India. These are hindering us from fulfilling our delivery obligations as expected and, in some cases, entirely.'[247] Around the same time, reports also confirmed that Apple's major supplier, Foxconn, which operates an iPhone assembly plant in the Indian city of Sriperumbudur, had been experiencing delays in the arrival of technicians and machinery from China.[248]

These reports vindicated the suspicion in India around China's willingness to weaponize trade vis-à-vis India. To be fair, the fears

[246]Sharma, Sukalp, 'Tunnel boring machines: Machines for India delayed, German firm flags bottleneck at Chinese customs', *The Indian Express*, 2 November 2024, https://tinyurl.com/4btj2bx8. Accessed on 16 November 2025.
[247]Ibid.
[248]Mohan, Rohini, and Yew Lun Tian, 'China's export ban on engineers and equipment disrupts manufacturing overseas', *The Strait Times*, 29 January 2025, https://tinyurl.com/y2ahk97r. Accessed on 16 November 2025.

of Chinese recourse to economic coercion weren't unfounded. The very fact that China is the world's biggest trading country, cornering over 14 per cent of global merchandise exports,[249] confers upon it the ability to weaponize trade. Beijing had, in the past, demonstrated its willingness to capitalize on this advantage by resorting to similar tactics against Japan in 2010, when it put restrictions on the export of rare earths to punish Tokyo after it detained a Chinese fishing trawler captain.[250]

In India, the cracking of the global trading order amid US-China tensions, the prolonged standoff with China in eastern Ladakh, and concerns around the security of supply chains that emerged during the pandemic had already galvanized thinking around economic dependencies, vulnerabilities and coercion. This was in line with the concern that had also gained currency across the West in the post-pandemic period.

It was in this light that the incident relating to the TBMs and Foxconn accentuated the urgency for an Indian de-risking strategy.

Interestingly, in parallel to this development, another key global concern centred around China's exports has been taking hold—the overcapacity problem.[251] China's industrial overcapacity—domestic production exceeds domestic demand—threatens to flood external markets with cheaper products and push foreign players out of competition. In 2024, China recorded a trade surplus of almost US$1 trillion,[252] an all-time high.

---

[249]'China remains top merchandise exporter in 2023 for 7th straight year', The State Council Information Office of the People's Republic of China, 15 April 2024, https://tinyurl.com/yca5wck3. Accessed on 16 November 2025.

[250]Branigan, Tania, 'China cuts Japan contacts over detained trawler captain', *The Guardian*, 19 September 2010, https://tinyurl.com/yucxf6mf. Accessed on 16 November 2025.

[251]Liu, Zongyuan Zoe, 'China's Real Economic Crisis', *Foreign Affairs*, 6 August 2024, https://tinyurl.com/5bntskx4. Accessed on 16 November 2025.

[252]'China's foreign trade hits new high in 2024', The State Council of the People's Republic of China, 13 January 2025, https://tinyurl.com/3v4c425n. Accessed on 16 November 2025.

One-tenth of this surplus is derived from exports to India. The dumping of Chinese goods has been a long-standing concern of the Government of India (GoI). New Delhi has repeatedly complained of Beijing's market-distorting practices and the denial of market access for Indian goods.[253] Several countries share similar grievances against cheap imports from China. These increasingly include other developing countries such as Indonesia, Brazil and Turkey. The issue of Chinese industrial overcapacity gained greater political salience amid the pandemic. In a strange way, pandemic-related disruptions resulted in popular policy discourse around the world appreciating China's manufacturing prowess while stoking anxieties around its industrial overcapacity simultaneously. The primary concern with the offloading of China's overcapacity in the external market is that it threatens to put people out of jobs and potentially de-industrialize other countries.

The fact that India is the fifth-largest importer of Chinese goods[254] makes New Delhi susceptible to China's offloading of excess capacity. And therefore, it has reasons to worry regarding dependence and dumping. These are likely heightened today given the intensification of the trade war between the US and China during the second Donald Trump presidency. To put things in perspective, India's trade deficit with China surpassed US$100 billion in 2023 for the first time, according to China's National Bureau of Statistics.[255] According to India's Ministry of Commerce and Industry, imports from China surpassed US$100 billion

---

[253]ET Bureau, 'Six countries including China, Japan and Russia dump steel in India: DGAD', *The Economic Times*, 13 April 2016, https://tinyurl.com/3hav3jeu. Accessed on 16 November 2025.

[254]Hong Kong is a separate economic entity within China but not a country. Thus, in terms of country, India is fifth.

World Integrated Trade Solution, https://tinyurl.com/2jxm6ujy. Accessed on 16 November 2025.

[255]National Bureau of Statistics of People's Republic of China, https://data.stats.gov.cn/english/index.htm. Accessed on 16 November 2025.

in FY 2024 for the first time, with the trade deficit reaching US$85 billion.[256] This is a huge contrast from the trade balance in 2000, when China's exports to India stood at US$1.4 billion, while India's exports to China amounted to US$734 million.[257] Furthermore, India's exports to China have remained stagnant at around US$16–18 billion annually over the last 10 years.[258]

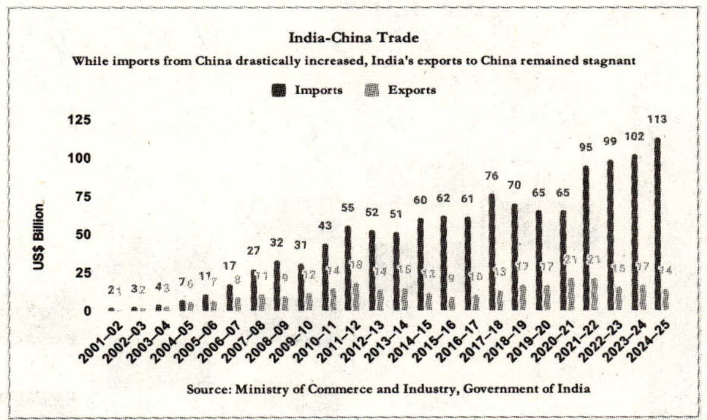

Figure 3.1: India-China Trade (2001–24)[259]

As the post-pandemic world woke up to the twin challenges of dependence and dumping vis-à-vis China, many including the US and the EU, have been thinking through policy permutations and combinations to deal with it.

It is in this context that this chapter recommends a pathway for India to approach trade with China. Very briefly, the chapter

---

[256]Ministry of Commerce and Industry of the Government of India, https://dashboard.commerce.gov.in/commercedashboard.aspx. Accessed on 16 November 2025.

[257]World Integrated Trade Solution, https://tinyurl.com/bdftvrft. Accessed on 16 November 2025.

[258]Ministry of Commerce and Industry of the Government of India, https://dashboard.commerce.gov.in/commercedashboard.aspx. Accessed on 16 November 2025.

[259]Ibid.

first picks up on the threat emanating from China's overcapacity and consequent dumping of goods in the Indian market, as it is relatively an easier problem to solve. It then proceeds to deal with the more intricate problem of identifying dependence-induced strategic vulnerabilities resulting from asymmetric trade. It outlines a framework to distil strategic vulnerabilities from dependencies. (See Figure 3.2)

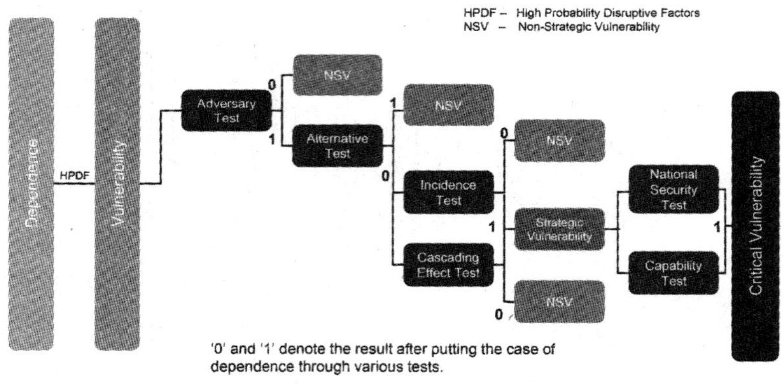

Figure 3.2: Strategic and Critical Vulnerability Framework[260]

Subsequently, it applies the framework to the three biggest import categories vis-à-vis China, i.e., organic chemicals, machinery and mechanical appliances, and electrical machinery and equipment. Together, these three product categories account for more than two-thirds of India's total imports from China. Finally, it provides possible de-risking options with respect to these product categories.

Clearing the Dumping Ground

[260]Kumar, Amit, 'Defining Dependence-induced Vulnerabilities in an Asymmetrical Trade Interdependence: A Conceptual Framework', *Takshashila Institution*, July 2023, https://tinyurl.com/4v2ystns. Accessed on 18 November 2025.

Since the launch of the 'Reform and Opening-up' under Deng Xiaoping's leadership in 1978, China has made tremendous strides in the field of manufacturing. This received a shot in the arm post its accession to the World Trade Organization in 2001. China's emergence as the world's global manufacturing hub (accounting for over 30 per cent of the global manufacturing output value in 2025 and 35 per cent by volume in 2020)[261] was fuelled by a range of policy decisions, such as opening up to trade and investment, fostering domestic competition, creating conducive conditions for businesses, upskilling its low-cost labour force, and cutting back on bureaucratism.

However, China has also been accused of subverting the rules of free and fair trade, and rightly so. Beijing's manufacturing preponderance is also owed to its unfair trade and market-distorting practices. The party-state has continuously engaged in suppressing interest rates, devaluing currency, floating heavy subsidies and tax rebates to keep its industries and exports competitive.

Thus, it isn't untrue that the Indian market has witnessed an influx of cheap Chinese goods over the years. Consequently, it makes sense for the Indian government to undertake measures to shield domestic players from unfair competition.

But a blanket ban by the government cannot be an answer. Even as it is an easy, perhaps even lazy, solution to discourage dumping, a broad-based ban can have adverse implications for the Indian economy. A complete prohibition, in some cases, may allow a few players to corner the market and engage in price fixing, a

---

[261]For output by value, see 'Measuring China's Manufacturing Might', *China Power*, https://tinyurl.com/yx9y9s6x. Accessed on 16 November 2025.

'China drives over 30 pct of global manufacturing growth during 2021-2025', *Xinhua*, 9 September 2025, https://tinyurl.com/mtepn97z. Accessed on 16 November 2025.

For output by volume, see Baldwin, Richard, 'China is the world's sole manufacturing superpower: A line sketch of the rise', *CEPR*, 17 January 2024, https://tinyurl.com/23zzt7et. Accessed on 16 November 2025.

situation in which sellers coordinate to raise prices collectively. Eventually, the buyers, or end consumers of the product, suffer. Furthermore, assured of a big domestic market share, existing players are likely to be discouraged from innovating. To make matters worse, the product quality may actually degrade in the absence of competition. The domestic players engaged in manufacturing and exporting commodities suffer too as imports of intermediate goods from China are critical to their business. Lastly, a strong trade can be a source of stability in the India-China relationship. As unpopular and counter-intuitive as it may sound, but the road to bridge the economic asymmetry vis-à-vis China flows through China.

It is important to address the point of failure in the process rather than eliminating the goods altogether. Influx of cheap Chinese goods below their cost price is bad for the Indian economy because it distorts the market by undermining competition. Thus, the correct policy response to correct this distortion is by restoring fair competition.

The appropriate policy solution for the government is to impose countervailing and anti-dumping duties. However, two key factors need to be considered before imposing duties on imports from China: *proportionality* and *domestic capability*. Any imposition of countervailing or anti-dumping duties must be proportionate to rival state support to compensate for the cheap influx of goods. This serves two purposes.

First, suppose there is an Indian-origin product A, which is trading at a selling price ~X in the Indian market. Suddenly, the market witnesses an influx of cheap Chinese origin product A at a selling price of X ±C-S, where 'C' represents the cost of comparative advantage or disadvantage and 'S' represents the cumulative unfair subsidies availed by the Chinese players. Here, the government must impose an anti-dumping or countervailing duty 'D' that is roughly equal to 'S' so as to bring the market price of product 'A' to its real price. It is to be noted that after correcting the price distortion, the Chinese-origin product 'A' may still trade at a market price which is lower than the Indian-origin product 'A', depending upon comparative advantage-or disadvantage-related cost. Not only does this allow for the correction of the distorted market prices of the imports from China and thereby protect domestic players against unfair competition, but it also offers domestic consumers a fair choice to still opt for Chinese products, based on their quality and price competitiveness. For an economy to continuously innovate, the empowerment of its consumers by fostering competition among businesses is a necessary precondition.

The second aspect to consider before imposing countervailing or anti-dumping duties on a commodity is assessing India's domestic capability in that segment.[262] In categories where domestic capability exists, duties can be justifiable. However, using the same remedy for commodity segments where India's domestic capability is non-existent punishes a category of manufacturers and traders who rely on cheap imports, including from China, to add value and gain competitiveness in both domestic and external markets. Such a policy also adversely impacts consumers by raising their cost of living. If India aims to bridge the wide economic asymmetry with China, it shouldn't hesitate to free-ride on its adversary's subsidies to aid domestic capability. Given that India's monetary and financial constraints are far greater than China's, it can act prudently by leveraging Chinese policies to subsidize its own development. In this way, India can ensure that the cost of its development stays as low as it can at a time when the world increasingly turns inwards—a factor that has certainly raised the developmental cost for emerging economies.

---

[262]Adapted from Pranay Kotasthane's Framework on Chinese investments in India. See Kotasthane, Pranay, 'India Policy Watch #2: A Framework for India's Approach Towards Chinese Firms', *Anticipating the Unintended*, 11 August 2025, https://tinyurl.com/4azkxvsm. Accessed on 15 November 2025.

Is Dependence Necessarily a Vulnerability?

Solving the vulnerability problem, however, is somewhat challenging. The world today has grown increasingly fractured, as geopolitical rivalries have intensified. A major fallout of the escalating great power competition has been an overhaul in how states think about trade and economic engagements. As trade wars have increasingly become a characteristic feature of great power competition, economic coercion has acquired greater salience in statecraft. While the US has been at the forefront of this campaign, China hasn't been far behind in employing similar tactics against its adversaries. In fact, China today has developed a rather sophisticated toolkit of economic coercion, entailing tariffs, regulatory hurdles, export controls, sanctions, financial restrictions and freezes, travel restrictions, etc. Some of these will impact trade with India even when targeted at other countries.

The sheer imbalance and persistent asymmetry in the trade relationship justify the concern relating to India's import dependence on China and the fact that this dependence renders India strategically vulnerable. But one may ask, does India's import dependence on China for soft toys or videogames make it vulnerable? Or, for that matter, does India's import of firecrackers from China render it strategically vulnerable? Even before one attempts to answer such issues, dealing with some fundamental and elementary questions becomes imperative. For instance, what is dependence? Further, is dependence the same as vulnerability? How is vulnerability different from strategic vulnerability? And finally, does dependence necessarily lead to strategic vulnerability?

Dependence is not the same as vulnerability. Vulnerability appears to be a consequence of dependence. In the context of asymmetric trade, dependence refers to a situation where an entity, say 'A', is reliant on another entity, say 'B', to carry out its business operations—broadly sales and purchases. Thus, dependency can be buyer-based (downstream) or seller-based (upstream). It is important to underline here that dependence is a two-way street.

For instance, consider a big grocery store in a small town. The people of the town rely on the store for some of the grocery items that no other stores in the town sell. The big store is thus the single stop for all grocery items, thereby increasing its appeal. While it is true that consumers of the town are more dependent on the single grocery store, the reverse is also true. The big grocery store depends on the demand from consumers for its sales. Suppose the big grocery store chooses to weaponize its dominant position and pushes the price up with an aim to inflate its profit. There is a high probability that this may force consumers to reduce their purchases from the big grocery store. Simultaneously, this could create an opportunity for the nearby small store to fill in the newly-created demand. Thus, dependence is indeed a two-way street.

The question then arises, what level of dependence is significant enough to investigate for the possible vulnerability? Deciding on a threshold is tricky and complicated, as there are no established formulae. India's Competition Act, 2002, regards a market share of above 40 per cent as dominant. While the law itself deals with competition, dominance and monopolies among companies, the threshold gives us an estimate to work with.

In our case, a threshold of 30 per cent with respect to China seems optimum for two reasons. This is so because the 30 per cent cut-off roughly corresponds to China's global production capacity, both by volume and by value. Thus, a dependence above this threshold highlights the upward standard deviation from the mean. Secondly, by its very nature, sufficient diversification already exists for items with dependence less than 30 per cent. Thus, by adopting this filter, the chapter focuses on items exhibiting significant dependence, subjecting them to maximum scrutiny.

Now, coming back to the issue of the distinction between dependence and vulnerability, as mentioned earlier, vulnerability appears to be a consequence of dependence. Now, the degree or severity of dependence can create conditions of vulnerability.

Vulnerability can be defined as a case of dependence tied to other disruptive factors that can render the dependence relationship untenable, fickle, or unreliable. In other words, it is a case of dependence that is susceptible to disruption due to the presence of High Probability Disruptive Factors (HPDF). These factors could range from recurrent tariff or non-tariff barriers and supply shocks to natural calamities and information asymmetry, among others.

Having decided on a threshold for significant dependence, we need to address the question of whether India's import dependence on Chinese videogames, soft toys or firecrackers constitutes a strategic vulnerability. To do so, one has to assess what kind of strategic cost can China inflict on India by disrupting the exports of such items. The only cost the Chinese can think of imposing is forcing Indians to celebrate Diwali with fewer firecrackers perhaps. Maybe we will go back to the good-old traditional way of celebrating Diwali by lighting oil lamps, distributing sweets and playing cards. Likewise, the only possible cost that the Chinese could impose by banning soft toys or videogames would be to nudge Indian toddlers and teenagers to perhaps explore the outside world a little more than before. But the question remains, does this offer China any strategic advantage vis-à-vis India? The answer is a resounding no.

One may ask, if dependence on imports of soft toys, videogames and firecrackers does not constitute a strategic vulnerability, then what does? The use of the adjective 'strategic' in this context offers some clues. Broadly, a strategic approach could be applied to various fields, such as domestic or international politics, business, or any other field characterized by competition among rivals.[263] In the context of international relations, the term is used to refer to a set of plans and actions that aim at furthering long-term

---

[263]Kumar, Amit, 'De-risking India's Trade with China: Identifying Strategic and Critical Vulnerabilities', *Takshashila Institution*, January 2025, https://tinyurl.com/zvcksaj8. Accessed on 16 November 2025.

national goals or for achieving an advantage over other actors. These could include the pursuit of economic, security or broader geopolitical objectives. In this process, a state can choose to deploy tools of compellence, deterrence, inducement and co-optation.

Thus, for a vulnerability to become a strategic vulnerability, it must fulfil two conditions. One, the driving factor, underlining the vulnerability, must be strategically motivated, i.e., the intention must be to extract some strategic benefit. Secondly, it should succeed in inflicting strategic cost on the player deemed as 'vulnerable' or 'dependent'. Thus, strategic vulnerability is a specific case of vulnerability, which is a function of strategic motivations.

The definition of strategic vulnerability discussed above is still too broad to arrive at a clear answer. Which criteria or tests should a case of import dependence fulfil to be classified as a case of strategic vulnerability? Drawing from the definition and expanding on the two conditions—the presence of a strategic motive and success in inflicting strategic cost—provides a starting point.

A strategic motivation to inflict a cost on India would only be harboured by any adversarial state. Of course, a friendly state could also resort to similar measures. However, given the congruence of interests, one expects that the motivation will be narrower rather than to impose broad-based, strategic costs. Thus, dependence vis-à-vis an adversarial state becomes a potential case of strategic vulnerability. The case of China fulfils this criteria.

But that's not all. The weaponization of dependence has to materialize in some form of strategic gain for the adversarial state. Conversely, the adversarial state must succeed in inflicting strategic pain on the dependent state. This can happen only if the dependent state fails to replace or substitute the imports, either from an alternative source or through an alternative product. If the imports from the adversarial state can be replaced within a short-term period, say six to nine months, the dependence is not much of a strategic vulnerability. However, if dependence exists on an imported item that can take substantially longer to replace, say medium to long term, it can be termed as a strategic vulnerability. Thus, the longevity of irreplaceability or the ease of substitutability is a critical determinant factor.

But lack of substitutability isn't the defining test. Let us again consider the example of imported firecrackers from China. Suppose India's dependence is to the tune of 90 per cent, and there is no way for India to replace the supplies from China, even in the long term. There exists no other alternative source to import firecrackers from. Does this enable China to impose a strategic cost on India? The answer is still no. But why?

It is because of the absence of any incidence effect on the general populace of India and, by extension, on the Government of India. To put it differently, the population isn't substantively impacted. Yes, Diwali might be less fun, but their daily lives would continue as usual even if India's imports of firecrackers suddenly came to a halt. Certainly, it wouldn't offer China any strategic gain; rather Beijing would alienate public opinion in India. In order for the adversary to gain a strategic advantage over the dependent state, that product needs to have two attributes: *ubiquity* and *utility*. This firstly means that the imported product must be widely consumed by the people. Secondly, the imported product must have a high utility for the consumers. Only goods that exhibit these two attributes can enable the adversary to impose a strategic cost on the dependent state by disrupting the lives of the people.

So, while imported goods like soft toys, firecrackers or decoratives may exhibit ubiquity, they certainly do not exhibit high utility for the consumers. In comparison, consumer electronics exhibit both ubiquity and utility for consumers, making them a potential candidate for a source of strategic vulnerability. However, do not forget that the test of alternatives, or ease of substitutability, still applies. Only if an imported product from China passes the two tests—substitutability and incidence test—can the dependence on the adversary be termed as a strategic vulnerability.

The incidence test, however, applies to products that are

directly consumed by the people, i.e., finished products. But there are goods which we indirectly consume. Consider a firm operating in India that imports key machinery from China to manufacture products that are consumed domestically and externally via exports. Now, people may not have a direct interface with the machinery being imported by this Indian firm, but they still benefit from it. Further, the incidence test also doesn't account for intermediate goods, such as raw materials, parts and spares, and chemicals. These aren't directly consumed by the people but go through various stages of value-addition before the finished product becomes accessible to consumers. The adversary can also leverage dependence in such segments to extract strategic advantage by halting the supplies of such capital goods. China's export restrictions on TBMs (tunnel-boring machines) fall into this category. Alternatively, the adversary can also place export restrictions on intermediate goods, such as rare-earth minerals and magnets, as China did to Japan in 2010 and again in 2025.

A disruption in the supply (import) of these types of goods can trigger a spill-over effect within and across the industry, impacting producers, workers, and finally consumers. This would certainly allow the adversary to inflict strategic cost on the dependent state. Thus, dependence on imported goods with high cascading effect or spill-over effect, usually intermediate or capital goods, can also be a source of strategic vulnerability.

To sum up, all goods of import must be assessed on these four criteria, i.e., adversary test, substitutability test, incidence effect and cascading effect, to determine whether dependence in their cases constitutes a strategic vulnerability. However, it is important to note that for any case of significant dependence to be a strategic vulnerability, it must clear the adversary and the alternative test and at least one of the incidence effect or cascading effect tests. The choice of test would depend on the type of commodity (finished, intermediate or capital goods).

It is plausible that some strategic vulnerabilities may be of a more severe or critical nature than others. Depending upon the severity of the challenge they pose, a different approach might be needed to deal with them. One such condition could be where the capability gap between the adversary and the rest of the world is so huge that substitutability seems impossible. Take China's capability deficit vis-à-vis the West with respect to photolithography equipment. The strategic vulnerability is so severe, owing to the capability gap, that it needs to be treated as a critical vulnerability.

By now, it must occur to you that all the tests discussed so far seek to identify such cases of dependence which could be leveraged by the adversary to impose costs on the population of the dependent state, and by extension on the government.

But the adversary can also resort to ways that impose cost directly on the government of the dependent state by taking down its critical infrastructure. One way to do so is through cyberattacks. Backdoors in imported hardware can also achieve this objective. Thus, an import dependence on the adversary for items like electronic parts, components, machines, etc., utilized in strategic infrastructure, like aviation, power grids, railways, nuclear facilities, communications, and advanced research facilities, amounts to an extreme kind of strategic vulnerability. In the framework discussed in this chapter, this is defined as a critical vulnerability.

Scrutinizing India's Import Basket

Having brainstormed the prerequisites of a strategic vulnerability underpinning asymmetric trade, it is time to dive into India's import basket vis-à-vis China. International trade between countries is governed by the Harmonised Systems (HS) of goods classification. The HS system refers to the universal and standardized numeric coding system used to categorize and classify goods for international trade. HS codes entail four layers of product classifications: HS2 (two-digit, indicating chapter), HS4 (four-digit, indicating heading within chapter), HS6 (six-digit, indicating subheading) and HS8 (eight-digit, indicating local classification). While the HS2 code is the broadest classification for traded goods, the HS6 and HS8 codes offer the most detailed, fundamental descriptions of individual goods. The HS4 code is an intermediate-level classification, which is more detailed than HS2 but relatively broader than HS6 or HS8.

For instance, consider a product 'A' with the designated HS code as 12345678. Here, the first two digits together will be called HS2 digits, which will indicate the chapter—the broadest classification of goods in the HS nomenclature. Let us assume, in this case, it represents wooden products. Similarly, the first four digits—1234—will combine to form the HS4 code that will further indicate the header within the chapter—further classification suggesting the type of wooden product. And so on, till HS8.

Now, of all the classifications, H6 is the most suitable for policy intervention. This is because the HS6 classification is nearly as detailed in capturing the description of traded goods and items as the HS8, allowing for reasonable and specific categorization of goods. At the same time, it eliminates unnecessary specifications that HS8 classifications often contain. Finally, the availability of corresponding data sets for goods classified under HS6 is greater than that for those classified under HS8. Furthermore, the amount or the value of imports at the HS8 level of classification is too low to employ economic coercion. For actions to be effective, restrictions need to be placed at an intermediate level of classification, either HS4 or HS6. Thus, from a policy perspective, it is more relevant to scrutinize dependence and vulnerabilities at the HS6 level.

If one glances through India's import basket vis-à-vis China, three HS2 product categories immediately grab attention. These are organic chemicals, machinery and mechanical appliances, and electrical machinery and equipment. Like many other product categories, these three also exhibit a percentage dependence (of India's total imports) of ~40 on China. But what sets them apart is their sheer size of import in aggregate terms. Each of these three categories had an import value greater than US$10 billion in 2023.[264] While organic chemicals imports were worth US$11.4 billion, machinery and mechanical appliances and electrical machinery and equipment imports were estimated at US$22.4 billion and US$31.3 billion, respectively. Together, these three categories comprised more than two-thirds of India's total imports from China in 2023. It is only logical, therefore, that these three categories be investigated for any possible strategic vulnerabilities.

However, at the HS6 classification level, there are at least 2,000 items across the three categories. Administering all the tests, especially the cascading and incidence effect test, to such a broad basket is challenging. Thus, while the Strategic Vulnerability Tests form the conceptual basis of assessment, it is essential to devise more practical and efficient methods to distil cases of import dependence-induced strategic vulnerabilities.

Modelling the Strategic and Critical Vulnerability Tests

In order to simplify the tests, it is necessary to have an estimate of two things to determine vulnerabilities associated with an imported commodity: the immediate shock on the economy as a consequence of the disruption and the duration of the disruption. The cascading and incidence effect tests seek to measure the shock on the economy, in terms of the impact on either consumers or the industry. This impact would be proportional to, or a factor of,

---

[264]Ministry of Commerce and Industry of the Government of India, https://dashboard.commerce.gov.in/commercedashboard.aspx. Accessed on 16 November 2025.

Kumar, Amit, 'De-risking India's Trade with China: Identifying Strategic and Critical Vulnerabilities', *Takshashila Institution*, January 2025, https://tinyurl.com/zvcksaj8. Accessed on 16 November 2025.

the value of the aggregate and percentage dependence. The higher the value, the higher the immediate shock. The duration of the disruption would depend on the relative ease of substitutability. If the product is substitutable, the disruption would be short-lived and wouldn't create conditions of strategic vulnerability. If disruption is long-term, it would create conditions of strategic vulnerability.

To sum up, there is a need to identify such items of import that can trigger immediate shock while exhibiting a relative lack of substitutability.

This could be achieved using two metrics calculated for each of the items, i.e., the Relative Impact Factor (RIF) and the Product Complexity Index (PCI).[265] The RIF for an item is a product of the values of its aggregate and percentage dependence on China. The greater the value, the greater the shock potential. For instance, consider an item 'I' that exhibits a percentage import of 60 per cent and import value of US$60 million. Its RIF would then turn out to be [(60x60)/10000 = 0.36] (Note: Division by 10,000 is used to limit the range of the values). The PCI is a measure of the technological complexity of a traded item and the diffusion of its knowledge or technology among countries. The Observatory for Economic Complexity and Harvard Atlas maintain data on PCI. PCI values range between -3 and +3. A higher score

---

[265]Kumar, Amit, 'De-risking India's Trade with China: Identifying Strategic and Critical Vulnerabilities', *Takshashila Institution*, January 2025, https://tinyurl.com/zvcksaj8. Accessed on 16 November 2025.

Hidalgo, C.A., and R. Hausmann, 'The building blocks of economic complexity', *PNAS*, Vol. 106, No. 26, 2009, pp. 10570–10575, https://tinyurl.com/3f9skars. Accessed on 15 November 2025.

The Atlas of Economic Complexity Glossary, https://tinyurl.com/y87sd2we. Accessed on 15 November 2025.

For the Harvard Atlas of Economic Complexity database, see https://tinyurl.com/4v8mxduv. Accessed on 15 November 2025.

For the OEC database, see https://tinyurl.com/y753pufx. Accessed on 15 November 2025.

means that the item is immensely complex to produce and only a handful of countries can produce it, and vice versa. The PCI score, thus, serves as an indicator of the relative ease/difficulty of the product's substitutability and, therefore, a measure of the period of disruption.

Based on these two metrics, this chapter uses the following classifications to distil items of import that might create conditions of strategic and critical vulnerabilities vis-à-vis China.

Table 3.1
Classification based on RIF value[266]

Impact Factor Description	*Insignificant*	*Substantially High*	*Exponentially High*
Range	RIF < 0.1	0.1 ≤RIF< 1	RIF ≥ 1

Table 3.2
Classification based on PCI value[267]

Complexity	*Low*	*Moderate*	*High*	*Very High*	*Extremely High*
Range	1 ≤ PCI < 1.25	1.25 ≤ PCI < 1.50	1.50 ≤ PCI < 1.75	1.75 ≤ PCI < 2	PCI ≥ 2
Substitutability/ Disruption	Short term (up to 9 months)	Short to medium term	Medium term (18 months)	Medium to long term	Long term (over 27 months)

[266]Kumar, Amit, 'De-risking India's Trade with China: Identifying Strategic and Critical Vulnerabilities', *Takshashila Institution*, January 2025, https://tinyurl.com/zvcksaj8. Accessed on 16 November 2025.
[267]Ibid.

Table 3.3

Classification for Strategic and Critical Vulnerability based on RIF-PCI Matrix[268]

Metrics *(RIF/PCI)*	*Low* *1 ≤ PCI < 1.25*	*Moderate* *1.25 ≤ PCI < 1.5*	*High* *1.5 ≤ PCI < 1.75*	*Very High* *1.75 ≤ PCI < 2*	*Extremely High* *PCI ≥ 2*
Substantially high 0.1≤RIF<1	Substantially high shock & short-term disruption	Substantially high shock & short to medium-term disruption	Substantially high shock & medium-term disruption	Substantially high shock & medium-to long-term disruption	Substantially high shock & long-term disruption
Exponentially high RIF≥1	Exponentially high shock & short-term disruption	Exponentially high shock & short-to medium-term disruption	Exponentially high shock & medium-term disruption	Exponentially high shock & medium-to long-term disruption	Exponentially high shock & long-term disruption

[268]Ibid.

Of course, even after identifying such items, a subjective filter to assess their value would be required. But this method will eliminate a lot of items that do not require attention from a strategic perspective.

Case Studies

Having devised a workable model based on the Strategic and Critical Vulnerability framework, let us now apply these tests on the three biggest import categories vis-à-vis China: organic chemicals, machinery and mechanical equipment, and electrical machinery and equipment.

1. Organic Chemicals

Organic chemicals find wide-ranging applications across industries, including agriculture, leather, textiles, polymers, chemicals, food and, most importantly, pharmaceuticals. The often-highlighted active pharmaceutical ingredients (APIs), key starting materials (KSMs) and drug intermediates (DIs) belong to the category of organic chemicals. India heavily depends on China (~70 per cent) to source these items that are critical to the country's pharmaceutical industry and healthcare. The cheap imports of APIs from China and the waiver of patents from the World Trade Organization (WTO) have allowed the Indian pharmaceutical industry to emerge as a low-cost option worldwide. This industry has been instrumental in keeping healthcare costs low in India, where the population's out-of-pocket health expenditure remains extremely high compared to the global average. It has also offered low-cost options to foreigners travelling to India, thereby powering the country's medical tourism industry. Accordingly, India has acquired the status of the pharmacy of the world. India's excessive dependence on China for APIs warrants an investigation of the plausible strategic vulnerability in this segment.

Organic chemicals also find extensive applications in material sciences, in the production of plastic, PVC, acrylic, nylon, polythene and several other complex materials in the polymer industry. They are also critical to the leather and textile industry, which uses organic chemicals to process raw materials into the final product. They also find applications as solvents, mixers, cleaners and degradable detergents across the chemical and environmental industries. The food industry uses organic chemicals as additives and preservatives to extend the shelf life of products. Some specific chemicals are also utilized in the manufacturing of explosives and ammunition. In the agricultural sector, organic chemicals find application in the preparation of agrochemicals, pesticides and insecticides. Thus, a disruption in this segment has the potential to trigger a cascading effect across other industrial sectors.

An analysis of the HS6 category organic chemicals, which lists around 300 items, highlights that the majority of items exhibit 'low' to 'moderate' product complexity. None of the organic chemicals imported from China with 'substantially high' immediate shock potential display 'extremely high' product complexity. Interestingly, only four items score either 'high' or 'very high' on product complexity, indicating relative difficulty in their substitution (medium to long term) in the event of a disruption. A total of 17 items under the organic chemicals category exhibit 'exponentially high' immediate shock potential. However, only one among them—a type of heterocyclic compound—exhibits a 'high' product complexity. A majority of items have a product complexity that is 'very low.' This suggests that their relative ease of substitutability will act as a countervailing factor and thus mitigate the impact of a shock in the case of disruption.

Nevertheless, India's import dependence on China for penicillin and other antibiotics is excessive, both in aggregate and percentage terms. Further, antibiotics are a strategic commodity given their utility in the health sector. Thus, even as their product complexity is fairly low (less than 1), suggesting easy substitutability in case of disruption, a de-risking strategy could be argued for.

Another class of organic compounds, called the heterocyclic compounds and their derivatives, warrants attention. Heterocyclic compounds act as ingredients for a range of pharmaceutical products that include drugs for inflammation, cancer and viral infections, among others. They also find application in agrochemicals, such as pesticides, insecticides, herbicides, etc. Thus, a disruption in the supply of heterocyclic compounds can trigger a huge cascading effect in a series of other sectors. Not only do heterocyclic compounds exhibit a 'substantially high' immediate shock potential, but they also exhibit relatively higher product complexity ('moderate' to 'high').

In addition to the heterocyclic compounds, carboxylic acids and epsilon-caprolactam, among others, also have applications in the pharmaceutical industry. Collectively, they also exhibit relatively higher product complexity compared to most. Organo-sulphur compounds, naphthols and their salts, ketones and quinones are other organic chemicals that warrant attention. Given their lack of relative substitutability (medium to long-term), a de-risking strategy to reduce dependence on China is warranted.

a. De-Risking by Stockpiling

The options to de-risk can range from diversification to domestic production. However, both of these are hampered by significant limitations. The ideal de-risking strategy in this regard is stockpiling reserves and mandating a buffer, as it is the most cost-effective strategy to brace against any shock induced by China. Given that the total annual import value from China stands at ~US$11 billion, strategic reserves to meet demands for a year would not cost much. This also allows Indian importers to avoid

Table 3.4

Distribution of Organic Chemicals on the RIF-PCI Scale[269]

Metrics	*PCI< 1*	*Low* *1 ≤ PCI < 1.25*	*Moderate* *1.25 ≤ PCI < 1.5*	*High* *1.5 ≤ PCI < 1.75*	*Very High* *1.75 ≤ PCI < 2*	*Extremely High* *PCI ≥ 2*
Substantially High 0.1≤RIF<1	48	30	9	2	1	0
Exponentially High RIF≥1	10	3	3	1	0	0

[269]Ibid.

any cost-escalation or demand-supply gap related to rerouting supply chains. Further, the government can explore either of the two options to secure this buffer. One, the government can itself maintain a buffer. But this would put a burden on the public exchequer. Alternatively, the government can mandate the Indian importers to create the buffer. This way, the cost would be distributed. Further, the government can pitch in with some form of insurance or financial assistance to support the buffer. Anyway, businesses tend to maintain weeks or months of contingency supplies. Thus, this de-risking strategy should not add too much in terms of a financial burden. Furthermore, it needs to be noted that not all organic chemicals, including APIs, are a priority area. Thus, the de-risking cost will further come down.

Nevertheless, the de-risking strategy should not drastically diversify supplies at this stage, as there are cost advantages of importing from China, which India should continue to leverage to support its domestic healthcare industry. Anyway, the nature of imports from China is substitutable in the short to medium term. India just needs enough stockpiles to see off that period of immediate shock.

2. Machinery and Mechanical Appliances

Machinery and mechanical appliances are India's second-largest import category vis-à-vis China. During FY 2024, India imported US$22.47 billion worth of machinery from China, which constituted around 39 per cent of its total imports in the category.[270] A scrutiny of India's dependence on China for 'Machinery and Mechanical Appliances' becomes crucial for several reasons. First, machines and machinery form the core of the entire industrial sector. As capital goods, they find widespread applications across the manufacturing sector. These

[270] Ibid.

include industrial robots, metal rolling machines, cyclotrons, complex air/gas/water turbines, industrial furnaces, automatic data-processing machines, critical machine tools, critical metalworking tools, machines used in metallurgy, pneumatic and hydraulic machines, laser/light/photon beam blasters, derricks, cranes, as well as various complex sorting and grinding machines. These are critical to value addition in the economy and producing finished goods for consumers. Second, the category also contains strategic machinery items like nuclear reactors, jet engines, broadcasting equipment and cyclotrons, which are key to a nation's infrastructure development. Strategic goods also include critical machine tools that are instrumental in manufacturing several dual-use components that find applications in the space, defence and cyber sectors. Finally, by virtue of being capital goods, a disruption in the supply of machinery can trigger a widespread cascading effect. A disruption will likely also have a pronounced incidence effect on the working class.

Overall, among the items with an RIF≥ 0.1 and PCI> 1, the majority exhibit 'low' product complexity. However, the number of items with 'moderate' and 'high' product complexity isn't insignificant either, suggesting relative difficulty in substitutability.

None of the items exhibit 'extremely high' product complexity. It suggests that India does not depend on China for items that can trigger a long-term disruption in this category. Two items score 'very high' on product complexity, indicating greater difficulty in their substitution in the event of a disruption. In total, there are 19 items across the three dependence categories with 'exponentially high' RIF. However, half of them exhibit PCI< 1. For such items, the potential high impact of disruption is mitigated by the relative ease of substitutability.

Table 3.5
Distribution of Machinery and Mechanical Appliances on the RIF-PCI Matrix[271]

Metrics	*PCI < 1*	*Low 1 ≤ PCI < 1.25*	*Moderate 1.25 ≤ PCI < 1.5*	*High 1.5 ≤ PCI < 1.75*	*Very High 1.75 ≤ PCI < 2*	*Extremely High PCI ≥ 2*
Substantially High 0.1 ≤ RIF < 1	62	23	11	12	2	0
Exponentially High RIF ≥ 1	10	5	3	1	0	0

a. De-Risking Strategy by Diversifying and Moving Up the Value Chain

India does not import any of the strategic goods such as nuclear reactors, jet engines or cyclotrons (minuscule) from China. However, India exhibits an extremely high dependence on portable automatic data-processing machines <10 kg. The resultant shock potential in this category is the highest both within (machinery) and across the categories (that include organic chemicals and electrical machinery and equipment). It makes India's dependence a source of potential vulnerability. Digital automatic data-processing machines (other than those mentioned in the severe dependence category) again figure in the high dependence category, thereby enhancing their combined significance. Like portable automatic data-processing machines (<10 kg), these machines also have a relatively high score on the RIF scale.

---

[271]Ibid.

A 'moderate' PCI score for automatic data-processing machines, however, suggests that enough diversification exists in terms of technological capability among countries. Additionally, in this segment, while imports are sourced from China, the manufacturing firms operating there include a range of foreign players. Thus, while an import ban, in this case, is not justified, state intervention to attract such foreign players to manufacture in India is a recommended de-risking strategy.

Metalworking and machine tools have a 'high' PCI score and, given their strategic significance in a range of manufacturing activities, emerge as a top priority area in India's de-risking strategy, thereby warranting state intervention of some form. The HS4 classification 8454-68 refers to the most critical machine tools or metalworking tools. Among them, India's dependence on China is significant only in the 8456 category at 57 per cent. The others exhibit a lesser degree of dependence. However, it is quite possible that single items with a higher degree of dependence at the HS8 level classification under HS4 categories exhibit a low degree of dependence. State intervention to encourage domestic capability in the select segments of the machine and metalworking tools is recommended.

Another priority area could be machines to extrude, draw and cut man-made fibres as they exhibit 'high' to 'very high' product complexity on the PCI scale. Textiles and knitting machines exhibit relatively high scores on the PCI and RIF scales, suggesting relatively difficult substitution and high shock potential. State intervention of some form (diversification coupled with domestic production incentives) can be justified in the textile machines segment. Tools with self-contained electric motors also consistently figure in the tables that exhibit RIF and PCI scores above the designated threshold. Thus, these segments also emerge as a priority area within the larger de-risking strategy.

Machines for making/finishing paper, pulp, paper boxes and paperboard have relatively high RIF and PCI, but when a subjective filter is applied, they do not appear to be strategic in nature. Thus, government intervention is strongly discouraged. State intervention isn't recommended for items that are not of strategic significance, such as rubber, plastic, glass working machines, vacuum pumps and compressors.

Overall, it is advisable to pursue a de-risking strategy entailing domestic production and diversification to an extent that is just enough to demonstrate India's ability to quickly switch suppliers. A drastic diversification or domestic production strategy has a higher probability of failure and cost-escalation.

Finally, India's reliance on 'parts and spares' can be a bigger source of strategic vulnerability than its reliance on machinery. Unlike capital goods and machine tools, which have longer lifespans, parts and spares need constant replacement at regular intervals. Thus, delays or disruptions in parts and spares, especially for machine tools and industrial machines and robots, can bring the entire production line to a halt. These measures are also the most effective from the adversary's viewpoint, as they allow the adversary to disrupt its rival's supply chain without imposing a huge economic cost on itself. A slump in exports of parts and spares would hardly make a dent in the adversary's finances, and yet it can achieve the desired outcome. Thus, a de-risking strategy must entail encouraging Indian private players to capture this segment. The capital investment required to jump-start production of parts and spares would be a fraction of the cost of laying down a production line for complex machinery. And as the backwards supply chain in India takes hold, the country will organically move up the value chain, further strengthening its manufacturing base. This could be a long-term de-risking strategy with minimal economic cost.

On the contrary, specializing in the manufacture of capital goods and machine tools from scratch could be difficult owing to a lack of complex process technology. Furthermore, the global competition from major players may render this segment unprofitable for Indian players. The parts and spares segment, however, is easy to capture, owing to the need for less complex technology and the presence of a readily available market in India.

3. Electrical Machinery and Equipment

The 'Electrical Machinery and Equipment' segment, classified under the HS85, is the largest import category for India vis-à-vis China. In FY 2024, India imported items worth US$31.3 billion in this segment, thereby accounting for over 30 per cent of its total imports from China. The category constitutes important electrical goods such as lasers/photon beams, signalling apparatus, electrons, capacitors, batteries, printed circuits, electric motors and generators, transmitters, receivers and amplifiers, memories as well as magnets (electrical and permanent), among others. These find application in broadcasting and telecommunications equipment, and thus are critical to the country's ICT infrastructure. Furthermore, lithium-ion batteries and solar photovoltaic cells, critical to the country's energy transition and climate goals, also belong to this classification of goods. Lastly, India's massive dependence on China for consumer electronics such as TVs, radio, microwave, flat panel displays, vacuum cleaners, etc., is also reflected in this category.

In general, India's import dependence (in aggregate and percentage terms) on China is highest in the 'electrical machinery and equipment' category. This is reflected in a significant number of items with 'exponentially high' RIF. However, none of the items in the category exhibit a product complexity higher than 'moderate'.

While items such as photovoltaic cells, flat panel displays, parts of radio and TVs, permanent magnets, electronic printed circuits, AC motors, etc., exhibit 'exponentially high' RIF, they display a product complexity of less than 1. This suggests that while most of the production for such items may be concentrated in China at present, it can quickly diffuse to other places. Lithium-ion has an 'exponentially high' RIF score of 16.5, but on the PCI scale it values just over 1, suggesting that there exists sufficient diversity with respect to technological complexity among nations to produce it if the market demands it. This suggests that China's dominance in lithium-ion is not a result of its technological or capability lead over others but a consequence of its competitive prices. However, given lithium-ion's strategic significance in India's clean energy transition, it might be prudent for India to diversify its imports and attract countries with the requisite economic complexity and incentives to produce the same on Indian soil.

Broadcasting and telecommunications equipment such as smartphones, parts for telephones, apparatus for transmission and receivers, etc., exhibit 'exponentially high' RIF, indicating massive dependence. However, they display 'moderate' product complexity, suggesting relative ease in their substitutability. Nonetheless, their massive RIF suggests a possibility for a huge shock, even if it is short-lived. Furthermore, given their significance in certain strategic sectors, there is a need for a de-risking strategy in the deployment of these equipment in sensitive areas.

Integrated circuits, memories and amplifiers also exhibit 'moderate' product complexity but 'exponentially high' RIF, indicating massive supply shock in the short to medium term. Processors (HS 854231) are absent from the list despite exhibiting an RIF of 8.7, as India's percentage dependence on China in this category is less than 30 (26 per cent).

A significant number of items with RIF≥0.1 exhibit a product complexity of less than 1. Among the items with an RIF≥0.1 and PCI>1, the majority exhibit 'low' to 'moderate' product complexity. None of the items exhibit 'high', 'very high' or 'extremely high' product complexity. More items (26) under the electrical machinery and equipment category exhibit an 'exponentially high' RIF score compared to those under organic chemicals and machinery and mechanical appliances. However, around two-thirds of them have a PCI< 1, suggesting relative ease in their substitutability in the event of a disruption. In general, electrical machinery and equipment exhibit 'exponentially high' shock potential but low product complexity. This means they are relatively easy to substitute in the short-to-medium term. Of course, there will be a price hit in ensuring alternatives. This is where the state can be supportive of entities in the segment.

Table 3.6
Distribution of Electronic Machinery and Equipment on the RIF-PCI Matrix[272]

Metrics	*PCI < 1*	*Low 1 ≤ PCI < 1.25*	*Moderate 1.25 ≤ PCI < 1.5*	*High 1.5 ≤ PCI < 1.75*	*Very High 1.75 ≤ PCI < 2*	*Extremely High PCI ≥ 2*
Substantially High 0.1 ≤ RIF < 1	49	9	1	0	0	0
Exponentially High RIF ≥ 1	17	3	6	0	0	0

a. De-risking by Deregulation

As highlighted above, the case of India's dependence on China with respect to electrical machinery and equipment is different from the case of dependence on the other two product categories, i.e. organic chemicals and machinery and mechanical appliances,

[272]Ibid.

in two ways. First, the severity of dependence is relatively much higher in electrical machinery and equipment than in the other two categories. This means that the potential for immediate shock in case of a disruption would be extremely high. Second, the product complexity exhibited by electrical machinery and equipment is relatively much lower. This means that the period of disruption is likely to be much shorter than in the case of organic chemicals and machinery.

In this light, steps can be taken to pursue some degree of diversification which does not increase the developmental cost by too much. But diversification beyond a certain degree may hurt businesses and consumers. Thus, an optimal long-term de-risking strategy should be to boost domestic manufacturing of electrical machinery and equipment.

However, the government should refrain from pursuing complete self-reliance or *atmanirbharta* by pumping subsidies and laying down industrial policies to support domestic players. That India's Production-Linked Initiative (PLI) schemes in several sectors, including electronics, failed to deliver the desired results, eventually forcing the government to allow the scheme to lapse, is a testament to the fact that such schemes are more likely to fail than succeed.[273]

Instead, the government should undertake measures to make India a more attractive destination for foreign investment. This would require shedding protectionist impulses and scaling back excessive bureaucracy and regulation, as these undercut India's position as a potentially massive consumer market. As the US-China trade war prolongs, India must capitalize on the urgency on the part of the businesses to double down on their 'China+1 strategy'.

---

[273]Singh, Sarita Chaganti, and Shivangi Acharya, 'India's $23 bln plan to rival China factories to lapse after it disappoints', *Reuters*, 24 March 2025, https://tinyurl.com/59acz7d3. Accessed on 15 November 2025.

Conclusion

This chapter addresses the question whether India's import dependence on China renders it strategically vulnerable. In that process, it deals with several fundamental issues, such as: Is dependence fundamentally bad? Does dependence necessarily lead to vulnerability? Are all vulnerabilities of similar intensity and impact? Or are there some that are of strategic and critical significance?

The assessment concluded that dependence is the product of comparative advantage. It is also a two-way street, with both buyers (importers) and sellers (exporters) being subject to it. Dependence and vulnerability are not the same. Specific conditions of dependence in certain situations can lead to vulnerabilities. For dependence to become a source of vulnerability, the severity of dependence has to be significant. Further, the case of dependence has to be tied to some disruptive factors that can render the dependence relationship untenable, fickle, or unreliable. These factors could include recurrent tariff or non-tariff barriers, supply shocks, natural calamities and information asymmetry, among others.

But vulnerabilities may not always be strategic in nature. For a vulnerability to become a strategic vulnerability, the act of inducing vulnerability must be strategically motivated, and the act should succeed in inflicting strategic cost on the player deemed as 'vulnerable' or 'dependent'. Thus, strategic vulnerability is a specific case of vulnerability, which is a function of strategic motivations.

To distil the cases of strategic vulnerability from the usual cases of vulnerability, this chapter proposed a four-stage test. This entailed the adversary test, the substitutability test, the incidence test and the cascading test. While the adversary test examines whether the case of dependence/vulnerability is vis-à-vis an adversary, the substitutability test checks for availability and affordability of existing alternatives. The incidence test is designed to approximate the impact of disruption on the general populace. Finally, the cascading effect test looks for the spillover effects of disruption within and beyond the supply chains. And only if the case of dependence passes the first two and at least one of the last two tests, can it be termed as a case of strategic vulnerability.

Yet, there may be cases of strategic vulnerabilities that are more severe than the others. Two types of such cases may emerge. First, a case of strategic vulnerability where the capability gap between the adversary and the rest of the world is so huge that substitutability seems impossible. This could induce chronic strategic vulnerability. The second one is a case of import dependence on the adversary for items like electronic parts, components, machines, etc., utilized in strategic infrastructure like aviation, power grids, railways, nuclear facilities, communications, and advanced research facilities, which amounts to an extreme kind of strategic vulnerability. Such cases of strategic vulnerabilities can be termed as critical vulnerabilities.

The chapter then modelled the framework to devise a simpler and practical test to identify cases of strategic vulnerability using two metrics—the Relative Impact Factor and the Product Complexity Index. The PCI was used as a metric for relative ease of substitutability of the imported item exhibiting high degree of dependence. This allows one to measure the longevity of the period of disruption. The RIF was used as a metric for gauging the immediate shock potential, which the incidence and cascading effect test seek to measure.

The test was then applied to the three largest import categories vis-à-vis China: organic chemicals, machinery and mechanical appliances, electrical machinery and equipment. Together, these accounted for over two-thirds of India's total imports from China in 2023.

Most of the items within the three product categories were eliminated for either exhibiting 'very low' potential for immediate shock or 'very low' product complexity. Of the items that remained, most within 'organic chemicals' exhibit low to moderate product complexity with substantially high shock potential. Only a handful exhibit either high product complexity or exponentially high shock potential. In general, electrical machinery and equipment exhibit high RIF, i.e., potential for substantially high and exponentially high shock potential, but score abysmally low on product complexity. Only a handful exhibit both substantially high to exponentially high shock potential along with low to moderate product complexity. Machinery and mechanical appliances, of the three product categories, have the most number of items that exhibit substantially high and exponentially high immediate shock potential and also high to very high product complexity. But even within this category, most of the items display low to moderate product complexity with either substantially high or exponentially high shock potential.

Based on this, this chapter recommended a variety of de-risking tools such as stockpiling, moderate diversification, capturing low-end items in the value chain like parts and spares, and boosting domestic capability by capitalizing on the opportunity presented by the 'China+1 strategy'. This would, in turn, require the government to pursue de-regulation and foster competition.

Lastly, it is important to underline the fact that if 'significantly high' RIF for items imported from China renders India susceptible to immediate and huge shock, and thus vulnerable, their respective 'low' to 'moderate' product complexity renders China equally vulnerable. As almost all of China's exports to India are relatively easily substitutable, Beijing's leverage over New Delhi is rather limited. Thus, one can argue that the nature of dependence equips India with leverage as well. It is to be emphasised that for China to extract any advantage of strategic value through economic coercion, the scale and impact of such a measure must be significant. This would require China to target multiple items that can inflict maximum shock or damage to India. But there exists a greater likelihood that any such incident would be a one-off interaction, as it is likely to push India towards forced diversification, thereby expending China's leverage forever.

4

Partners for Power: How India Must Engage China and the World

MANOJ KEWALRAMANI AND
VANSHIKA SARAF

The rise of China has emerged as one of the most critical strategic challenges for India in the 21st century. As Asia's two preeminent powers, India and China are bound not only by geography but also by history and ambition. Their coexistence is complicated by a paradox: both countries share an interest in regional and global stability, multipolarity, technological advancement and economic growth. In fact, there is a strong case to be made for India-China cooperation across several domains. However, the fact is that there are significant divergences in the two countries' approaches towards these goals and their visions for the international order.

For instance, as mentioned earlier, while both countries seek global multipolarity, India believes that a multipolar world order must be underpinned by a multipolar Asia. Likewise, both India and China agree on the need to maintain the UN-centred international institutional architecture. They also concur that this architecture has not necessarily kept pace with the times and needs significant reform to reflect the new geopolitical and geoeconomic realities. However, there are sharp differences on the direction of this reform, with the Chinese side unwilling to accommodate India's aspirations at forums like the Nuclear Suppliers Group and the UN Security Council.

On the more narrow issues, too, such as data privacy and security, climate change negotiations and the evolution of groupings like BRICS, the two sides have differing approaches. Under Indian law, privacy is a fundamental right, having implications for data governance. This is a very different framework than China's more state-centric and national security-focused approach to data governance. On climate change, differences in technological capabilities, development levels and state capacity have resulted in China adopting more ambitious or proactive commitments while India has taken a more cautious, development-first posture. Finally, while China and Russia have sought to drive the BRICS towards a more anti-Western agenda, India has resisted, framing its approach as non-West rather than anti-West. These differences are sources of tension and discord.

With this in mind, this chapter argues that India must pursue dialogue with China where interests coincide while forging and deepening counter-balancing partnerships as a strategic imperative. The framework for such a policy should be one of self-strengthening. This is key to further India's developmental transformation, expand its national power, and shape a new regional equilibrium that ensures stability and predictability.

India's China dilemma is multi-dimensional. China is a neighbour, an economic partner, a military threat, and a geopolitical enigma. The asymmetry between the two countries is stark. China's GDP is nearly five times India's;[274] its defence budget is over three times India's; and it is a permanent member of the United Nations Security Council, while India continues to aspire for that status. Militarily, China's advances in infrastructure, technology and force projection, particularly through its Western Theater Command, border fortifications along the Line of Actual

---

[274]Mujib, Mashal, and Alex Travelli, 'India Is Passing China in Population. Can Its Economy Ever Do the Same?', *The New York Times*, 19 April 2023, https://tinyurl.com/mpjmfva6. Accessed on 12 November 2025.

Control (LAC) and its expanding presence in the Indian Ocean Region are altering the regional balance of power. China's ambitions are not limited to its borders. Under President Xi Jinping, Beijing has sought to position itself as the preeminent power in Asia, if not a peer competitor to the United States globally. It envisions a hierarchical regional order with China at the apex, an aspiration India inherently resists.

To this end, Beijing has increasingly resorted to coercion and containment to gain India's acquiescence and constrain its room for manoeuvrability. This has been evident through its growing assertiveness along the disputed boundary over the past 15 years. It has also consistently used its position at the UN Security Council to block the listing of Pakistan-backed terrorists under the UN sanctions committee. In addition, Beijing has increasingly employed economic coercion, as seen in the recent disruption of exports of tunnel-boring machines and fertilizers to India. Chinese efforts to inhibit India's rise are also reflected in the strengthening military cooperation with Pakistan. China today is the largest weapons supplier to Pakistan, accounting for 81 per cent of arms procurement.[275] In particular, China is invested in beefing up the Pakistani navy.[276] Over time, the expansion of Pakistan's navy along with its Sinicization can potentially erode the Indian navy's advantage. Apart from this, China has also been extremely cautious in its approach to Indian multinational initiatives, refusing to endorse them. Its decision to not join the India-led International Solar Alliance is a case in point. On the other hand, Beijing has lashed out at India for its deepening partnerships with other countries, such as the US,

---

[275]SIPRI, 'Trends in International Arms Transfers, 2024', https://tinyurl.com/4d2xp43e. Accessed on 16 November 2025.

[276]PTI, 'China Delivers Second of Eight Modern Submarines to Pakistan Navy', *The Economic Times*, 16 March 2025, https://tinyurl.com/2fxev45y. Accessed on 16 November 2025.

Japan, Australia and France. This has been evident in Beijing's displeasure[277] over India's participation in forums such as the Quadrilateral Security Dialogue (Quad) and the Indo-Pacific Economic Framework (IPEF). By casting these arrangements as instruments of 'encirclement' or containment,[278] China seeks to deter India from pursuing engagements that are forged by strategic convergence. Another recent example of this is Beijing's reported demand that India guarantee that heavy rare-earth magnets imported from China would not be re-exported to the US and would be used only to meet local needs.[279] In essence, the Chinese approach amounts to desiring a veto, formal or informal, over India's foreign policy choices.

Yet India, as a rising power, cannot afford to limit the breadth and depth of its strategic engagements. India today is not only the world's fourth-largest economy but also among the fastest growing major countries in the world. Foreign trade accounts for around 45 per cent of the country's GDP.[280] It is a key destination for foreign investment and is increasingly integrating with global supply chains and markets. Tens and millions of Indian citizens and persons of Indian origin live and work around the world, forming a vibrant and influential diaspora. In addition, India possesses one of the world's largest and youngest populations,

---

[277]'Foreign Ministry Spokesperson Mao Ning's Regular Press Conference on January 22, 2025', Ministry of Foreign Affairs of the People's Republic of China, 22 January 2025, https://tinyurl.com/3vnpw7zs. Accessed on 9 December 2025.
[278]'The Quad Taking China as a Target Is Destined Not to Go Far', *Global Times*, 23 September 2024, https://tinyurl.com/34tdzytk. Accessed on 16 November 2025.
[279]Mukherjee, Sharmishtha, and Dipanjan Roy Chaudhary, 'China seeks India's assurance on no heavy rare earths diversions to US', *The Economic Times*, 9 October 2025, https://tinyurl.com/bdhchnde. Accessed on 16 November 2025.
[280]Ministry of Commerce & Industry, 'The cumulative exports (merchandise & services) during FY 2024-25 (April-March) is estimated to grow by 5.50% at US$ 820.93 Billion, as compared to US$ 778.13 Billion in FY 2023-24 (April-March)', *PIB*, 16 April 2025, https://tinyurl.com/4dr74hu7. Accessed on 16 November 2025.

offering a demographic dividend that can fuel innovation, labour competitiveness and consumer demand for decades. India is also a leading player in critical sectors like information technology, pharmaceuticals and space technology, and is emerging as a significant actor in global climate diplomacy and green energy transition. With this backdrop, an inward-looking approach would not only constrain India's global ambitions but also undermine its long-term national interests in an interconnected world. India, therefore, must retain the agency to choose its partners, pursue its interests, and shape its external environment.

However, this autonomy must be exercised in a calibrated manner. In fact, one key aspect of this exercise of strategic autonomy is engagement with China because despite the differences discussed above, there are several points of commonalities that the two countries can build on. This argument does not draw from some form of Asian or developing-world romanticism, akin to the 1950s. Rather, it is based on having a clear-eyed understanding of national interests and pursuing them with pragmatism.

To this effect, Indian policymakers must adopt a two-pronged strategy. On the one hand, India must focus on building comprehensive national power through external partnerships, across military, economic and technological domains. The objective of these partnerships is not to engage in some sort of grand containment of China. Indian policymakers must assiduously guard against the country becoming a frontier state in what could be a new Cold War. Rather, the goal is to fortify India's defence capabilities and build interoperability, boost economic linkages and supply chain integration, and catalyse technological innovation while weaving India more tightly into the fabric of global innovation ecosystems. This self-strengthening through external balancing is critical if New Delhi has to blunt Beijing's coercive capabilities.

On the other hand, it is equally vital for India to engage China. Sporadic or unstructured dialogue with Beijing is insufficient and, in fact, counterproductive to India's long-term interests. India and China are not just neighbours; they are civilizational states and rising major powers whose actions reverberate across Asia and the world. What is, therefore, needed is consistent and structured dialogue. Moreover, in the international arena, New Delhi must navigate the shifting landscape and leverage the opportunities created by China's rise. On certain issues, this might require India to work in partnership with China. Of course, structuring such a bilateral dialogue requires both sides to play ball. What then should India do if China refuses to engage in meaningful dialogue? The answer lies in focusing on sustained economic growth, investing in domestic capabilities, and strengthening comprehensive national power through external balancing. Bringing Beijing to the negotiating table is not a matter of rhetorical or moral persuasion; it requires influencing China's perception of its relative balance of power. Once that shifts, Beijing will likely deem dialogue necessary.

The rest of this chapter expands on this strategy. Before that, however, it is important to outline what strategic autonomy means in a world that is between orders.

Understanding India's Strategic Autonomy

Strategic autonomy, as both a doctrine and in practice, has been integral to India's foreign policy since Independence. Traditionally, it has referred to the capacity of a state to pursue its national interests and make sovereign choices without being constrained by external powers or commitments. In the first few decades after India's Independence, strategic autonomy meant the decision to not formally align with either of the two competing Cold War blocs. Among other factors, the imprint of colonialism on the Indian psyche, the developmental challenges before the country, and a sense of idealism—even a belief in India's manifest destiny as a great power—shaped this approach.[281] India was, therefore, wary of dependencies on external powers, although it deeply engaged the US, Soviet Union, the UK, France and China. Writing in 1963, Indian Prime Minister Jawaharlal Nehru described non-alignment as 'freedom of action' in the international arena, arguing that this was an extension of independence.[282]

In practice, of course, developmental imperatives and the shifting balance of power in the 1960s led to India partnering much more closely with the Soviet Union. In the end, this resulted in the signing of the Indo–Soviet Treaty of Peace, Friendship and Cooperation in 1971. In other words, even during the early decades, Indian policy was partly focused on engaging and seeking partnerships with all major powers in order to maintain a broad bouquet of options. This was the case until, of course, it became untenable to do so. Towards the end of the Cold War, India began to revert to this posture in response to shifts in great power competition. So in that sense, historically, there has been far greater continuity in Indian policy than one would ordinarily assume.

The post-Cold War era saw a seismic shift in India's foreign policy, as the country grappled with the collapse of the Soviet Union and the emergence of American unipolarity. In the decades that followed, successive Indian administrations strengthened ties with the United States while maintaining a diversified suite of relationships. In more recent years, this policy position has come to acquire the nomenclature of multi-alignment. India's External Affairs Minister S. Jaishankar defines multi-alignment as 'the approach of engaging all major centers of power', given

[281]Pande, Aparna, *From Chanakya to Modi: The Evolution of India's Foreign Policy*, HarperCollins, India, 2017.

[282]Nehru, Jawaharlal, 'Changing India', *Foreign Affairs* Vol. 41, No. 3, 1963, pp. 453–65, https://doi.org/10.2307/20029632. Accessed on 16 November 2025.

the emerging reality of global multipolarity.[283] He contends that India today is pursuing 'multi-vector and multi-aligned policies', which entail issue-based engagements and partnerships.[284]

This is *the* core facet of the concept of strategic autonomy, i.e., the ability to determine the nature of one's engagement with others based on one's own interests with regard to a particular issue. However, the exercise of such autonomy depends on two key pillars. First, it is substantially a product of one's own capabilities. In other words, it is the cultivation of economic heft, military power and domestic stability that endows a country with the capacity to exercise meaningful strategic autonomy. In large part, this is because such capabilities strengthen a country's ability both to endure external pressure and impose costs on others. Second, at its heart, strategic autonomy is about maintaining flexibility in policy options. For one to be in a position to enjoy this flexibility, a certain degree of diversification is critical. This is necessary in terms of ideological approach, diplomatic engagements, military systems and equipment and economic partnerships. In fact, the current fragmented global order characterized by uneven distribution of power and the breakdown of the normative rules-based order facilitates the practice of flexibility. Compared to any other time since the end of the Cold War, states today are largely limited by their own objectives, political will, power and imagination.

That said, the exercise of strategic autonomy does not mean either impunity in action, equidistance from different power centres or indecision in foreign policy. From an Indian

---

[283]Ministry of External Affairs, 'Remarks by External Affairs Minister, Dr. S. Jaishankar at MIREX, Dominican Republic', Government of India, 30 April 2023, https://tinyurl.com/bddsu8m3. Accessed on 16 November 2025.

[284]Ministry of External Affairs, 'Transcript of External Affairs Minister, Dr. S. Jaishankar, in Conversation with Mariano-Florentino (Tino) Cuéllar of Carnegie Endowment, Washington, DC (October 2, 2024)', Government of India, 2 October 2024, https://tinyurl.com/4nbvev7r. Accessed on 18 November 2025.

perspective, it implies taking positions that are in India's national interests. On some occasions, this requires pulling off an ungainly balancing act, such as the one New Delhi engaged in following the Russian invasion of Ukraine in 2022. At other times, it involves confronting difficult trade-offs and prioritizing one set of interests over others. The Indian government's decision to phase out any crude oil imports from Iran amid American sanctions is a case in point. The severity of the trade-offs that one has to confront is often a reflection of a country's national power, either real or as perceived by its own leadership. Likewise, the capacity of a country to mitigate the adverse effects of a potential trade-off is also a product of the estimation of its power and utility—current and future—by others. The American government's 2022 decision to approve an India-specific waiver for punitive Countering America's Adversaries Through Sanctions Act (CAATSA) sanctions following New Delhi's decision to go ahead with the S-400 missile defence system deal with Russia is an example of this. Similarly, the Trump administration's use of economic coercion against India reflects its calculation of relative dependence. It believes that current geopolitical and geoeconomic trends give Washington greater leverage over New Delhi.

If one is to suggest a pragmatic yet bold path forward for Indian policy, it is essential to apply this understanding of strategic autonomy. As we have discussed earlier, the world today appears to be adrift, with the international order being in a state of tremendous flux. It simultaneously engenders aspects of unipolarity, bipolarity and multipolarity.[285] Within this context, the US and China are seeking to compete with each other by investing in domestic capacity, constraining and delegitimizing

---

[285]This framework was first articulated by Dhruva Jaishankar in The Great Power Show podcast 'India's Tryst with Destiny: Time to Get Real', *Tracking People's Daily (Substack)*, 6 February 2025, https://tinyurl.com/msvejzac. Accessed on 16 November 2025.

each other's actions and expanding influence. Other actors, meanwhile, are eyeing capability enhancement, autonomy of action and greater bargaining power. In essence, what we are witnessing today is in an era of great power competition in an increasingly multipolar world.

In this environment, it is essential that India eschew binary choices. Rather, it must seek robust partnerships with the US and a range of major powers, while simultaneously engaging China. The aim of this policy is not simply capability enhancement but also for India to enjoy better relations with the US and China than they have with each other. This can potentially lend New Delhi significant leverage. That said, given the nature of Sino-US competition, the volatile churn in American domestic politics and structural cleavages in India-China ties, it is highly likely that this goal is simply unfeasible. Under such circumstances, India must seek to leverage the opportunities created by US-China competition, even as it avoids being drawn into a new Cold War-style confrontation. This not only requires New Delhi to engage Beijing in meaningful dialogue but also the strengthening of carefully calibrated economic and civil society bonds. The approach must be one of cooperation without submission, and resistance with escalation if needed. To this end, one must always keep in mind that engagement is a double-edged tool; it creates the potential to both benefit the other and impose costs on them.

Engaging Like-Minded Partners

To effectively leverage its external partnerships and buttress national capabilities, India must prioritize the three pillars of defence, economy and technology. Deepening defence cooperation facilitates modernization, improves deterrence and operational readiness and creates new instruments of leverage. In addition, China's rise has created opportunities for India to expand economic engagement with key partners through new trade agreements, strategic investments and technology cooperation. Making the most of these can enable India's developmental transformation and expand national power. The rest of this section details specific approaches in each of the three domains.

a. Building Fire Power

India's military posture is undergoing a structural transformation. This is driven by the goal of strengthening the country's overall military power to meet a diverse set of interests. One subset of this is the recognition that it must be prepared to deter and, if necessary, defend against an assertive China. The growing threat perceptions along the Line of Actual Control and in the Indian Ocean Region have also catalysed changes in force distribution and posture, along with an emphasis on investing in indigenous capabilities. In addition, there is greater openness today to building strong, flexible and issue-based military partnerships with like-minded states. The aim of these military partnerships has been to function as force multipliers that serve common interests rather than alliance commitments. As the world moves toward a new age of warfare dominated by cyber threats, space militarization and precision strikes, India must ensure its firepower is backed by strong friendships.

In regard to dealing with the China challenge, India's external military partnerships should be guided by two broad goals, i.e., capability enhancement and supporting the strengthening of forces that balance China's growing power. In this context, it is a priority for India to continue pursuing modernization of firepower through acquisitions and leveraging partners in the development of equipment and weapons systems. In other words, India's approach must be driven by capability enhancement. Foreign partnerships provide India with access to advanced technologies, combat platforms and logistical infrastructure that are crucial for modernizing its armed forces. The Defence Technology and Trade

Initiative (DTTI) with the United States,[286] having commenced in 2012, not only enabled joint development of critical technologies like UAVs but also led to the signing of foundational agreements in the latter part of the decade, expediting information sharing between the armed forces. The DTTI eventually gave way to the Initiative on Critical and Emerging Technologies (iCET), which itself has now been renamed Transforming Relations Utilizing Strategic Technologies (TRUST). Since 2008, India has contracted for at least $24 billion worth of US-origin defence goods.[287] These include transport and maritime aircraft, attack helicopters, anti-ship missiles, howitzers, and the P-8I Poseidon maritime patrol aircraft. The two countries also launched INDUS-X in 2023 to expand strategic technology and defence industrial cooperation.

Similarly, defence cooperation with France has resulted in the most recent acquisition of 26 Rafale Marine, making the Indian Navy the first user of the aircraft outside France.[288] In fact, India is the leading partner for France when it comes to the latter's defence exports. India accounts for nearly 29 per cent of French defence exports; imports from France account for nearly 33 per cent of India's defence purchases.[289] Another key Indian partner is Israel. Indian imports account for nearly 37 per cent of Israel's overall defence exports.[290] While India has begun to reduce its dependence on Russia gradually, New Delhi

[286]Congressional Research Service, 'India-U.S.: Major Arms Transfers and Military Exercises', 17 March 2025, https://tinyurl.com/4346t9f4. Accessed on 16 November 2025.

[287]Congressional Research Service, 'U.S.-India Trade Relations', 8 May 2025, https://tinyurl.com/5t32rm5u. Accessed on 16 November 2025.

[288]'Signature of the Rafale Marine Contract for India', *Dassault Aviation*, 28 April 2025, https://tinyurl.com/45hjtk3c. Accessed on 16 November 2025.

[289]Wezeman, Pieter D., Katarina Djokic, Mathew George, Zain Hussain, and Siemon T. Wezeman, 'Trends in International Arms Transfers, 2023', SIPRI Fact Sheet, Stockholm International Peace Research Institute, March 2024, https://tinyurl.com/57y5w9xe. Accessed on 16 November 2025.

[290]Ibid.

still sources around 36 per cent of its defence hardware from Moscow.[291] This partnership has been instrumental in boosting India's strike and deterrence posture through the BrahMos missile system and the S-400 air defence platform, the latter proving to be exceptionally effective during Operation Sindoor in May 2025.[292] Meanwhile, collaboration with South Korea brought in K9 Vajra-T howitzers,[293] part of India's artillery modernization drive, intended to replace older field guns with modern 155 mm systems. These are designed to meet the Indian Army's specific needs for diverse terrains, including deserts, plains and high-altitude areas.[294]

Going forward, however, it is imperative to also continue to infuse defence acquisition with a de-risking approach. This means investing substantially in indigenous capabilities, while diversifying import partners and stressing on joint development and technology transfers. Already, policy appears to be moving in a desirable direction. The Defence Acquisition Procedure (DAP) 2020 encourages foreign direct investment and co-development under the 'Make in India' framework.[295] As China's military modernization outpaces India's in several areas, such as hypersonics, space and cyberwarfare, New Delhi cannot close the gap alone. Collaborative ventures with Israeli radar systems,

---

[291]Ibid.

[292]Tarapore, Arzan, 'Operation Sindoor and the Evolution of India's Strategy Against Pakistan', *War on the Rocks*, 19 May 2025, https://tinyurl.com/33cp2vaw. Accessed on 16 November 2025.

[293]'Embassy Hosts Signing Ceremony of K9 Vajra Phase 2 Project Agreement between Hanwha Aerospace and L&T', Embassy of the Republic of Korea to the Republic of India, 3 April 2025, https://tinyurl.com/mr2hhktv. Accessed on 16 November 2025.

[294]Larsen & Toubro, 'L&T Precision Engineering & Systems Wins Major Order for K9 Vajra-T Artillery Platforms', 23 December 2024, https://tinyurl.com/ycy8nc4u. Accessed on 16 November 2025.

[295]Ministry of Defence, 'Defence Acquisition Procedure (DAP) 2020', Government of India, 30 September 2020, https://tinyurl.com/szwc25vz. Accessed on 16 November 2025.

American drones, European avionics and Russian heavy platforms can help in boosting composite deterrence. That said, technology transfers and joint development, particularly with regard to sensitive and critical domains, are products of political alignment. In that sense, they entail some costs on the exercise of strategic autonomy.

In addition to acquisitions, the approach to deepening military partnerships should focus on building interoperability, boosting domain awareness and intelligence sharing. Over time, the Indian armed forces have expanded their joint exercises and information-sharing arrangements with key partners. The annual Yudh Abhyas exercise with the US, now in its 20th iteration, exemplifies this progress. India now conducts more exercises and personnel exchanges with the United States than with any other country.[296] Over time, these drills have expanded in terms of domain coverage, assets deployed and emphasis on real-world scenarios. In 2022, the Yudh Abhyas drill was held in Uttarakhand, around 100 kilometres away from the LAC with China, ruffling feathers in Beijing.[297] With Australia, the Austrahind exercise helps build coordination in sub-conventional operations in urban and semi-urban settings, and the Varuna naval exercise with France strengthens maritime cooperation through cross-deck operations and anti-submarine warfare drills. Beyond bilateral engagements, India has also hosted large-scale multilateral exercises such as Tarang Shakti 2024, its first multinational air combat exercise, involving air forces from 11 countries and observers from 18 others, thereby broadening its strategic partnerships.[298] With

[296]Kronstadt, K. Alan, 'India-U.S.: Major Arms Transfers and Military Exercises', *Congress.gov,* 17 March 2025, https://tinyurl.com/ytfnye47. Accessed on 16 November 2025.

[297]Krishnan, Ananth, and Dinakar Peri, 'India-U.S.exercise near LAC irks China', *The Hindu,* 1 December, 2022, https://tinyurl.com/ve3m248z. Accessed on 16 November 2025.

[298]Chopra, Anil, 'Exercise Tarang Shakti – Largest Multilateral Air Exercise in

trusted partners like the Quad countries, there is a broader approach being adopted beyond warfighting to encompass maritime law-enforcement.

The Indian Ocean is the theatre of both opportunity and vulnerability. Naval partnerships enhance India's ability to secure its sea lines of communication and project power in response to Chinese naval forays. For example, after securing access to the Duqm Port in Oman, India opened its first off-shore military logistics facility, enhancing its operational reach in the western Indian Ocean Region and counterbalancing China's military presence in Djibouti.[299] Domestically, India has invested in surveillance systems like the Information Management and Analysis Centre (IMAC) and the Integrated Coastal Surveillance System (ICSS)—developed by Defence Research and Development Organisation (DRDO)—which constitutes a radar and sensor network across the coastline. These systems provide real-time situational awareness, enabling the detection of unauthorized vessels and strengthening coastal security. The IMAC is currently being upgraded to the National Maritime Domain Awareness centre. Likewise, India has expanded cooperation on domain awareness with partner countries, with the Quad's Indo-Pacific Partnership for Maritime Domain Awareness being critical to this process. But such domain awareness and intelligence cooperation is not just critical in the seas. Even along India's land borders, intelligence sharing with partners can prove critical to effective actions. This was underscored by reports that the US government provided 'real-time details' of Chinese positions and force strength ahead of an incursion in the eastern sector in 2022.[300]

India', *Indian Aerospace & Defence Bulletin*, 5 September 2024, https://tinyurl.com/2uvbubcy. Accessed on 16 November 2025.

[299]Martin, Peter, et al., 'China Piles the Pressure on India in Its Own Backyard', *Bloomberg*, 12 March 2025, https://tinyurl.com/47wr8fx6. Accessed on 16 November 2025.

[300]Shinkma, Paul D., 'U.S. Intel Helped India Rout China in 2022 Border

Expanding such engagements remains crucial for several reasons. Apart from being force multipliers, they improve collaboration, enable exchanges of threat assessments and adversary strategies, facilitate equipment testing, support training and skill development, and provide opportunities to learn from the operational practices of other countries. Importantly, they also help build joint capabilities to address humanitarian challenges. In the context of China, joint operations with like-minded partners significantly extend the reach of India's maritime power. Operating east of the Malacca Strait in coordination with partners lends greater weight and strategic value to even a modest Indian presence. Increasing the frequency and duration of Indian maritime deployments in China's neighbourhood sends a strong signal to Beijing. Likewise, expanding defence ties with countries in China's periphery, such as the Philippines and Vietnam, is strategically significant. In 2022, the Philippines signed a $375 million contract with India for the acquisition of BrahMos supersonic cruise missiles.[301] With Vietnam, defence relations include naval training, hydrographic surveys, and a $300 million line of credit to support its defence procurement and capacity-building efforts.[302] More recently, India has also developed security dialogue mechanisms with Singapore, Vietnam, Indonesia, the Philippines, Thailand and Malaysia.[303] This visible projection of

---

Clash: Sources', *U.S. News & World Report*, 20 March 2023, https://tinyurl.com/4f6s8f3m. Accessed on 16 November 2025.

[301]Peri, Dinaker, 'India delivers first batch of BrahMos to Philippines', *The Hindu Aerospace*, 20 April 2024, https://tinyurl.com/3mxfyxss. Accessed on 16 November 2025.

[302]Sang, Huynh Tam, 'Eyeing China: Vietnam–India Defense Ties on the Upswing', *F.A.C.T.S. Asia*, 19 August 2024, https://tinyurl.com/4zhmhtmw. Accessed on 16 November 2025.

[303]Pradhan, S.D., 'India's Security Dialogues with Southeast Asian Nations: Strategic Manoeuvres to Strengthen Maritime Security for Economic Prosperity', *Chanakya Code Blog*, *The Times of India*, 21 January 2025, https://tinyurl.com/3chchzp8. Accessed on 16 November 2025.

power also strengthens India's position in diplomatic and strategic negotiations.

b. Strengthening Economic Ties

The goal of developmental transformation must lie at the heart of Indian diplomacy. External Affairs Minister S. Jaishankar has underscored this through the framing that 'if today our aspiration at home is to become a Viksit Bharat, surely there must be a foreign policy for Viksit Bharat.'[304] The purpose of this developmental ambition is to enhance the well-being of all Indians. To this end, sustaining a rapid growth rate is essential. This, however, cannot be achieved simply through self-reliance or by closing oneself from the world. Rather, what is required is for the Indian economy to be far more deeply integrated into global supply chains, enjoy access to foreign markets, capital and technologies, and emerge as a haven for high-skilled talent. In short, global engagement is indispensable to enhancing India's economic competitiveness and national prosperity.

However, this pursuit is unfolding against a backdrop of shifting global dynamics. Protectionism is on the rise and strategic and political considerations are increasingly shaping economic decisions. Indian policymakers, therefore, must navigate this complex environment. At the same time, they need to balance security concerns with developmental priorities. In this process, while national security concerns must be factored into discussions on trade, investment and technology, they must not be allowed to override development imperatives. After all, long-term security rests on the foundation of sustained growth and development. To that end, this section argues that India must deepen its economic partnerships on trade, capital, technology

---

[304]'Remarks by External Affairs Minister, Dr. S. Jaishankar, at the Launch of India's World Magazine', Ministry of External Affairs, 15 December 2024, https://tinyurl.com/tmf58cz5. Accessed on 16 November 2025.

and talent, not only to accelerate growth and development but also to mitigate certain security concerns.[305]

India is the world's fourth largest economy and is projected to be the third largest by 2030, yet it has historically been extremely cautious when it comes to trade agreements. India's decision to exit the RCEP at the last minute is a case in point. The current era, with the fragmenting and re-ordering of the global economy, opens certain opportunities that were hitherto less accessible. These opportunities, however, will not be open for long. Indian policy must, therefore, not be inward-looking; rather it must be proactive in leveraging the congruence of geopolitical interests and geoeconomic concerns to cut deals that build strength.

In terms of trade and investment, the approach should translate to lowering of tariffs and non-tariff barriers, particularly when dealing with trusted partners. Data inform that despite the substantial growth of Indian imports over the past decade, the country's trade-weighted average tariffs on imported goods has doubled to 12 per cent during the same period.[306] This is not only far higher than the figures for the US and European Union countries but also in comparison to BRICS countries like Brazil, Russia, China and South Africa, and others like the Republic of Korea and Vietnam. This needs serious reconsideration, not only in light of the impact that tariffs have on Indian businesses and consumers but also broader strategic partnerships. Reciprocity—along with trade complementarities and creation—must continue to underpin India's approach to trade deals and market access. However, it is imperative to not hold a narrow like-for-like definition of the principle of reciprocity. It needs to be looked

---

[305]Kumar, Amit, 'De-risking India's Trade with China: Identifying Strategic and Critical Vulnerabilities', *Takshashila Institution*, 1 January 2025, https://tinyurl.com/mr4cf4b7. Accessed on 16 November 2025.

[306]World Trade Organization, 'World Tariff Profiles 2024', June 2024, https://tinyurl.com/ynkmv5c4. Accessed on 16 November 2025.

at from the perspective of broader strategic gains and impact on the overall goal of self-strengthening.

In this context, at least one aspect of Indian trade policy appears to be moving in a desirable direction over the past five years. After nearly a decade's lull, the Indian government has inked a series of Free Trade Agreements (FTAs) with Mauritius and the UAE in 2021 and 2022, respectively. Also in 2022, India and Australia signed an early harvest trade deal. The Economic Cooperation and Trade Agreement (ECTA) provides competitive tariff elimination and reduction on a wide range of goods and services for both countries. It has laid the groundwork for a broader FTA. Subsequently, in 2024, India concluded a comprehensive Trade and Economic Partnership Agreement (TEPA) with Iceland, Liechtenstein, Norway and Switzerland, who are members of the European Free Trade Association. In July 2025, India and the United Kingdom also inked a Comprehensive Economic and Trade Agreement (CETA). Current signalling seems to indicate that an FTA with the EU is also increasingly likely soon.

Finally, India is also reportedly negotiating a Bilateral Trade Agreement with the United States. This is likely to be a phased and challenging process, given the flux in US economic and trade policy under President Donald Trump. Following the February 2025 meeting between Trump and Prime Minister Narendra Modi, the two countries have set themselves a trade target of $500 billion by 2030. A comprehensive trade agreement is critical to achieve this goal. The US's imposition of 50 per cent tariffs on select Indian exports in August 2025 has obviously complicated this situation. Political trust is certainly damaged. Regardless, pursuing a mutually acceptable deal is still in the strategic interest of both sides.

Leveraging these deals, however, requires a holistic approach that improves India's overall FTA utilization rate. Estimates of FTA utilization by Indian exporters vary from 5 per cent to 25 per cent. This is well below that of developed countries. Addressing this requires a series of measures, starting from improving awareness, reducing compliance costs and documentation, cutting regulatory hurdles, and reducing broader tariffs, which hurt the competitiveness of Indian exports.

Beyond this, the trade agreements that are being discussed now are likely to have a new, important dimension, which has been opened up with the India-UAE FTA, i.e., the Comprehensive Economic Partnership Agreement (CEPA) of 2022. Under this deal, both countries have agreed to reciprocal national treatment and non-discrimination when it comes to government contracts. This is the first such deal that India has signed with any country. It is worth noting that India has not signed the Government Procurement Agreement (GPA) as a member of WTO. The CEPA deal opens up 34 Indian central government entities for UAE-based firms, while Indian firms can bid for contracts with 41 central government entities. Both sides have also set certain restrictions, particularly with regard to 'essential security interests'. In addition, New Delhi's concerns regarding the impact on smaller Indian players has resulted in the retention of preferential policies for domestic industries and the setting of a significant threshold for such contracts. India's commitments to opening of government procurement apply only when the value of goods, services or construction services exceeds ₹200 crore. In contrast, the UAE has set significantly lower thresholds, with its obligations covering all government procurements above ₹1.6 crore for goods and services and ₹60 crore for construction services.[307] Along with this, rules of origin restrictions also have been retained. Likewise, the CETA with the UK has also opened up government procurement for firms of both countries, with specific thresholds and exclusions. These agreements provide a template for future negotiations, and could open up a broad range of deals with European countries, the US and Japan.

[307]Ministry of Commerce, 'INDIA-UAE CEPA (FAQs)', Government of India, https://tinyurl.com/t4tfmanv. Accessed on 16 November 2025.

Of course, this policy shift has sparked concerns in some quarters about growing dependencies and its impact on domestic industry. Often, government procurement has been used as a tool to cultivate and nurture domestic industries. That said, in principle, this approach to create a competitive market with a broader set of players from like-minded partner countries is sound. It fits with the logic of self-strengthening. Concerns around corruption and impact on domestic industry should not derail these efforts. Protectionism does not equate to lack of corruption or cronyism; rather it limits competition, thereby adversely impacting price and quality. Concerns around dependence and impact on investment, meanwhile, can be addressed through higher local content requirements. That said, it is important for the government to ensure transparency and stakeholder engagement in the process of finalizing such deals to identify and mitigate potential economic and security risks.

c. Tech and Talent Cooperation

On technology, it is important to acknowledge that the world increasingly appears to be moving in a bipolar direction. While there are differences between the US and its allies, there is a broader bifurcation between China and the West that appears to be taking place on technology goods and services, capital, talent and research. This is a challenging environment, but it presents important opportunities. Although the global science and technology ecosystem is splintering, transnational linkages continue to be essential. In that sense, the science and technology ecosystem isn't de-globalizing; rather it is re-globalizing. Just given the complexity and cost implications, the new world that is emerging will still feature cross-border linkages with regard to supply chains, capital flows, movement of high-skilled talent, intermediate products and specialized equipment, along with interconnections between research and development ecosystems. In this world, the quest for narrow self-reliance is an expensive and perhaps even a losing proposition. Consequently, the objective for India must again be self-strengthening.

To that end, this section proposes a three-point agenda. First, India must closely align with like-minded partners to expand access to key technologies, deepen supply chain integration and co-develop frontier technologies. Second, India must promote open technology. Third, India must expand and leverage its high-skilled talent pool as an asymmetric advantage to embed itself into global supply chains. What goes unstated in this is the need to ensure that domestic regulation supports innovation, ease of doing business, and greater spending on research and development.

First, India must remain an attractive destination for global capital and innovation. Protectionism and techno-nationalism, while politically popular, often undermine long-term competitiveness. The challenge lies in balancing openness with national security. India's digital economy, for instance, has benefited from FDI and technological inputs from both Western and East Asian firms. Regulatory clarity, improved ease of doing business, and better dispute-resolution mechanisms will be key to sustaining investor confidence. Talent mobility is another key area of engagement, despite the deepening of anti-immigration politics in the developed world.[308] India must facilitate the movement of high-skilled labour and knowledge workers through digital economy agreements, mutual recognition of qualifications, and co-innovation platforms. This is particularly crucial in AI, green tech and advanced manufacturing.

The more open the world remains to India, and the more open India remains to trusted partners, the more robust its balancing power vis-à-vis China becomes. India needs to harness external

---

[308]Sahu, Satya, Vanshika Saraf, Adya Madhavan, Rijesh Panicker, and Arindam Goswami, 'The Geopolitics of Indian Talent', *Takshashila Institution*, 2 September 2024, https://tinyurl.com/nhm22fb3. Accessed on 16 November 2025.

partnerships in the development of cutting-edge technologies. The 2021–24 Quad summits resulted in initiatives around semiconductor supply chain resilience, open RAN collaboration, AI and cyber standards development, green shipping and clean energy.[309] India's participation in the Quad aligns with its broader vision of digital sovereignty and trusted innovation. The Quad's working groups enable India to harmonize its standards with like-minded partners. The challenge in this regard, however, is the pace of delivery, and the increasing vacillation in US policy. Political turmoil in Washington must not derail India's efforts to work with other Quad partners on some of these critical issues. Moreover, India's climate goals, including net-zero by 2070, hinge on access to green technologies. Strategic partnerships with countries like Germany, under the Green and Sustainable Development Partnership,[310] and with the EU, under the Clean Energy and Climate Partnership,[311] are vital. India's ongoing development of indigenous supercomputing, under C-DAC, AI ethics frameworks via the NITI Aayog,[312] and quantum research, under the National Mission on Quantum Technologies and Applications, positions it well in strategic tech domains, if backed by smart partnerships.[313]

Second, as our colleagues have argued elsewhere, India

---

[309] 'Unclassified Quad Brief – February 2025', Ministry of External Affairs, February 2025, https://tinyurl.com/y8t92hdb. Accessed on 16 November 2025.

[310] Press Information Bureau, 'Joint Statement: 7th India-Germany Inter-Governmental Consultations (IGC)', Prime Minister's Office, Government of India, 25 October 2024, https://tinyurl.com/4mjjs3ez. Accessed on 16 November 2025.

[311] Ministry of External Affairs, '10th Meeting of the India-EU Energy Panel and 3rd Phase of the Clean Energy and Climate Partnership', Government of India, 22 November 2024, https://tinyurl.com/33y7c9z7. Accessed on 16 November 2025.

[312] NITI Aayog, 'National Strategy for Artificial Intelligence', 2018, https://tinyurl.com/5n95r92n. Accessed on 16 November 2025.

[313] 'The National Quantum Mission: An Unprecedented Opportunity for India to Leapfrog in Quantum Computing Technologies', Department of Science & Technology, https://tinyurl.com/yc5pmw73. Accessed on 16 November 2025.

urgently needs a well-defined open-source technology strategy.[314] Such a strategy is vital for achieving techno-strategic autonomy, fostering economic growth, advancing technology leadership, and promoting skill development. Crucially, it also aligns with India's democratic values. Open-source technologies naturally encourage transparency, inclusivity and collaboration, reinforcing India's potential role as a global technology leader. By actively promoting open platforms, standards and models, India can position itself as a key contributor to shaping global technology norms. Open standards, in particular, enhance interoperability, efficiency, competition, accessibility, cost-effectiveness and fairness. To fully realize these benefits, a comprehensive policy framework is essential. This framework must nurture a culture of contribution and provide incentives to sustain a thriving open-source ecosystem.

To address the fragmented nature of open-source software adoption and development, India should establish a statutory Open Source Programme Office under the Ministry of Electronics and Information Technology. In the domain of open-source hardware, India should pursue strategic collaborations with like-minded global partners. Platforms like RISC-V demonstrate how international open-source projects efforts can yield shared benefits. Open-source hardware should also form a key part of India's engagement in the India-EU Trade and Technology Council and others who are keen on prioritizing greater technological autonomy. This can be critical even in the context of the semiconductor challenges that India faces. As Pranay Kotasthane has pointed out, India's endorsement of open-source systems at the Paris AI Action Summit illustrates

---

[314]The recommendations are drawn from the work done by our colleagues at Takshashila. For a deeper dive, see Gupta, Apar, et al., *An Open Tech Strategy for India (A Working Draft), Takshashila Institution*, Bengaluru, 2022.

a strategic alignment with this viewpoint.[315]

Finally, it is self-evident that manpower, particularly high-skilled talent, is a current and future advantage that India can leverage. In fact, India is soon expected to overtake the US as the largest hub for software development.[316] Despite the rapid advancements in artificial intelligence, estimates still indicate a growing demand for tech talent across industries. However, maintaining this advantage requires a broader approach in terms of investment in education and opening up new partnerships in education and research and development with like-minded actors. Recent reports on the establishment of new campuses by foreign universities in India are a positive development.[317] It is essential to continue down this path of collaboration. From a strategic perspective, it is imperative that India leverages its talent pool of engineers and technologists to expand Indian participation in all major technology ecosystems.[318] This can create dependencies, which can make it extremely difficult for others to isolate or coerce. At a policy level, therefore, rather than being overly concerned about brain drain, New Delhi must focus on enhancing India's attractiveness through partnerships and facilitating two-way talent mobility.

---

[315]Kotasthane, Pranay, 'Tech Atmashakti, Not Tech Atmanirbharta: Four Pathways to Technological Sovereignty', *India's World*, 14 May 2025, https://tinyurl.com/34wfztmr. Accessed on 6 November 2025.

[316]ET Team, 'India to Turn Largest Hub of Software Developers by 2027: Thomas Dohmke, CEO, GitHub', *The Economic Times*, 2 September 2024, https://tinyurl.com/yznsz75d. Accessed on 16 November 2025.

[317]India Today Education Desk, '15 Foreign Universities to Set Up Campuses in India This Academic Year', *India Today*, 27 May 2025, https://tinyurl.com/4xmjtu8s. Accessed on 16 November 2025.

[318]Kotasthane, Pranay, 'Tech Atmashakti, Not Tech Atmanirbharta: Four Pathways to Technological Sovereignty', *India's World*, 14 May 2025, https://tinyurl.com/34wfztmr. Accessed on 16 November 2025.

Dealing with China

The second aspect of the dual-track strategy we propose involves sustaining continuous and purposeful engagement with China. This engagement serves multiple functions, including preserving open channels of communication, managing expectations, clarifying mutual red lines, building strategic empathy, preventing inadvertent escalation, and identifying areas of shared interest. Most importantly, however, it is indispensable for cultivating new equities in the bilateral relationship, which can function as foundations that foster stability, predictability and opportunity. These, in turn, are vital for enhancing India's strategic autonomy. To this end, this section details four recommendations. These do not cover the domains that are already under discussion, such as enhancing direct flight connectivity, expanding and easing the issuance of visas, expanding the Kailash Mansarovar Yatra, and other people-to-people engagement initiatives.

a. Strategic and Economic Dialogue

First, instead of the framework of informal summits or sporadic dialogue, the two countries need to establish a broad-based Strategic and Economic Dialogue. This should involve annual bilateral engagements between foreign, commerce, finance and defence ministries, with the agenda being set by the top leadership. This dialogue can be based on the broad commonalities between the two countries' worldviews. Let's refer to these as the 'three agreements'. The first point of agreement is that both sides believe that the UN-centred global institutional architecture is a net positive that must be sustained. Both countries also agree that this architecture has not kept pace with the times, and needs significant reform to address modern-day challenges and reflect the new geopolitical and geoeconomic realities. Such reform will be rendered unfeasible if the rights and interests of a large country and major economy like India are not taken into account.

The second point of agreement is that both countries believe that the world order is moving towards inevitable multipolarity. But what should be the shape of this new multipolar order? Are the dispersion of power and the fruits of development generating greater stability or engendering instability? Is global multipolarity feasible without multipolarity in Asia? What should be the contours of this regional order—its rules and norms? At the core of this, of course, should be the insistence on respecting sovereignty, territorial integrity and autonomy of decision-making of countries, along with practical action against the use of terrorism as an instrument of statecraft. These are philosophical but real-world issues that both sides need to deliberate.

Finally, the third agreement is on economic globalization. It is self-evident that both India and China have been the beneficiaries of the historic process of economic globalization, and both have a stake in maintaining an open global economy. But it is also true that the headwinds to economic globalization are strengthening. While decoupling is not feasible and must not be pursued, the fact is that security today is a crucial vector in economic decision-making for all countries, including China and India. It is a reality that both sides must contend with as they work to enhance trade and investment ties and people-to-people engagement.

Manifesting these 'three agreements' into tangible actions, however, will depend on how the two countries address the differences that lie beneath. There are already several measures that have long been agreed upon but that have not been implemented. For instance, Prime Minister Narendra Modi's 2015 visit to China had resulted in 24 deals.[319] Several of the MoUs have not been implemented. Likewise, India and China already have a Strategic

---

[319]Ministry of External Affairs, 'List of Agreements Signed during the Visit of Prime Minister to China (May 15, 2015)', Government of India, 15 May 2015, https://tinyurl.com/3f7z3365. Accessed on 16 November 2025.

Economic Dialogue (SED) which was established in 2010. The last SED was held in 2019. This platform, however, needs to be upgraded. In its present form, it is co-chaired by the Vice-Chairman of NITI Aayog and Chairman of China's top planning body, the National Development and Reform Commission. This platform needs to be re-imagined to focus on issues related to maintaining smooth functioning of key supply chains, export controls, trade imbalance and barriers, technological cooperation in agriculture and investment issues. China is likely to experience a contraction in external demand. This creates opportunities that India can leverage as part of the trade dialogue. Similarly, China's expanding toolkit of economic coercion, including export controls, sanctions, licensing requirements, etc., can have downstream effects for Indian industry, even if not targeted at Indian entities. A broader economic dialogue should encompass these issues.

Beyond this, it is essential to infuse India-China bilateral engagement with a regional and global perspective. This includes the two sides working with each other on multilateral forums, cooperating on transnational issues, and talking about countering extremism and terrorism. In particular, New Delhi must not shy away from engaging Beijing on the issue of cross-border terrorism emanating from Pakistan. The relationship with Pakistan is a strategic bet that China made several decades ago. Today, China increasingly shares a patron-client relationship with Pakistan. So it is highly unlikely that Beijing will fundamentally distance itself from Islamabad. That said, as much as China leverages Pakistan to constrain India, there are evident concerns in Beijing about being caught in a situation wherein the tail wags the dog. This concern is likely to intensify as Pakistan diversifies its patron network, with deepening ties with the US, Saudi Arabia and others. In other words, China's objective is to leverage Pakistan to further the Chinese regional and even global agenda rather than getting caught in serving Pakistan's goals. This is not an easy balance for Beijing to strike, and there have been moments when it has demonstrated a willingness to impose costs on Pakistan. Moreover, despite Xi Jinping being far more risk-tolerant in leveraging the military instrument compared to his immediate predecessors, Beijing remains extremely wary of getting caught in conflicts that don't impact its core interests. The cost of such entanglement can be deeply detrimental in terms of the broader goal of national rejuvenation. These dynamics can create openings for India to discuss the Pakistan problem with Beijing.

At the global level, both sides need to discuss the potential of supporting some of each other's international proposals, such as India's International Solar Alliance and China's Global Development Initiative. This can potentially lead to further conversations on aspirations, such as India's bid for the Nuclear Suppliers Group and the UN Security Council. Such cooperation, of course, will be neither easy nor straightforward. It will require a calibrated process of give and take, and one will have to consider the ripple effect on ties with other partners too. That said, there are clearly some low-hanging fruits among the areas outlined above. Achieving progress in these domains could help build momentum and confidence in the relationship, effectively exercising the muscles of engagement while allowing space to grapple with more contentious issues. Even so, it is important not to harbour any illusions that Beijing will readily shift its position on India's global ambitions. Changing this calculus will be a long and arduous process. It necessitates both the cultivation of meaningful equities in the bilateral relationship and the steady augmentation of India's comprehensive national power. Only by doing so can India create the conditions necessary to nudge Beijing to reconsider its approach to India's international aspirations.

b. Reviewing Chinese Investments

One key part of the economic agenda with regard to China is the issue of Chinese investments in India. Framing this as a binary is not the most effective approach. What is needed instead is a well-considered strategy. Being open to Chinese capital and talent, particularly those that aid the development of India's manufacturing sector and deepen linkages with global value chains, is a pragmatic and prudent approach. It is, in fact, in India's larger strategic interest to do so. This is not to argue that there isn't any need for scrutiny. However, this should not be an ad hoc process. Rather, it is far more prudent to establish a new investment review mechanism with clear guidelines, conditions and timelines. The goal of this effort is to engender greater predictability for industry, boost domestic capacity, and ensure adequate democratic oversight. In this, India can draw from the experiences of others. Two key points must further be considered in this process.

First, the nature of investment, i.e., whether the investment is focused on short-term financial gain or the creation of long-term productive assets and industrial capacity. In the case of financialized investment that is driven by the former logic, greater scrutiny is warranted. This is even more so the case if the sector or entity that is attracting the investment has broader social or strategic significance. For instance, Chinese entities buying stakes in Indian banks or investing in real estate or agricultural assets for speculative purposes must be scrutinized to differing extents. On the other hand, Chinese investment that enables industrial capacity development or research and development in India should be considered favourably. However, it is important to establish clear pathways for such investments, which include strict joint venture requirements. The objective of this approach is to ensure diffusion of technology know-how and managerial approaches, and incentivize the establishment of the full industrial chain through expansion of domestic content requirement over time. Likewise, India should expedite investment by Chinese entities that are serving global brands looking to establish manufacturing facilities.

Second, a traffic-lights approach at sectoral and sub-sectoral levels should be adopted. In simple terms, this involves creating a framework that assesses national security concerns across a range of sectors and even within sectors. Doing this, of course, requires proactive government engagement with industry bodies. The goal is to classify a narrow set of sectors and sub-sectors as strategic and/or critical from a national security perspective and therefore walled off from Chinese entities. These fall within the red category. Then there would be a range of areas that fall into the green category. These are domains where Chinese entities can invest via the old automatic route. At the most rudimentary level, this would imply opening up areas such as textiles, garments, shoes and other consumer goods manufacturing, along with sectors like retail, construction and even transport to some degree. Even in the energy sector, while nuclear and hydel energy projects should ideally be denied to Chinese entities, investments in certain areas of the solar and wind power supply chain can be welcomed. Finally, there will be a whole range of sectors that should be classified in the orange category. These are the kind of investments that call for a thorough assessment via the new investment scrutiny mechanism. This assessment must be time-bound and based on clearly-defined parameters, specifically focusing on the national security and strategic impact of accepting the investment. Intuitively, tech-related investments, connected elements of certain sectors, domains where there are data security or social impact concerns and investments that impact India's relations with trusted partners, would fall within this category. These lists, of course, should be periodically reviewed.

c. Climate Change Dialogue

Climate change offers a pragmatic area for cooperation between India and China, both of which face severe climate-related challenges and share interests in green financing, clean technology and biodiversity conservation. To this end, we propose the establishment of a dedicated India-China

Climate Change Dialogue. This mechanism should take the form of an inter-ministerial framework that brings together key environment and technology ministries from both sides. Its objectives would include fostering mutual understanding on international climate negotiations, coordinating positions in multilateral forums particularly around common concerns like financing and carbon taxes, and identifying priority areas for collaboration in green technologies. The dialogue should also facilitate the exchange of best practices in pollution control, adaptation strategies and sustainable development. In addition, the Climate Change Dialogue can also facilitate discussions on climate adaptation in the Himalayan region, glacial monitoring, environmental impact of hydel projects, and transboundary river-water data sharing.

Given the size of their populations, energy needs and developmental advancements, India and China have a unique responsibility in shaping the global climate agenda. The proposed dialogue platform can help the two sides better leverage existing platforms like the BASIC group, which has committed to scaling up joint action,[320] the BRICS climate working groups, and the G20's green finance frameworks. It can also help harmonize differences and create opportunities for joint action in international negotiations and standard setting. Agreements on common principles in areas such as solar photovoltaic supply chains, hydrogen energy innovation and sustainable finance definitions could attract broad-based support from other developing countries, allowing them to jointly shape global standards rather than merely adapt to them.

Importantly, a climate dialogue would also serve as a low-politics, high-impact domain for confidence-building

---

[320]'BASIC Ministerial Joint Statement on Climate Change', Ministry of Foreign Affairs Federative Republic of Brazil, 16 October 2023, https://tinyurl.com/k2v724da. Accessed on 18 November 2025.

amidst strained bilateral ties. Dialogue with adversaries on non-traditional security issues can often create an institutional ballast in the relationship, reducing the risk of uncontrollable spirals during crises. A bilateral climate forum would be a pragmatic step, signalling that even amidst the strategic competition between the two sides, cooperation is possible where interests converge.

d. Managing the Boundary

Finally, we recommend that the Indian security establishment must prepare for a more volatile land boundary and competitive Indian Ocean Region. As has been mentioned earlier, there is little evidence that the Chinese leadership is interested in a resolution of the boundary dispute in the near term. Instead, it appears that given the power asymmetry between the two sides, Beijing is keen on testing New Delhi's resolve through transgressions and incursions, the building of infrastructure and military facilities, and the deployment and use of new technologies. The entire boundary with China, therefore, is likely to be far more contentious for the foreseeable future. Such a grim prognosis might lead some to contend that this underscores the futility of talks at the Special Representatives' level.

On the contrary, the more volatile a situation is likely to be, the better it is that established lines of communications are maintained. India must pursue an annual SR-level dialogue. While a resolution of the boundary issue may be a long way away, New Delhi must insist on clarity with regard to Chinese territorial claims, including exchanges of maps. What is, therefore, necessary is resetting expectations about what these talks can achieve. Likewise, the Indian Ocean is the gateway for China's global ambitions. Given the expanded Chinese economic footprint in this region, particularly investments in key port facilities, increased naval presence through intelligence and surveillance vessels and warships is inevitable. Given this, apart from investing in military capabilities as discussed in an earlier chapter, it is essential to engage in a sustained and expanded military and security dialogue with China.

On the boundary issue, New Delhi must not accept the altered status quo in eastern Ladakh as final. It is essential to insist on restoration of all patrolling and grazing rights. In doing so, it is important to appreciate that this will be a long-drawn process. Indian policymakers must, therefore, not let time become a pressure point that Beijing can exploit. Doing this of course requires a degree of transparency from the government and building of some base-level concurrence with the country's broader political elite. Further, this process of negotiations with China should also entail the pursuit of new confidence-building measures (CBMs) across the land boundary.

The 1996 and 2005 agreements on CBMs have generally served the two sides well. Among other things, they placed restrictions for 'preventing dangerous military activities' and 'large-scale military exercises' near the LAC, discussed modalities related to aircraft movement, established two new border meeting points and outlined the process to de-escalate face-to-face encounters. The 2013 Border Defence Cooperation agreement built on these, stipulating the need for flag meetings or border personnel meetings at designated places, and periodic meetings between officers of the relevant military personnel, departments and ministries. It also called on both sides to set up border meeting point sites in all sectors and establish telephone contacts and telecommunication links at mutually agreed locations along the LAC. In addition, both sides talked about establishing a hotline between the military headquarters of the two countries. The agreement also envisioned joint drills and training, disallowed troops following or tailing patrols of the other side in areas where there is no common understanding of the LAC, and warned against 'exchange of fire or armed conflict'. In general, these methods of management have served the two sides well. It is, however, important to update these accords to take into account the new realities, particularly related to technological changes—such as the use of UAVs—and infrastructure development on both sides.

The intensified challenge in the continental domain should, however, not be permitted to derail the expansion of India's maritime power. Naval capacity enhancement should be accompanied by dialogue. In 2016, the two countries held the first India-China Maritime Affairs Dialogue. The second and final edition of this dialogue was held in 2018. It might be worthwhile reviving and reimagining this mechanism to cover engagement between the two foreign ministries, navies and maritime law-enforcement agencies. The objective of this is to engage in consultations on maritime issues including piracy, drug and human trafficking, sea-bed mining and illegal, and unreported and unregulated fishing, address concerns around military and research activities in each other's peripheries, establish clear red lines, and discuss potential HADR and blue economy cooperation.

Conclusion

This chapter has recommended a two-pronged approach for Indian foreign, economic, technology and security policies in order to deal with the challenges of China's rise. It contends that in dealing with the multi-dimensional challenges and potential opportunities that China's rise presents, the Indian strategic response cannot be one based on binaries. A more nuanced and adaptive posture is required. Further, instead of pursuing a narrow vision of self-reliance, this chapter has emphasised the importance of self-strengthening. This objective must be pursued through targeted external partnerships in defence, the economy, and technology, alongside purposeful and calibrated engagement with China. As argued above, such an approach is not at odds with the framework of strategic autonomy. Rather, it is the very means by which India can expand the scope of its choices and effectively exercise strategic autonomy in a contested international environment.

5

Confident, Not Coy: Why Openness Is an Asset for India

RAKSHITH SHETTY

Historically, India and China enjoyed multiple vectors of interconnection. Travellers and scholars traversed the vast expanse between the two ancient civilizations, understanding and recording their experiences and wisdom. Buddhism and religious exchanges carried ideas and philosophies beyond the Himalayas, and trade facilitated material and cultural interactions. However, with the advent of Western colonialism and the subsequent emergence of modern nation-states, these civilizational neighbours were fundamentally transformed into sovereign entities with distinct modern political systems and often competing national interests. The mid-20th century, marked by decolonization and the imperative to assert territorial sovereignty, redefined the terms of engagement. It replaced centuries of fluid cultural interaction and porous frontiers with rigid state-centric frameworks anchored in borders, ideologies and strategic rivalries.

In their contemporary relationship, India and China have oscillated between camaraderie and contention. But a series of border clashes in the last five years crystallized a rupture in trust that had been widening since the Doklam standoff in 2017.[321] Yet,

[321]Haidar, Suhasini, Ananth Krishnan, and Dinakar Peri, 'Indian Army Says 20 Soldiers Killed in Clash with Chinese Troops in the Galwan Area', *The Hindu*,

even as military tensions persist along the 3,488-kilometre Line of Actual Control (LAC), bilateral trade hit a record $127.7 billion in FY 2024–25, underscoring an uncomfortable interdependence between the two nations.[322]

Post-Galwan, India adopted a tough stance: no normalcy without border peace.[323] This policy froze cultural exchanges and academic interactions, halted direct flights, and restricted visas affecting travel and tourism, snapping the threads of engagement between the two societies. These policy measures were essentially signalling tools, emphasising Indian anger with the events in eastern Ladakh. However, long-term retrenchment of this nature risks further deteriorating a relationship already hampered by mutual mistrust and misperceptions.

Today, a handful of Chinese students study in India, while Indian students who want to study in China currently face bureaucratic hurdles. In 2022, India's inbound tourism from China was negligible, with only 0.18 per cent of foreign tourists coming from there.[324] Additionally, India does not rank among China's top ten sources of tourists.[325] This is striking, given that Chinese travellers have been among the top contributors to global tourism. The bilateral relationship is fundamentally characterized by a securitization of openness, where political mistrust overshadows societal engagement. Media narratives in

---

16 June 2020, https://tinyurl.com/36ak2szw. Accessed on 16 November 2025.

[322]Khan, Md Zakariya, 'US Is Top Trading Partner of India in FY25; Trade Deficit with China Widens', *Business Standard*, 16 April 2025, https://tinyurl.com/49skdepn. Accessed on 16 November 2025.

[323]Ministry of External Affairs, 'Statement by External Affairs Minister, Dr. S. Jaishankar in Lok Sabha', Government of India, 3 December 2024, https://tinyurl.com/488nt2s4. Accessed on 16 November 2025.

[324]Ministry of Tourism, 'India Tourism Statistics 2023', Government of India, https://tinyurl.com/457afkdy. Accessed on 18 November 2025.

[325]World Tourism Alliance and KULV Data Marketing, 'WTA Data Analysis Report of China's Inbound Tourism', 2019, https://tinyurl.com/2983w7vx. Accessed on 16 November 2025.

both countries tend to be disinterested in the other, reinforce existing biases or amplify nationalist sentiments. At the same time, limited tourism and student exchanges and the dearth of journalistic interactions reflect a stark asymmetry: India and China, home to over a third of humanity, share fewer people-to-people (P2P), cultural and educational bonds than either does with Western nations.[326]

This chapter contends that India's strategic positioning vis-à-vis China necessitates a fundamental recalibration that reconceptualizes societal openness as a strategic asset, rather than a security liability. India's post-Galwan approach of compartmentalizing and constricting cross-civilizational engagement has yielded an epistemic paradox: even as bilateral trade flourishes, the atrophying of cultural, academic and journalistic exchanges has created critical blind spots in India's understanding of Chinese domestic dynamics. This information asymmetry leaves India increasingly dependent on Western analytical frameworks that may not align with its distinct historical experience and regional imperatives.

The resulting knowledge deficit manifests in two dimensions: first, in the realm of policy formulation, where decisions are increasingly based on mediated assessments rather than indigenous insights; and second, in the domain of strategic autonomy, where India's capacity to develop independent evaluations of Chinese intentions, capabilities and internal contradictions becomes progressively constrained. By abandoning what Chinese scholars term 'relational capital' (guānxì zīběn)—the advantage gained through sustained, trust-based relationships—India risks not only misreading critical inflection points in China's political economy but also relinquishing control of its strategic narrative to external

---

[326]Ministry of External Affairs, 'A Shared Vision for the 21st Century of the Republic of India and the People's Republic of China', Government of India, 14 January 2008, https://tinyurl.com/4s36r558. Accessed on 16 November 2025.

actors whose assessments and interests may diverge from India's developmental priorities and security imperatives.

Frameworks of Trust

At its core, trust in international relations is the expectation that a nation-state will behave in a predictable manner aligned with shared interests, even when there are no enforceable guarantees. This concept is best understood through three key theoretical lenses: rationalist calculations of interest, social constructivist notions of shared identity, and psychological perceptions of intent. From a rationalist perspective, trust emerges from repeated interactions and careful assessment of costs and benefits. Political scientist Andrew Kydd suggests that states invest in trust when they believe (based on available information and incentives) that the other side is likely to act cooperatively.[327] In this view, trust is less about sentiment and more about weighing the probability of reciprocal actions.

In the India-China context, this trust calculus is fundamentally shaped by realism, with both weighing strategic costs and benefits amid persistent informational asymmetries. While liberal economic interdependence, evidenced by record bilateral trade, creates shared interests, it has proven insufficient to overcome underlying strategic mistrust. Both countries remain locked in a posture of cautious rationalism, where cooperation is contingent on demonstrable alignment of interests rather than ideological affinity or normative commitment.

Constructivism, by contrast, emphasises the role of shared norms and identities in fostering trust. Trust, in this context, is a social construct cultivated through cultural exchanges, institutional

---

[327]Kydd, Andrew H., *Trust and Mistrust in International Relations,* Princeton University Press, New Jersey, 2007.

dialogues, and narratives of commonality.[328] While both nations invoke ancient ties rhetorically, the absence of sustained societal engagement hollows out the epistemic basis for mutual trust. In the India-China context, this framework illuminates how pre-2020 mechanisms like the India-China High-Level Dialogue on Cultural Exchanges[329] and collaborative Buddhist heritage projects such as the Nalanda revival initiative[330] sought to somewhat codify civilizational commonality. These efforts hinged on the belief that cross-border pilgrimages, academic partnerships and cultural festivals could normalize mutual engagement as a natural extension of historical linkages.

Finally, the psychological approach delves into perceptual dynamics, where trust is an emotional belief shaped by cognitive biases and historical memory. Deeply-held Indian beliefs around Chinese perfidy following the experience of the 1962 war and China's suspicion of a Western-aligned India along with hostile media narratives exemplify particularized distrust. This refers to a belief in the inherent untrustworthiness of the other.[331]

Particularized distrust also manifests in how both nations increasingly view the other's citizens, institutions and initiatives through a security-focused lens. Asymmetric information flows and limited P2P contact reinforce this dynamic, forcing both publics to rely predominantly on state-filtered narratives. The absence

---

[328]Hurd, Ian, 'Constructivism', *The Oxford Handbook of International Relations*, Christian Reus-Smit and Duncan Snidal (eds.), Oxford Academic, Oxford, 2008.

[329]Ministry of External Affairs, 'First Meeting of the India-China High Level Mechanism on Cultural and People-to-People Exchanges', Government of India, 14 December 2018, https://tinyurl.com/4rcsfkef. Accessed on 16 November 2025.

[330]PTI, 'China Donates One Million $ for Nalanda University Revival', *The Economic Times*, 15 November 2011, https://tinyurl.com/3j6359e9. Accessed on 16 November 2025.

[331]ETV Bharat English Team, 'Five Chinese Nationals Among Eight Foreigners Held In Bihar In Just Ten Days', *ETV Bharat*, 18 May 2025, https://tinyurl.com/3ax2tpsk. Accessed on 16 November 2025.

of independent, on-ground reporting and sustained bilateral interaction creates fertile ground for misinformation to proliferate. The September 2022 rumours surrounding a supposed coup against Xi Jinping, widely misreported[332] in Indian media, primarily due to the lack of resident Chinese correspondents and a tendency to amplify viral social media content, exemplify how information vacuums enable false narratives to gain traction in contexts of mutual suspicion.

Therefore, understanding trust in the India-China context requires an epistemological synthesis of the above three frameworks. Trust is not merely an objective condition but a contested knowledge claim, shaped by how each state, and even society for that matter, interprets the other's intentions. Unfortunately, in the India-China dyad over the past 15 years, the erosion of trust has followed a cyclical pattern—episodic crises rupturing nascent confidence, followed by tactical engagements to stabilize ties. The two sides have historically engaged in calculated trust-building, yet their interactions remain overshadowed by a structural deficit of mutual assurance.

Theoretical insights suggest that rebuilding trust requires multi-level engagement. Rationalist models advocate for confidence-building measures (CBMs), like clarified border protocols or trade dispute mechanisms, which reduce uncertainty through institutionalized reciprocity. Constructivism stresses the need to resurrect shared narratives, reviving academic exchanges or collaborative projects, such as initiatives focused on climate resilience in the Himalayas. Finally, psychological approaches recommend graduated reciprocity, where small cooperative steps, such as resuming direct flights, accumulate to potentially enable a recalibration of perceptions. However, the epistemological divide

---

[332]Yang, Zeyi, 'How the false rumor of a Chinese coup went viral', *MIT Technology Review,* 27 September 2022, https://tinyurl.com/3929bwkd. Accessed on 18 November 2025.

poses a challenge. Trust-building assumes a shared understanding of what constitutes credible commitment, a premise absent in India-China relations. For trust to transcend rhetoric, both states must reconcile their epistemic frameworks. India must acknowledge China's developmentalist and major power self-perceptions. China, meanwhile, must appreciate India's desire for status and development along with its postcolonial sovereignty sensitivities.

Networks for Empathy and Stability

Global precedents validate the efficacy of societal exchanges in mitigating interstate hostilities. This remains true even when profound structural and historical differences exist between nations. One can look at the post-World War II Franco-German reconciliation or Japan-South Korea cultural diplomacy as examples. These, of course, carried their own peculiarities. Likewise, the India-China relationship operates within a context quite distinct from other historical examples. These differences stem from several factors. Asymmetric power dynamics shape strategic calculations between Delhi and Beijing. Contrasting political systems create divergent approaches to governance and the nature of international balance of power.

Despite these differences, the fundamental principle remains salient. Grassroots engagement serves several constructive purposes in even contested bilateral relations. It fosters empathy between the populations on both sides, whose primary exposure often comes through state-filtered narratives. Such exchanges gradually dilute antagonistic framings that dominate popular discourse. P2P contact creates constituencies for engagement and peace in both societies. These constituencies can eventually facilitate the transcending of state-level discord. The interpersonal connections formed through cultural, educational and commercial exchanges establish resilient networks. These networks frequently persist even when official diplomatic channels experience friction. Historical precedents from other regions demonstrate the transformative power of institutionalizing such grassroots exchanges, particularly in overcoming rivalries and fostering lasting reconciliation.

The Franco-German Youth Office (FGYO), established in 1963, exemplifies institutionalized societal engagement as a tool for post-conflict reconciliation.[333] At a time when mutual suspicion dominated—rooted in two World Wars and centuries of rivalry—the FGYO facilitated over nine million youth exchanges, embedding shared experiences in education, sports and cultural collaboration. This bottom-up approach cultivated a generation of leaders and citizens who viewed cooperation as inevitable rather than aspirational. Crucially, it decoupled societal ties from political volatility; even during disagreements over NATO or EU policies, P2P bonds ensured that dialogue persisted. Similarly, Japan-South Korea relations demonstrate how cultural soft power can circumvent historical grievances.[334] Despite unresolved issues like the abuse of women as sex slaves during wartime and territorial disputes, the organic proliferation of K-pop and Japanese anime has created a transnational cultural commonality, particularly among millennials. For India and China, which lack a comparable bilateral mechanism, replicating such structured exchanges—despite the persistent nature of the boundary dispute—could insulate societal engagement from geopolitical flare-ups.

However, critics argue that such models are incongruent with the India-China context. Unlike post-WW2 Europe, where US-led institutions enforced reconciliation, India and China

---

[333]Germond, Carine, 'War, Peace and Memory: Franco-German Reconciliation', *The Cambridge History of the European Union*, Mathieu Segers and Steven Van Hecke (eds.), Cambridge University Press, Cambridge, 2023, pp. 481–507.

[334]Ashley, Ryan, and Joseph Su, 'Mending Historical Memory: Improving People-to-People Ties Between Japan and South Korea', *Foreign Policy Research Institute*, 1 May 2024, https://tinyurl.com/54phst9n. Accessed on 16 November 2025.

operate in a multipolar arena with competing strategic alliances. There is merit to this argument. Societal exchanges alone cannot resolve territorial or strategic rifts. However, they do generate the *relational capital* necessary for crisis management. They help cultivate constituencies committed to mutual advancement and strategic stability; these are actors who can maintain dialogue during periods of tension and foster an enduring recognition that even fractured relationships require collaborative solutions in domains of shared interest. The imperatives of geography make this critical in the India-China dyad.

Openness and Vulnerabilities

The Indian discourse surrounding engagement with China is increasingly dominated by narratives that conflate openness with vulnerability. Such a conception frames societal exchanges as vectors for espionage, disinformation and ideological subversion. These fears, while rooted in legitimate security concerns, are often amplified to justify isolationist policies, which undermine India's long-term strategic interests. Within India, the 2020 Galwan clash and subsequent border tensions intensified suspicions about China. Increasingly, questions were raised about the threat of espionage being carried out through public diplomacy and the use of low-profile actors such as educators, students and business people.[335] The heightened concerns over China's influence efforts have increasingly steered policy toward restricting P2P ties, academic cooperation and media access.[336] Paradoxically, such

[335]Mayal, D.C.S., 'Chinese Human Intelligence (HUMINT) Through Public Diplomacy in South Asia: A Critical Assessment', *Journal of Defence Studies*, Vol. 19, July-September 2025, pp. 5–24, https://tinyurl.com/nhk83prr. Accessed on 16 November 2025.

[336]*Bloomberg*, 'India slaps new curbs on visas, schools to stem China's influence', *The Times of India*, 21 August 2020, https://tinyurl.com/2wz64cm7. Accessed on 16 November 2025.

apprehensions mirror Beijing's own rhetoric about Western infiltration and increasing paranoia with regard to foreigners, revealing the shared echoes of a siege mentality that stifles mutual understanding.[337]

Historical precedents, however, suggest that openness need not compromise security. During the 1980s and 1990s, despite unresolved border disputes, India and China fostered academic exchanges and trade links following the Rajiv Gandhi-Deng Xiaoping dialogue, which prioritized engagement over confrontation.[338] These interactions allowed for greater scholarly exchanges and cross-pollination of ideas on issues of economic reform and development.

Critics of cross-border educational initiatives frequently point to China's Confucius Institutes—state-funded language and cultural centres—as vehicles for espionage and ideological influence. However, India's decision to avoid establishing analogous joint universities or cultural institutions with China, unlike Western nations that host Confucius Institutes while also operating their own counterparts (e.g. Germany's Goethe-Institut), represents a strategic oversight. By abstaining from reciprocal soft power mechanisms, India forfeits opportunities to project its civilizational diversity, its pluralistic traditions, democratic ethos, and linguistic heritage on Chinese soil. The resulting perception gap persists because engagement remains restricted to elite diplomatic and business circles, denying public access to grassroots interactions that could humanize the *other*. This cycle becomes self-reinforcing. In other words, restricted exchanges breed caricatured perceptions, which in turn legitimize

---

[337]Gan, Nectar, 'China sees foreign threats 'everywhere' as powerful spy agency takes center stage', *CNN*, 21 April 2024, https://tinyurl.com/48yc33jr. Accessed on 16 November 2025.

[338]'For Peace and Friendship, Win-Win Cooperation and Common Development', Ministry of Foreign Affairs of the People's Republic of China, 9 September 2008, https://tinyurl.com/5896cb96. Accessed on 16 November 2025.

policies that deepen isolation, perpetuating mutual distrust.

The Indian security establishment's concerns about Chinese cyberespionage and disinformation campaigns are valid but require calibrated responses. In this scenario, Taiwan offers a useful example to learn from. Openness, when paired with institutional safeguards, strengthens India's capacity to navigate an asymmetric rivalry while preserving a democratic ethos. Despite facing relentless cyberattacks and influence operations from Beijing, Taipei has maintained vibrant academic and commercial ties with the People's Republic of China.[339] Its success lies in pairing openness with robust countermeasures. These include a dedicated cybersecurity agency, real-time rumour-debunking platforms, and stringent transparency laws for Chinese investments.

India, by contrast, has oscillated between reactive bans and bureaucratic inertia. For instance, at one level, national security concerns, including data security issues, resulted in the Indian government banning hundreds of Chinese apps since 2020. On the other hand, many state governments until recently continued procuring Chinese surveillance technology, such as CCTV cameras.[340] This is a contradiction that exposes the incoherence of current policies. Rather than blanket restrictions, India needs a framework that distinguishes between malign actors and legitimate exchanges. At the same time, it should develop regulatory approaches that tackle clearly defined risks rather than defaulting to broad bans and restrictions.

The narrative that openness necessarily correlates with Chinese territorial assertiveness also represents a mischaracterization of Beijing's strategic calculus. In reality, a complex set of factors

---

[339]Sang, Huynh Tam, Tong Thai Thien, and Le Thi Yen Nhi, 'How Taiwan Fights the Disinformation War | Lowy Institute', *theinterpreter*, 20 June 2024, https://tinyurl.com/tn66zrw5. Accessed on 16 November 2025.

[340]Dalmia, Vinayak, 'China's Hikvision Controls India's Surveillance Market. Modi Needs to Do More than Ban Apps', *The Print*, 1 July 2020, https://tinyurl.com/y4jhfh8u. Accessed on 16 November 2025.

animate Chinese policies. These include assessments of balance of power, complexities of domestic politics including contestation between different interest groups, economic objectives, public perception and nationalism, and the nature of information flow to the leadership along with the quality of that information.[341] What becomes evident upon closer examination is that information restrictions do not necessarily deter Chinese assertiveness. Instead, they inhibit others, such as the Indian state, from developing a fuller and more robust understanding of Chinese behaviour, which can lead to adverse assessments and compound crisis management. During moments of heightened tension, precisely when clarity is most crucial, having constrained avenues for communication and interpretation creates dangerous information vacuums. Bridging these informational vacuums requires not only official communication channels but also the presence of independent observers and mediators within each other's societies.

In this context, the role of journalists is indispensible. However in the current bilateral climate, these vital informational channels have been significantly eroded. Visa restrictions and bureaucratic obstacles have dramatically reduced the presence of Indian journalists in China and vice versa. This mutual retrenchment forces both countries to rely increasingly on second-hand interpretations, often filtered through Western media perspectives.

India's espionage concerns vis-à-vis China differ fundamentally from those of Western nations—a distinction that should inform policy approaches to bilateral engagement. Unlike the United States or European countries, India does not face significant industrial

---

[341]Menon, Shivshankar, 'Internal Drivers of China's External Behaviour: Working Paper', *Centre for Social and Economic Progress (CSEP)*, 12 January 2022, https://tinyurl.com/5765jnep. Accessed on 16 November 2025.

Jost, Tyler, *Bureaucracies at War: The Institutional Origins of Miscalculation (Cambridge Studies in International Relations)*, Cambridge University Press, England, 2024.

espionage threats, given its current technological positioning relative to China's advanced manufacturing base. Likewise, unlike the West, India is not home to a sizable Chinese diaspora. But it does host the Dalai Lama, along with a large Tibetan population and the Central Tibetan Administration. Therefore, Western restrictions, predicated on protecting intellectual property and industrial advantages and related to diaspora politics, are conceptually misaligned with India's strategic context. The pathway forward lies in devising policies tailored to India's specific security concerns rather than borrowed Western frameworks. For instance, this could take the form of some sort of visa pre-verification for certain academics and entrepreneurs before visa issuance or the issuance of short-term visas with mandatory requirements for registration with local law-enforcement.

The most significant rethinking that needs to take place is in the information domain. Ensuring direct access for Indian journalists, businesses, academics and analysts to a range of Chinese information sources, like newspapers, policy documents, economic data, government platforms, academic publications and business forums, is critical to build a strong knowledge base. It would enable them to develop a deeper understanding of internal dynamics and interpret policy debates and bureaucratic contestation. Likewise, Indian journalists working in China can also play a crucial role in making sense of the country's complex political and social environment. Through continuous reporting, they could help demystify the inner workings of China's policymaking process, offering the Indian public and officials a nuanced, real-time view that transcends simplistic or monolithic portrayals of Chinese intent.

When Indian scholars and analysts can directly observe social media discourse on Weibo and WeChat, they stand to gain invaluable insights into how popular nationalism exerts bottom-up pressures on Chinese leadership. These dynamics would otherwise be invisible from external vantage points. For instance, during periods of economic adjustment, such as the ongoing property market contraction, journalists with local contacts can discern whether provincial officials are faithfully implementing central directives or quietly resisting them. They can track regional variations in policy implementation, identify emerging social tensions before they escalate into protests, and gauge public sentiment. Such inputs are crucial for anticipating political and policy shifts that could affect the Indian economy, bilateral trade, investment flows and national security.

a. Bridging the Disconnect

The question of whether P2P ties can operate independently of state-level tensions depends fundamentally on addressing entrenched structural barriers across four critical domains: media, think tanks, academia and tourism. These sectors have become increasingly paralysed by institutional suspicion and bureaucratic calcification.

A structured media fellowship programme, drawing inspiration from the Australia-China Journalist Exchange model, offers a practical pathway to gradually recalibrate distorted perceptions.[342] Such a programme would facilitate reciprocal access for Indian and Chinese journalists, creating opportunities for direct observation and sustained reporting. However, this approach must be grounded in realistic expectations: expanded access alone will not immediately transform reporting frameworks, particularly given the constraints Chinese journalists operate under domestically. Similarly, Indian journalists in China will continue to face significant access limitations and self-censorship pressures. Yet, from an Indian strategic perspective, establishing this presence is a long-term investment in developing deep expertise and sustained influence over a generation of

---

[342] 'Five senior Australian journalists visit China on first post-COVID exchange', *Asia Pacific Journalism Centre*, 15 December 2023, https://tinyurl.com/2duzn5p7. Accessed on 16 November 2025.

engagement, rather than seeking immediate narrative shifts.

The gradual exposure of more Chinese professionals to India's complex realities also creates opportunities for multidimensional perspectives to emerge over time. The primary objective is not short-term narrative management but cultivating constituencies with potentially favourable dispositions. More importantly, from India's perspective, the informational asymmetry created by journalistic absence in China constitutes a vulnerability that outweighs concerns about continued negative coverage by Chinese media. Access, even at the cost of criticism, ultimately serves India's long-term interest in developing autonomous analytical capacity regarding its most consequential neighbour. While increased professional exchange enhances mutual understanding at the individual level, sustained progress also depends on structured institutional efforts, such as think tank dialogues.

Unfortunately, think tank dialogues between India and China still remain constrained by their elite-centric focus. The India-China Think Tanks Forum, launched in 2015 to foster policy-relevant research, has met less than six times as of 2025, with minimal impact on bridging perceptual gaps.[343] Track 1.5 dialogues, featuring retired diplomats and military officers, and Track 2 dialogues have likely been useful in discussions on crisis management and ideation, but their ad hoc nature limits their ability to cultivate sustained societal trust. Joint initiatives such as future labs on global issues, like governance of global commons, climate change, AI ethics and governance, urban planning, pollution, or disaster management, offer a pragmatic pathway to reframe the relationship from zero-sum rivalry to conditional collaboration. This structural shift would broaden the scope of bilateral dialogue beyond elite circles while expanding the pool

---

[343]'First India China Think-Tanks Forum, New Delhi', Ministry of External Affairs, Government of India, 10 December 2016, https://tinyurl.com/3the8y4v. Accessed on 16 November 2025.

of engagement to include diverse institutional stakeholders. The challenges facing elite dialogues are not unique; similar headwinds have impeded progress in educational exchanges, another pillar of India-China engagement.

Prior to the Galwan Valley clash of June 2020, approximately 23,000 Indian students were pursuing higher education in China, with a significant concentration in medical programmes. This robust educational exchange collapsed rapidly under the combined weight of geopolitical tensions and the COVID-19 pandemic. While the global pandemic disrupted student mobility worldwide through border closures and travel restrictions, the India-China relationship faced a compounded crisis: post-Galwan visa restrictions and institutional barriers further constrained educational access. The result has been dramatic. Indian student enrolment in Chinese institutions has plummeted to approximately 8,580, representing a decline of nearly 63 per cent and signalling the broader erosion of bilateral engagement channels.[344]

The asymmetry in bilateral educational exchange remains striking. Chinese student presence in India has historically been minimal, with fewer than 1,000 students primarily engaged in short-term Hindi language instruction at Agra's Kendriya Hindi Sansthan.[345] While health protocols during the pandemic necessitated temporary restrictions, the persistent imbalance reflects deeper structural issues. The 2006 Education Exchange Programme (EEP), despite its renewal in 2015, exemplifies this underinvestment in bilateral educational infrastructure, allocating merely 25 annual scholarships per country—a fraction of the

[344]Ghai, Neil, and Prachi Verma, 'Diplomatic Thaw Sparks Renewed Interest from Indian Students in Chinese Universities', *The Economic Times*, 30 January 2025, https://tinyurl.com/3yaawxyu. Accessed on 16 November 2025.

[345]News Desk, 'Chinese students want to learn Hindi and apply for admission to the Central Hindi Institute', *Amar Ujala*, 4 July 2020, https://tinyurl.com/u8stnzpd. Accessed on 16 November 2025.

30,000+ scholarships India extends to Western students.[346]

Unlike China's substantial academic integration with Western institutions, evidenced by more than 15 university partnerships with American counterparts, Sino-Indian joint academic ventures remain conspicuously absent. This institutional void persists despite the pandemic catalysing innovative virtual exchange models elsewhere. The absence of robust academic partnerships transcends pandemic-related disruptions, reflecting deeper mutual suspicions regarding ideological influence, a dynamic that continues to constrain knowledge production and human capital development across both societies. This pattern of minimal P2P exchange extends beyond academic corridors into tourism, where bilateral flows remain equally anaemic despite both nations being major global travel markets.

In 2022, Chinese tourists accounted for just 0.18 per cent of India's inbound tourism, while Indian visits to China remained confined to a niche Buddhist pilgrimage.[347] The suspension of direct flights following the Galwan clash compounded this disconnect, disrupting business travel and familial visits. However, recent diplomatic breakthroughs signal a potential reversal of this trend. Following high-level discussions between External Affairs Minister S. Jaishankar and Chinese Foreign Minister Wang Yi, and subsequent meetings in January and March 2025, both nations agreed to resume the Kailash Mansarovar Yatra in summer 2025 after a five-year suspension.[348] The Ministry of External Affairs announced that 750 pilgrims would undertake the sacred journey between June and August 2025, travelling in batches via two

---

[346]'Education Relations', Embassy of India, Beijing, China, https://tinyurl.com/3m7hnwps. Accessed on 16 November 2025.

[347]Ministry of Tourism, 'India Tourism Statistics 2023', https://tinyurl.com/457afkdy. Accessed on 16 November 2025.

[348]Ministry of External Affairs, 'Kailash Manasarovar Yatra, 2025 – Draw of Lots (May 21, 2025)', Government of India, 21 May 2025, https://tinyurl.com/mtfsr3es. Accessed on 16 November 2025.

routes: the Lipulekh Pass in Uttarakhand and the Nathu La Pass in Sikkim. The first batch was flagged off in June 2025, marking the restoration of the first major people-to-people mechanism between India and China since the pandemic and border tensions.

Building on this momentum, further measures are being discussed, including reciprocal visa-on-arrival schemes for accredited professionals and tourists, modelled on arrangements trailed during the 2024 Hangzhou Asian Games. India could strategically promote the Buddhist Circuit tours to attract Chinese pilgrims, while China could market heritage sites to Indian history enthusiasts. While the two countries restored direct flight connectivity in October 2025, expanding linkages to more sectors would not only facilitate religious tourism but also catalyse broader regional economic and cultural exchanges, which could gradually help rebuild trust through sustained interaction.

b. Cultivating a Uniquely Indian Perspective

One of the challenges of restricting the avenues of interactions is that India's understanding of China then tends to get mediated through reportage and analytical frameworks originating in the West. A substantial body of insightful scholarship on China has emerged, and continues to emerge, from academics, journalists and policy institutions across the US, western Europe, Australia, Japan and Taiwan. Some of the most rigorous and nuanced analyses of China's political, economic, social and security dynamics originate from educational institutions and policy think tanks based in these countries. While such assessments significantly enrich India's understanding of China, they are inevitably shaped by particular national and cultural vantage points.

Western scholarship, media narratives and policy paradigms on China, at times, fall into the binaries of democracy versus authoritarianism or of containment versus engagement. Likewise, Western analyses of China can often emphasise ideological and security narratives, which might not necessarily align with India's security concerns or socio-cultural impulses. From a geopolitical standpoint, increasingly, much of the Western discourse tends to interpret China's rise primarily as a threat to the liberal international order or the primacy of the US as the global hegemon. Simply accepting such frameworks can be detrimental to India's interests. For instance, it can result in overlooking areas where Indian and Chinese interests converge, such as on the issue of centrality of the norm of sovereignty in international relations or the reform of global financial institutions and governance structures to reflect new power realities. Likewise, adopting the simplified prism of authoritarianism or top-down governance can colour the understanding of China's economic development and decision-making, overlooking the adaptive governance mechanisms that have enabled China's poverty alleviation or its hybrid economic model, which blends state-led infrastructure development with market dynamism. Another example is the criticism of China's Belt and Road Initiative (BRI) as debt-trap diplomacy, which tends to ignore its impact in fostering South-South connectivity. From an Indian perspective, studying the different project models under the BRI umbrella can provide some useful insights that might inform India's own initiatives like the International North-South Transport Corridor (INSTC).

More importantly, from a strategic perspective, the lack of intellectual connectivity and indigenous insights coupled with the dependence on Western institutions can create a perceptual straitjacket, obscuring Indian understanding of China. The absence of robust Indian scholarly and societal engagement with China, therefore, can leave policymakers dependent on filtered interpretations, which can often be misaligned with India's strategic imperatives. This can have tangible consequences. For instance, during the 2020 Galwan clash, Western media's focus on wolf warrior diplomacy overshadowed nuanced analyses of China's domestic nationalist pressures, the interpretation of performance incentives by China's foreign affairs officials, and the

PLA's internal dynamics. Indian policymakers, drawing on these narratives, risk misjudging Beijing's motivations and intentions along with opportunities for tactical cooperation. This asymmetry extends to economic analysis. Western think tanks dominate studies on China's technology sector, while India's dependency on solar panels and EV battery components remains understudied. Therefore, cultivating a uniquely Indian lens to analyse China's polity, economy and society is not just an intellectual exercise but a strategic necessity in a multipolar world where India's interests demand autonomy in perception and action.

An Indian perspective, however, should not be confined to India's own interests. It must also foreground an understanding of China's development within its own context. In other words, such a perspective should dispassionately examine China's distinctive path of modernization—its achievements, constraints and contradictions—and consider what lessons, if any, India might draw from that experience. India and China share post-colonial trajectories of nation-building, albeit through divergent political systems. China's approach towards modernization can offer lessons for India's developmental goals. For instance, China's Township and Village Enterprises (TVEs), which drove rural industrialization in the 1980s, could inform India's MSME sector. Likewise, it can be instructive for Indian scholars and policymakers to understand how China has cultivated a research and development ecosystem to support hard technology advancement. Pollution control and urbanization are also domains where significant learnings can be gained. On the flip side, India's digital public infrastructure development and its thriving software and services industries can offer lessons for Chinese technocrats.

Geopolitically, India's non-Western position allows it to interrogate China's actions without ideological baggage. Doklam and Galwan revealed China's territorial assertiveness but also its aversion to full-scale conflict. This is a nuance that might be better understood through Kautilyan realism than Huntingtonian clash of civilizations. On matters related to the South China Sea, stability in the Taiwan Strait, and maintaining the balance of power in the Indo-Pacific, India shares a commonality of interests with the US and its allies. However, these interests are not identical. Therefore, contemplating China's approaches to these issues through the lens of Indian interests, rather than that of India's partners alone, is crucial.

Economically, India must dissect China's dual circulation strategy not as isolationism but as a recalibration toward self-reliance and de-risking. In this context, the India-China trade deficit demands a granular analysis of supply chain dependencies and opportunities for sectoral reciprocity, such as IT services or generic drug exports. Indian economists could also draw lessons from China's experience in managing state-owned enterprises (SOEs). Likewise, there is an urgent need to study the impact of Chinese economic actions in response to the trade war with the US on the Indian economy and supply chains. Building this nuanced perspective requires dismantling structural barriers in information access, academia, media and policymaking. India's China studies ecosystem remains woefully under-resourced compared to the West. Supporting the blossoming of this ecosystem and enabling the building of bridges with international and Chinese institutions is necessary. And this is not just incumbent upon the government but also private sector actors, who must fund deeper knowledge cultivation.

Once again, it is important to grasp that the absence of an Indian perspective on China is not merely an academic issue but a strategic one. By not investing in this effort, India risks outsourcing policy thinking to actors with divergent priorities. Cultivating an autonomous analytical framework, which is rooted in India's developmental agenda and geopolitical experience and imperatives, will enable nuanced engagement.

Conclusion

India's strategic engagement with China requires a fundamental reorientation, viewing openness not as a vulnerability but as a calculated strength. The current strategy of restricting information flow and P2P exchanges inadvertently empowers adversarial narratives and limits India's ability to develop an independent and more textured understanding of its neighbour. To rebuild trust and foster a more balanced relationship, India must adopt a multi-dimensional approach that blends geopolitical realism with the institution of confidence-building measures, the revival of shared narratives, and the gradual implementation of reciprocal engagement.

Bridging the epistemological divide between the two nations will require reconciling their distinct frameworks to cultivate a shared understanding of credible commitments. Societal exchanges are indispensable in this process, serving to humanize interactions, dilute antagonistic perceptions, and create constituencies for peace that extend beyond the confines of state-state relations. Addressing structural impediments in media, academia, tourism and think tanks is essential to insulating P2P ties from geopolitical tensions. By fostering sustained engagement in these domains, India can lay the groundwork for more meaningful and enduring connections. At the same time, cultivating a uniquely Indian perspective on China's polity, economy and society emerges as an urgent priority. This entails dismantling barriers within academia, media and policymaking to build an autonomous analytical framework that aligns with India's interests.

This recalibration demands targeted investments in language training, the revival and sustainment of Track 2.0 and 1.5 dialogues, and the use of India's diaspora networks in China. These measures would not only enhance India's capacity for independent analysis but also foster channels of communication that can potentially withstand political turbulence. Ultimately,

India's approach should reflect strategic autonomy, a confident ability to navigate the complexities of its relationship with China while safeguarding its core interests and values.

List of Contributors

Manoj Kewalramani (Chapter Author and Book Editor)

Manoj Kewalramani is the chairperson of the Indo-Pacific Studies Programme at the Takshashila Institution. His research interests range from Chinese politics, foreign policy and great power competition to addressing questions of how India can work with like-minded partners to address the challenges presented by China's rise. Manoj is the author of *Smokeless War: China's Quest for Geopolitical Dominance* (2021), which discusses China's political, diplomatic, economic and narrative responses to the Covid-19 pandemic. Manoj writes a daily newsletter tracking Chinese political and policy discourse in the *People's Daily*, the Communist Party's flagship newspaper. He is also the host of a leading International Relations podcast—'The Great Power Show'. Manoj's work has been widely covered in Indian and international media outlets. He has also testified before the US Congress' US-China Economic and Security Review Commission as an expert witness in 2022 and 2024.

Amit Kumar (Chapter Author)

Amit Kumar is a Staff Research Analyst with the Takshashila Institution's Indo-Pacific Studies Programme. With a broader focus on China, he primarily studies issues at the intersection of economy, security and technology. He keenly tracks the geopolitical and geoeconomic trends emerging from China. His writings encompass themes such as India-China border relations, India-China trade and economic relations, and the Chinese economy and financial system.

Anushka Saxena (Chapter Author)

Anushka Saxena is a Staff Research Analyst with the Takshashila Institution's Indo-Pacific Studies Programme. She is also a Doctoral Scholar with the Manipal Institute of Social Sciences, Humanities and Arts, Manipal Academy of Higher Education, Manipal, India. Her research focuses on the Chinese People's Liberation Army and its reforms, China-Taiwan relations, and India's foreign policy. She also curates the weekly newsletter, *Eye on China*.

Vanshika Saraf (Chapter Author)

Vanshika Saraf is a Research Analyst with the Indo-Pacific Studies Program at the Takshashila Institution. She has also been a fellow of the Global Leaders' Alliance Fellowship and a research fellow at the Alliance Centre for Eurasian Studies at Alliance University, Bengaluru. She curates the newsletters *The Indian Radius* and *Quad Bulletin*.

Rakshith Shetty (Chapter Author)

Rakshith Shetty is an independent researcher who previously worked with the Takshashila Institution as a Research Analyst. His research focused on the evolution of China's green energy ecosystem. Rakshith's writings have been published in leading national and international media outlets. He holds a Master's in Diplomacy, Law and Business from O.P. Jindal Global University.

Index